Northwestern University
STUDIES IN *Phenomenology &*
Existential Philosophy

The Phenomenology
of the Social World

Alfred Schutz

Translated by

With an Introduction by

The Phenomenology of the Social World

GEORGE WALSH
and
FREDERICK LEHNERT

GEORGE WALSH

NORTHWESTERN UNIVERSITY PRESS

1 9 6 7

Northwestern University Press
www.nupress.northwestern.edu

Originally published in German under the title *Der sinnhafte Aufbau der sozialen Welt.* Copyright © 1932 by Julius Springer, Vienna; copyright © 1960 by Springer-Verlag, Vienna. English translation copyright © 1967 by Northwestern University Press. First published 1967. First paperback edition 1972.

Printed in the United States of America

10

ISBN-13: 978-0-8101-0390-0
ISBN-10: 0-8101-0390-7

Acknowledgments

THE PRESENT WORK is a translation of Alfred Schutz's *Der sinnhafte Aufbau der sozialen Welt*, first published in Vienna by Julius Springer in 1932, and again, in unaltered form, by Springer-Verlag in 1960. The book is Schutz's major systematic work, setting forth his attempt to provide a phenomenological foundation for the basic concepts of the social sciences.

The development of Schutz's later thought is to be found in his *Collected Papers*, published in three volumes by Martinus Nijhoff, The Hague, in 1962, 1964, and 1966 under the editorship of Maurice Natanson, Arvid Brodersen, and Ilse Schutz, respectively. An English adaptation by Thomas Luckmann of Chapter 4 of the present work has previously appeared in the second volume of *Collected Papers*.

At the time of his death in 1959 Schutz was preparing a final systematic statement of his position. This manuscript, edited by Thomas Luckmann, will be published in German under the title *Die Strukturen der Lebenswelt* and will be followed by an English translation.

The translators have sought at all times to follow the terminology established by Schutz in his English publications or otherwise used in *Collected Papers*. Where Schutz himself used alternative terms, we have felt free to exercise our discretion. Since many readers will wish to follow Schutz's arguments more closely by reading his many quotations in context, we have used readily available English translations for the latter, taking the liberty of correcting them only in cases where we judged that Schutz's point would otherwise be lost. In this matter our decision was based on what we believed would be a major advantage for the reader who might come to know some of the writings of Husserl or Weber only through the present work.

[ix]

We wish to express our thanks first of all to Mrs. Ilse Schutz, who rendered kindly encouragement and concrete assistance at every stage of our work. We owe a special debt also to our colleague at Hobart and William Smith Colleges, Professor Helmut Wagner, a former student of Schutz, who read the first chapter and made a number of suggestions which we have adopted, and who gave scholarly assistance at many other points. Professor Thomas Luckmann, a former colleague of ours at Hobart and William Smith Colleges, was also very helpful with advice both general and specific. Detailed and careful advice was also given to us by Professor Fred Kersten, of the University of Montana. Others who rendered assistance on specific points or who were kind enough to send us their suggestions were our colleagues Professors Daniel Petrizzi and John S. Klein and Messrs. Eugene Miller and Perrell Payne; also Professor Kurt H. Wolff, of Brandeis University, Cathy Walsh, Olga and Hans Frank, and Robin Trail. Of course, none of these should be held responsible for any errors in the final product. Our colleague Professor Donald Scherer rendered much-appreciated assistance of an indirect nature. Nor can we forget the conscientious help given us over a period of two and a half years by Miss Muriel Hodge, Mrs. Edna Farnsworth, and other members of the library staff at Hobart and William Smith Colleges and also the members of the library staff at Cornell University. For extraordinarily competent and patient secretarial and stenographical assistance we are grateful to Mrs. Jane Corcoran and Mrs. Rosemary Currie.

To Hobart and William Smith Colleges we are indebted for a grant which greatly facilitated our work.

Finally we wish to express our special thanks to Professor James M. Edie, our former colleague and now an editor of the Northwestern University Studies in Phenomenology and Existential Philosophy, and Professor Lewis White Beck, of the University of Rochester. It was their kindly encouragement that helped us decide to undertake the translation of the present work.

GEORGE WALSH
FREDERICK LEHNERT

Geneva, New York
September, 1966

Contents

INTRODUCTION

ALFRED SCHUTZ IS GRADUALLY achieving recognition as one of the foremost philosophers of social science of the present century. Recognition of Schutz's importance coincides with an awareness —extending far beyond the academic world—of the centrality of the problems which he discussed. Two of these problems are the role of objectivity versus subjectivity in the social sciences and the nature of human action. The present work contains a thoroughgoing analysis of both of these questions from the phenomenological point of view. But the book goes far beyond that. It presents a philosophical analysis of the nature of social science as such, and raises as well as answers the fundamental question of whether and to what extent the social sciences can provide us with a genuine understanding of human beings.

The problem of objectivity versus subjectivity is emerging with dramatic importance in our contemporary culture. If objective knowledge of human beings can only be achieved by regarding them as "types" which one must not "fold, spindle, or mutilate," is not objectivity by definition, then, precisely the attitude and approach which misses the human reality? Is not the true understanding of human beings to be achieved rather in face-to-face encounter, in interpersonal relationship, in "dialogue," in "commitment"? This problem, which is so urgent today, is discussed by Alfred Schutz, not in the prophetic fashion in which it has so often been expressed, as by Buber—however valuable such an approach might be—but in a manner which is systematic, exhaustive, and analytic.

The problem of the nature of human action, which of course is tied up with the problem of freedom, is today receiving special attention from more than one philosophical school. It is part of the more general question of what distinguishes the human being as such, and in this

[xv]

sense it belongs to philosophical anthropology. Schutz, in an original and extended analysis, relates action to the rest of our experience, to meaning, and to our time-consciousness. His contribution here, including his now classic distinction between "in-order-to motives" and "because-motives," has stimulated considerable philosophical discussion.[1]

Der sinnhafte Aufbau der sozialen Welt—"The Meaning-Construction (or, more literally, the 'Meaningful Construction') of the Social World"—amounts *in substance* to a phenomenological study of the basic concepts of the social sciences. But the *form* in which it is cast is that of a phenomenological "preface to interpretive sociology," namely, the sociology of Max Weber. It is this form which may make the book somewhat difficult for the Anglo-American reader whose acquaintance with Weber may be limited to his monumental concrete historical studies. Likewise, the reader who is ignorant of phenomenology will experience his own difficulties. It would be impossible within the scope of an introduction of this nature to expound the basic concepts of either Husserl or Weber, not to speak of expounding them both together. Happily, Schutz is a master expositor, and the careful following of his argument will itself give even the completely innocent reader, if he is in earnest, an elementary grasp of the two positions in question. As we have, throughout, used readily available English translations of both Husserl and Weber, every quotation can be found, read in context, and used as the starting point for further study.

Since the purpose of this Introduction is to render all possible assistance to the reader who is first approaching Schutz, it will be divided into three parts, of unequal length. The first will deal briefly with Schutz's life and intellectual career, the second will outline, however sketchily, the background of the problem involving the distinction between the *Geisteswissenschaften* and the *Naturwissenschaften* as conceived by Dilthey and the Southwest German School, and the third will give an analytical synopsis of Schutz's first four chapters. The material in the second part is intended to orient the reader to the manner in which Schutz poses the problem in Chapter 1. The material in the third part is meant as a guide to help the reader find his way through a highly involved but cumulative argument. This synopsis is, of course, meaningless without the text but will, I believe, prove valuable to the reader both as a means of cross-reference and as a means of checking his progress. Once the concepts of Chapter 4 are grasped, Schutz's central methodological position will be understood, and the argument in the important final chapter will unfold with ease.

1. Cf. Lewis W. Beck, "Agent, Actor, Spectator and Critic," *The Monist*, XLIX, No. 2.

The expository approach of this Introduction is rendered necessary by the fact that the book presupposes a background not easily available to the Anglo-American reader of today. This is far less the case with Schutz's later writings. The Introduction is, then, purely a tool which the reader may use or lay aside according to his need.

[I] SCHUTZ'S LIFE AND CAREER

ALFRED SCHUTZ WAS BORN in Vienna in 1899. He studied law and the social sciences at the University of Vienna. Among his teachers were the celebrated scholars Hans Kelsen, the philosopher of law, and Ludwig von Mises, the economist of the Austrian marginalist school, both of them later well known in this country. He also studied under the eminent sociologists Friedrich von Wieser and Othmar Spann. Schutz became interested quite early in the work of the greatest of German sociologists, Max Weber, especially in the latter's attempt to establish a consistent methodological foundation for the social sciences. Weber's early statement of his position on this matter [2] had roused Schutz's teacher, Ludwig von Mises, to an acute polemical criticism.[3] Schutz regarded this criticism as in part justified but as one which also pointed the way to a more defensible concept of "ideal types," toward which Weber himself seemed to be working. The perception of the logical problems involved in the notion of ideal types and in several other of Weber's key ideas drove Schutz to a thorough philosophical analysis of Weber's whole methodological position. He began to see this as harboring serious ambiguities. Weber's approach was dependent on his central concept of meaning (*Sinn*), which was supposed to be distinctive of human action as opposed to mere reactive behavior and which was also supposed to be open to interpretive understanding (*Verstehen*) by the sociologist. Schutz found this notion, and all its dependent ideas, ambivalent. Seeking for a consistent theory of meaning, he found it in Husserl. By applying Husserl's concept of meaning to action he was able to recast the foundations of interpretive sociology, in other words, to give the latter a phenomenological grounding. The present work is the study in which this task was carried out. Although his main debt was to Husserl, Schutz also drew heavily upon Bergson's analysis of the way in which the stream

2. Cf. " 'Objectivity' in Social Science and Social Policy" in *Max Weber on the Methodology of the Social Sciences*, trans. and ed. by Edward A. Shils and Henry A. Finch (Glencoe, Ill., 1949).

3. An idea of Mises' position can be gained from his *Human Action* (New Haven, 1963), pp. 30–32, 59–64, and esp. pp. 61–62, 251–55, and 126.

of consciousness is modified by the phenomenon of attention. On this point Schutz was attracted to Bergson's dualism between life and thought, which he shared to some degree. However, he was basically a phenomenologist and in no way oriented to the Bergsonian metaphysics. When Schutz finished the work, he dedicated a copy of it to Husserl, who replied on May 3, 1932: "I am anxious to meet such a serious and thorough phenomenologist, one of the few who have penetrated to the core of the meaning of my life's work, access to which is unfortunately so difficult, and who promises to continue it as representative of the genuine *philosophia perennis* which alone can be the future of philosophy." Although Schutz frequently thereafter visited Husserl at Freiburg and joined in many discussions with the phenomenological circle there, and although he corresponded with Husserl until the latter's death, he was unable for personal reasons to accept the offer to become his assistant. Schutz left Austria in advance of the Nazi occupation, staying in Paris one year before emigrating to the United States. He arrived here in July, 1939, and shortly after that took a position on the Graduate Faculty of the New School for Social Research in New York. He also became a member of the editorial board of the journal *Philosophy and Phenomenological Research*. In his new life in America he not only had the pleasure of constant contact with other scholars who had studied with Husserl, such as Aron Gurwitsch and Dorion Cairns, but also found other sources of inspiration. Among these was the thought of the eminent pragmatist George Herbert Mead, whose concern with the analysis of meaning in social interaction paralleled that of Schutz, although it had been arrived at by a completely different road. Schutz's mind was broadened by the American scene, and he was able to synthesize to a unique degree the rigor and discipline of his European background with the greater informality and openness to experience characteristic of his new environment. This, combined with a warm and delightful personality, made him an object of admiration and affection to his students and colleagues. Schutz's career was cut short by untimely death in 1959 as he was preparing a final statement of his position as it had developed in the many years since the publication of the present work.

[II] THE DISTINCTION BETWEEN THE GEISTESWISSENSCHAF-
TEN AND THE NATURWISSENSCHAFTEN

THE NINETEENTH CENTURY had witnessed a great flowering in Germany of historical scholarship, economics, and the study of languages and institutions. It is not surprising that basic questions began to be raised about the "lack of certainty" and therefore allegedly unscientific character of these studies in contrast to the natural sciences. Other questions, equally basic, were asked about their relations to one another and to philosophy. Did some or all of them, for instance, deal in general laws? Could they be truly objective and free of value assumptions (*wertfrei*)? Some were attracted to the answer of the positivists and their allies as expressed by John Stuart Mill in the uncompromising statement at the head of Book VI of his *System of Logic:* "The backward state of the moral sciences can only be remedied by applying to them the methods of physical science duly extended and generalized."

Mill's "logic of the moral sciences" and the whole ideology surrounding it, although it was, as we have said, attractive to some minds, nevertheless encountered opposition of a very basic and fundamental nature. The leaders of this opposition were Wilhelm Dilthey, Wilhelm Windelband, and Heinrich Rickert. The first was an essentially solitary thinker, who combined in his outlook elements of the romantic humanism of Lessing, Novalis, and Goethe with elements of neo-Kantianism. The other two were leaders of the so-called "Southwest German (or Baden) School," which, because of its extreme stress on the activity of the mind in knowledge and on the priority of value, is sometimes called neo-Fichtean. The works in which they first made their distinctive views known were: Dilthey, *Einleitung in die Geisteswissenschaften,* 1883; Windelband, *Geschichte und Naturwissenschaft,* 1894; and Rickert, *Die Grenzen der naturwissenschaftlichen Begriffsbildung,* 1902.

All three of these thinkers agreed that there was a fundamental difference between the natural sciences, on the one hand, and studies such as history, jurisprudence, and economics, on the other. But they disagreed as to where that distinction lay. Dilthey and Rickert are the most important of the three, and we shall confine our attention to them.

Dilthey maintained that the distinction was one of *content.* For this reason he insisted on using the term *Geisteswissenschaften.* History, economics, and jurisprudence study man's mind (*Geist*) in contrast to physics and chemistry, which study external processes. Of course it is man's mind as objective (*objektiver Geist*), in other words, as a system of cultural products and institutions, together with the meanings they bear, that is the object of these "sciences of mind." But the important thing from Dilthey's point of view is that the mind is central. In turn, what is most important in the mind is *Erlebnis*—lived experience or immediate experience. This intimate inner life achieves an outward expression (*Ausdruck*), as in art. By interpreting this outward expression in terms of what lies behind it, we come to understand (*verstehen*) others. We do this by reconstituting our own inner experience "in" the other person by "reading" him. Understanding is thus a "rediscovery of the I in the Thou" (*das Verstehen ist ein Wiederfinden des Ich im Du*).[4] This insight into others is, therefore, the paradigm, so to speak, of the knowledge that is proper to the social sciences.

While it is possible that Dilthey had some influence on Schutz, it seems to have been more of a suggestive nature, since Schutz was in agreement with Weber that Dilthey's basic approach was unscientific.

Weber, however, was influenced to a considerable degree by Rickert. We must now try to sketch (however inadequately, as must be the case in a treatment confined to a few paragraphs) Rickert's fundamental position.[5] Rickert rejected the term *Geisteswissenschaften* and substituted for it the term *Kulturwissenschaften*. The object of the cultural studies is not mind as such, he pointed out, for mind can just as well be studied by the procedures of experimental psychology. Rather, that object is cultural products and institutions. It is these and their *meanings* that the cultural sciences seek to understand, not inner psychological processes. In fact, the natural and cultural sciences are merely two different ways of imposing the network of conceptual knowledge upon an originally "immeasurable manifold." When data are organized in terms of abstract general laws, we have the natural sciences. When they are organized in terms of understanding concrete individual cases that are suffused with *meaning,* the cultural sciences are the result.

But such meanings cannot be understood except in terms of values. The cultural sciences must, therefore, deal with values. But they can deal with them adequately only in terms of an objective science of values. This in turn can only be supplied by a philosophy of history. Values are not real, they merely have validity (*Geltung*). In a sense, value may be regarded as the polar opposite of actuality. It is in terms of value that we approach actuality and organize it. Our values determine our standpoint.

Rickert's influence upon Weber lay chiefly in the notion of actuality as an unorganized manifold which is then approached from the standpoint of certain interests or values and so organized into a conceptual system. However, Weber insisted, as Schutz makes clear, that in quite another sense science is perfectly objective and value-free (*wertfrei*). It is one thing to ask questions in terms of a value or interest. It is quite another thing to *answer* them in such terms.

4. Wilhelm Dilthey, *Gesammelte Schriften* (Stuttgart and Göttingen, 1958), VII, 191.
5. Cf. Heinrich Rickert, *Science and History,* trans. George Reisman, ed. Arthur Goodard, (Princeton: Van Nostrand, 1962).

The general structure of the intellectual background against which Schutz poses his basic problems ought now to be clear to some extent. We can at this point pass to our synoptical study of the major theses which Schutz advances in his first four chapters.

[III]   Synopsis of Schutz's Fundamental Theses [6]

Schutz's book is divided into five chapters. Chapter 1 is concerned with the sociological background of the basic problems which he intends to attack. The question as first stated is the nature of sociology and the methodology which is appropriate to that science. Schutz sketches briefly the ways of putting the question and the various answers offered in German sociology up to the time of Max Weber. He then analyzes critically the fundamental concepts in the methodological introduction to Weber's *Wirtschaft und Gesellschaft*. He accepts Weber's axiom that the social sciences must be value-free. He likewise accepts Weber's methodological individualism and his contention that social phenomena are properly to be understood in terms of ideal types. And he not only accepts but emphasizes Weber's view that the social sciences are concerned essentially with *social action*, the concept "social" being defined in terms of a relationship between the behavior of two or more people, and the concept "action" being defined as behavior to which a subjective meaning is attached. A social action is, therefore, an action which is oriented toward the past, present, or future behavior of another person or persons. The specific mode of orientation is its subjective meaning; revenge is an example. But Schutz's agreement with Weber's fundamental point of view renders all the more acute his dissatisfaction with what he regards as systematic ambiguities in the latter's basic concepts. It is not our purpose here to give a detailed outline of Schutz's critique of Weber. Rather the whole book has to be read, and the sections dealing directly with Weber analyzed closely, before the full force of the argument is appreciated. Suffice it to say that, while agreeing with Weber that it is the essential function of social science to be *interpretive*, that is, to understand the subjective meaning of social action, Schutz finds that Weber has failed to state clearly the essential characteristics of understanding (*Verstehen*), of subjective meaning (*gemeinter Sinn*), or of action (*Handeln*). This imprecision is so considerable in Schutz's

6. This section is indebted in both inspiration and detail to the justly famous abstract, "A New Approach to the Methodology of the Social Sciences," by Alfred Stonier and Karl Bode, *Economica*, IV (1937), 406–23. It differs, however, in approach and diverges radically on some points of terminology.

opinion as to weaken seriously the foundations of interpretive sociology. For the concept of subjective meaning is so ambiguously stated that it is not at all clear whether the point of view sought is that of the *actor* himself, or that of the anonymous sociological *observer*. Inasmuch as the hallmark of science is objectivity, how can social science pursue subjective meaning? By being objective about that which is by its nature subjective? But the very attempt to do this involves a host of problems. First there is the insistence of Weber that objectivity in the social sciences is made possible only through the use of ideal types. But how can ideal-typical concepts penetrate to the subjective meaning of individuals? How can the concept "entrepreneur" lead us to understand what an eighteenth-century Boston merchant had in mind when he purchased a ship? And does it help the situation any to add the adjective "Calvinist" before the noun "entrepreneur"? And then there is the question of the unit which is to be understood, namely, the action. When does the action begin and when does it end? In short, what is its span? Can we discover this just by observing a person's physical motions, as he turns a doorknob, for instance? Is he "opening the door"? But he might be a locksmith "checking the latch." Or an actor practicing for a part in a play. Or a man simply exercising his wrist. How long do we have to wait before we can say that we have "observed his action"? Perhaps we had better ask the man what he is doing with the knob. He might even answer that he didn't know he was turning it. And so, unless we had asked him, we should never have known that this was no true action at all but a piece of absent-minded behavior. Is it possible that we cannot even define a specimen object-unit of a science of action without thus abandoning the role of observer and becoming a participant in a social relationship? What is gained and what is lost by such a change of role? If we become participants, do we lose our objectivity? If we remain mere observers, do we lose the very object of our science, namely, the subjective meaning of the action? Is there any way out of this dilemma? What is the epistemological status of the *interview*? In order to understand the subjective meaning of an action, must we understand its motive? But by "motive" do we mean the balance of environmental and hereditary factors behind the action, or do we mean the plan which the agent had in mind at the time of the action? In what sense is an individual "free"? Is his action somehow determined by his ideal type, or is there a sense in which it can be "type-transcendent"?

All these questions Schutz puts to the basic concepts of interpretive sociology, and he finds that they fail to supply any coherent account of themselves. It is obviously an external and mechanical account of action which regards the latter as a mere "course of behavior" to which "subjective meaning" is somehow "attached." Since we cannot even trace the temporal outline of the external behavior without already presupposing its meaning, it is clear that a *thoroughgoing philosophical investigation of the nature of action is essential to a coherent statement of the proper subject matter and methodology of the social sciences.*

Now, since Schutz agrees with Weber that action is defined through *meaning,* the first positive step of his theory is to formulate a concept of meaning. At this stage he relies heavily upon Husserl. His originality becomes apparent at the next stage, when he proceeds to formulate the more specific concept of "the meaning of an action."

Drawing not only upon Husserl but also very heavily upon Bergson, Schutz turns in Chapter 2 to the "stream of consciousness" in his quest for the origin of meaning. "Here and here only," he says, "in the deepest stratum of experience that is accessible to reflection, is to be found the ultimate source of the phenomena of meaning [*Sinn*] and understanding [*Verstehen*]." What is primordially given to consciousness is an unbroken stream of lived experiences (*Erlebnisse*)—heterogeneous qualities without boundaries or contours which wax, wane, and pass gradually into one another. The contents of this stream of consciousness have no meaning in themselves. However, they may be divided into passive and active. An example of a passive experience would be a sensation of red. An example of an active lived experience would be a turning of the attention to the sensation of red or perhaps a recognition of it as something experienced before. Schutz, following Husserl, uses the term "behavior" (*Verhalten*) for such "spontaneous" experiences. He also constantly refers to them as "Acts" (*Akte*), which we always render in capitalized form.

All such lived experiences, whether passive or active, are lacking in meaning and discrete identity. At the time they are actually lived through, they are not given to us as separate and distinct entities. However, once they have receded a slight distance into the past, that is, once they have "elapsed," we may turn around and bring to bear upon them one of the aforementioned Acts of reflection, recognition, identification, and so forth. Once it has been caught in the "cone of light" emanating from the Ego, an experience is "lifted out" of the stream of duration and becomes clear and distinct, a discrete entity. It is at this moment and by virtue of the Act of turning-toward (*Zuwendung*) that the experience acquires meaning (*Sinn*). The process of endowing with meaning may be compared to the making of a microscopic slide. Just as something is lost to the specimen in the making of the slide, namely, life itself, so, in the taking-on of meaning, the experience loses something of its living, duration-immersed concreteness. And it is important to realize that not only passive but also active experiences may be thus focused upon and frozen in the gaze of attention. Thus, from an original duality within the stream of consciousness, namely, the duality between passive and active experiences, Schutz sees another duality rising, that between experiences which are meaningful or meaning-bearing and those which are without meaning.

To none of its experiences while they are actually occurring may the Ego ascribe meaning. There are, indeed, some experiences, those closest to the core of one's personality, to which one may never ascribe meaning. But to most experiences meaning may be ascribed *in retrospect*. Happily, however, we may also ascribe meaning *prospectively* to future experiences. We cannot reproduce here Schutz's highly complex treatment of the problem of how we anticipate future experience. However, this looking-forward into the future is essential to the concept of action (*Handeln*). Action is behavior directed toward the realization of a *determinate* future goal. But, as we have seen, that which is pictured as determinate, that is, as complete and well-defined, must possess an element of *pastness*. The goal of the action must, then, possess both an element of futurity and an element of pastness. Schutz borrows a term from grammar in order to express this complex situation. He says that we picture the goal of the action "in the future perfect tense" (*modo futuri exacti*). That is, the goal, or completed action, is pictured as over and done with even while it is still anticipated. An example would be leaving the house in order to visit a friend. The visit to the friend is pictured as over and done with even while I am on my way to his house. The visit thus pictured Schutz calls the "act" (*Handlung*), which we render throughout without capitalization. Another duality thus appears: that between the action in progress and the completed act. Borrowing a term from Heidegger, Schutz speaks of the completed act thus pictured in the future perfect tense as the project (*Entwurf*) of the action. "What is projected," Schutz says, "is the act which is the goal of the action and which is brought into being by the action."

The project is thus a complex of meaning or context of meaning (*Sinnzusammenhang*) within which any one phase of the ongoing action finds its significance. It is convenient to consider the purpose of the whole action apart from any given phase. The former is called the "in-order-to motive" (*Um-zu-Motiv*) of the action. Schutz sharply distinguishes this, in turn, from the "because-motive" (*Weil-Motiv*), an event lying in my past which led me to project this particular act. The because-motive is only grasped retrospectively; whereas my completed act now really lies in the past, its because-motive is seen as lying still further back in the past, or, as Schutz puts it, it is pictured in the pluperfect tense (*modo plusquamperfecti*). For instance, if I open my umbrella as it begins to rain, my because-motive is the perception of the rain added to my knowledge about the effect of rain on clothing, and so forth. The in-order-to motive, on the other hand, is "to keep dry." Schutz's whole treatment of the distinction between the two kinds of motives is particularly interesting in view of the contemporary discussion of the nature of human action [7] in connection with the problem of determinism and free will.

In Chapter 3 Schutz passes to the problem of intersubjective understanding. He emphasizes that he does not intend to give a solution to the crucial philosophical problem of how we know there are other minds. This is the *transcendental problem of intersubjectivity*. Rather Schutz is concerned with the way in which we know other people's lived experiences once we have postulated and taken for granted the *general thesis of the alter ego*. We are concerned here with the mode of understanding of that which is other or alien to us (*Fremdverstehen*). Now it is important to note here that Schutz makes the sharpest distinction between *the genuine understanding of the other person* and the abstract conceptualization of his actions or thoughts as being of such and such a type. This distinction surely corresponds to a distinction we all make in everyday life. The caricature of the social worker in the famous song in *West Side Story* is a vivid picture of the understanding of human beings that is limited to this second kind of approach. Merely to understand the general kind of action in which another is engaging is merely to order one's own experiences into categories, or what Schutz calls "self-elucidation" (*Selbstauslegung*). On the other hand, the genuine understanding of the other person is a more concrete thing. It is a type of *perception*. This does not mean that we can directly intuit another person's subjective experiences. What it does mean is that we can intentionally grasp those experiences because we assume that his facial expressions and his gestures are a "field of expression" for his inner life. This is what Schutz calls the "bodily presence" or "corporeal givenness" of the partner. The crucial factor here is *simultaneity*. We sense that the other person's stream of consciousness is flowing along a track that is temporally parallel with our own. The two duration-flows are synchronized, and, in social interaction, they can become interlocked. This is the essence of the interpersonal relationship, and it is basic to our knowledge of other people. Of course, we are at a certain disadvantage in our knowledge

---

7. Cf. Lewis W. Beck, *op. cit.* For a general treatment from the point of view of analytic philosophy see Stuart Hampshire, *Thought and Action* (New York, 1960).

of other people's inner life. In a certain sense this knowledge is indirect and discontinuous. But Schutz makes the interesting observation that there is another sense in which we can know other people better than we can know ourselves. For we can "watch" other people's subjective experiences as they actually occur, whereas we have to wait for our own to elapse in order to peer at them as they recede into the past. No man can see himself in action, any more than he can know the "style" of his own personality.

Fremdverstehen, then, is the true comprehension of *subjective meaning*. As we saw, it must be carefully distinguished from the comprehension of objective meaning. All cultural objects or "products" can be interpreted objectively or subjectively. If someone utters, for instance, the judgment $2 + 2 = 4$, this judgment is interesting both from the point of view of its logical "content," which is a timeless mathematical proposition, and from the point of view of why this particular person made this particular statement at this particular time. Only by understanding the motives of the speaker do we grasp his subjective meaning.

The distinction between objective and subjective meaning has definite implications for the methodology of the cultural sciences. The meaning-content of a cultural product is independent of its creator. It can be regarded as something that can be created or enacted repeatedly by anyone or everyone. This is what Schutz, following Husserl, calls *"the ideality of the 'I-can-do-it-again.'"* The creator of such a product is conceived as an anonymous "one." The concepts and laws of pure economics have this anonymous character. On the other hand, the concepts of economic history, such as "Western capitalism" or "the caste system," can only be understood in terms of the motives of particular individuals or groups. The former concepts have universal validity; the latter do not. In advancing this thesis, Schutz is trying to take a mediating position between the polemically opposed outlooks of Max Weber and Ludwig von Mises. What emerges so far is that all of the cultural sciences are concerned with meaningful products and that some of them understand these products in a more objective and anonymous way than others. Whether any of the cultural sciences actually grasp subjective meaning in itself is another question.

This brings us to the crucial fourth chapter, which gives us in the true sense a *phenomenology of the social world*. It is set forth only in outline, of course, for Schutz was in this book merely laying the foundations for the more detailed investigations which he hoped that he or others would later carry out.

As Weber had showed, the social world is properly understood in terms of the concept "social action," which Schutz now defines as an action whose in-order-to motive contains some reference to another's stream of consciousness. The motive of the action may be merely to observe or understand the other. Or it may be to affect the other. Communication is an example of the latter kind of social action. If the situation is such that there exists an objective probability of a reciprocal intentional transaction or "cross-reference," then a *social relationship* exists. There are three basic types of social relationship: a relationship in which the two partners merely observe each other, a relationship in which the first partner affects the second while the latter merely observes the first, and a relationship in which the two partners affect each other. However, there is a fourth case, in which one person observes the other without trying to affect him in any way and in which the second person is unaware of the first. This is *not* a social relationship but is *social observation* in the strict sense.

We now come to the crux of Schutz's theoretical contribution. He believes that our social experience makes up a vast world (*soziale Welt*) that is constituted in an immensely complicated network of dimensions, relations, and modes of knowledge. First of all, he distinguishes between directly experienced social reality and a social reality lying beyond the horizon of direct experience. Directly experienced social reality (*Umwelt*) consists of my immediate consociates, whom I am directly perceiving in the sense already noted. Those whom I am not directly perceiving fall into three classes. First comes the world of my contemporaries (*Mitwelt*), then the world of my predecessors (*Vorwelt*), and finally the world of my successors (*Folgewelt*). My contemporaries are distinguished from the other two by the fact that it is in principle possible for them to become my consociates.

The modes of our relatedness to others differ greatly according to the social realms which the latter "inhabit." For instance, toward a consociate I have what Schutz calls a "Thou-orientation" (*Dueinstellung*). If this is reciprocated, a *face-to-face* situation results, and we have a "We-relationship" (*Wirbeziehung*). Within the world of directly experienced social reality there is a unique connection between observation and social relationships. First of all, of course, I can observe my consociates in *simultaneity*, and this gives me an advantage over anyone who is conducting merely indirect observations upon them. For instance, being present while a friend talks is very different from reading his letter. I not only can grasp the objective meaning of his words, but I can hear the tone of his voice and watch his gestures and other bodily movements. But the difference is not merely that these concrete symptoms are present to me. There is an additional advantage: I can look into his eyes and ask him what he means. In other words, I can transform direct social observation into a direct social relationship.

My knowledge of my contemporaries, predecessors, and successors is, on the other hand, indirect. As for my contemporaries, they coexist with me in objective time, to be sure, but I must picture them in a *quasi-simultaneity* rather than perceive them in a real simultaneity. I do not see their actual bodily movements but only their products, such as letters, etc. I cannot comprehend them with a direct grasp (*in Selbsthabe*) but at a distance and by means of a peculiar inferential process. We interpret the products as being the result of such and such an inner process, such and such an emotion, such and such an in-order-to motive, and we interpret the contemporaries in question as being persons of such and such a *type*. In short, when interpreting the behavior of our contemporaries, we are resorting to *ideal types*, either course-of-action types or personal types. The use of ideal types does not, then, enter at the stage when we pass from prescientific to scientific observation. It enters rather when we pass from direct to indirect social experience.

My contemporaries are therefore something less than fully concrete persons for me. Their degree of concreteness may vary. My friend, whom I saw last week and who has just sent me a letter, is almost as concrete to me as if he were present in person. But the postal clerk who will cancel my letter and whose existence I merely assume when I drop the letter in the box is almost completely "anonymous." With a contemporary we can have only a relationship at a distance, a *They-relationship*,[8] based on a corresponding relatively abstract They-orientation, which is in turn made possible by the use of ideal types.

Ideal types can be arranged on a scale of increasing anonymity. There is, for instance, my absent friend, his brother whom he has described to me, the professor whose books I have read, the postal clerk, the Canadian Parliament, abstract entities like Canada itself, the rules of English grammar, or the basic principles of jurisprudence. As the types get more and more abstract, we are, of course, getting further and further away from the actual subjective meaning-complexes or contexts of individuals. We are making more and more use of objective contexts of meaning. But these refer by their very nature to subjective meaning-contexts of greater or lesser anonymity. We have at last arrived at the answer to the crucial question "What is social science?" Social science, Schutz replies, is an objective context of meaning constructed out of and referring to subjective contexts of meaning. The fundamental tool of social science is, as Weber claimed,

8. Schutz's term is *Ihrbeziehung*, *Ihr* being a formal second-person pronoun in German as opposed to the informal *Du*. We have, following Luckmann, rendered the "distancing" involved by shifting to the third person, "They."

the ideal type. Although the ideal type is present in all cases of indirect understanding of another person, it has a special function in social science. It must be fitted into a whole hierarchy of other objective concepts making up the total complex of scientific knowledge.

The reader now has at his disposal an outline of the conceptual apparatus which Schutz in his final chapter brings to bear on "the basic problems of interpretive sociology." The outline, of course, is merely a guide and can only be understood by a careful reading of the text. However, once the conceptual apparatus itself is grasped, Schutz's proposals for clearing up the ambivalences lying at the root of Max Weber's concepts will be seen to follow quite easily and to be well worth the exhaustive phenomenological analysis that has gone before. The reader will then have at his disposal what is truly a phenomenological prolegomenon to the social sciences.

GEORGE WALSH

Geneva, New York
January, 1967

Preface

THE PRESENT STUDY IS BASED on an intensive concern of many years' duration with the theoretical writings of Max Weber. During this time I became convinced that while Weber's approach was correct and that he had determined conclusively the proper starting point of the philosophy of the social sciences, nevertheless his analyses did not go deeply enough to lay the foundations on which alone many important problems of the human sciences could be solved. Above all, Weber's central concept of subjective meaning calls for thoroughgoing analysis. As Weber left this concept, it was little more than a heading for a number of important problems which he did not examine in detail, even though they were hardly foreign to him. Almost all these problems are closely related to the phenomenon of the lived experience of time (or internal time-sense), which can be studied only by the most rigorous philosophical reflection. Only when we have grasped the nature of the internal time-consciousness can we attack the complicated structure of the concepts of the human sciences. Among these concepts are those of the interpretation of one's own and others' experiences, meaning-establishment and meaning-interpretation, symbol and symptom, motive and project, meaning-adequacy and causal adequacy, and, above all, the nature of ideal-typical concept formation, upon which is based the very attitude of the social sciences toward their subject matter. All this must be accompanied by very detailed and laborious investigations, which are, however, unavoidable if one is to become clear about the basic theme and methodology of the social sciences. Only such a clarification of the hitherto obscure nature of the ---- phenomenon of social being can guarantee a precise grasp of scientific method. Only a philosophically founded theory of method can exorcise the pseudo-problems which today hinder research in the social sciences, and especially in sociology.

In this work I have attempted to trace the roots of the problems of the social sciences directly back to the fundamental facts of conscious life. Of central importance for this investigation are the studies of Bergson and Husserl on the internal time-sense. Only in the work of these two thinkers, especially in Husserl's transcendental phenomenology, has a sufficiently deep foundation been laid on the basis of which one could aspire to solve the problem of meaning.

Holding, as I do, these great philosophers in the deepest admiration, I am very mindful of the high degree to which the present study and all my thinking are dependent upon their work and that of Max Weber.

I wish to express my deep gratitude to Professor Tomoo Otaka of the University of Keijo, Japan, for the deep understanding which he has brought to my thought and for his active assistance, without which the appearance of this work in these difficult times would have been indeed questionable. I also wish to thank Dozent Felix Kaufmann (Vienna) who shared and furthered these studies in their incipient stages, always with the most indefatigable interest, who rendered me the laborious service of reading the proof sheets, and, finally, who was a constant source of stimulation.

ALFRED SCHUTZ

Vienna
March, 1932

Preface to the Second German Edition

TWENTY-SEVEN YEARS after the appearance of the first edition, which meanwhile had long since been out of print, the author decided to issue a second edition. The determining factor in this decision was the recognition of the fact that after almost three decades the book still had a significance that transcended the merely historical. Rather, it had become clear that its methods and ideas could yet further enrich contemporary research in the social sciences.

The author intended to bring the book up to date by a comprehensive presentation of developments since the first edition. His unexpected death made the realization of this aim impossible. The publisher, therefore, submits to the public an unaltered second edition in the conviction that it will shed important light upon the basic problems faced by sociology today.

ILSE SCHUTZ

New York
October, 1959

Glossary

(Note distinction between capitalized and lower-case English terms.)

Akt	Act
Anzeichen	indication
Aufbau	construction
Chance	probability
Ego	ego
Einstellungsbeziehung	orientation relationship
Entwurf	project
Erfahrung	experience
Erfahrungsvorrat	stock of knowledge (at hand)
Erfahrungszusammenhang	context of experience
Erlebnis	lived experience, subjective experience
Erzeugnis	product
Folgewelt	world of successors
Fremdeinstellung	Other-orientation
Fremdverstehen	intersubjective understanding
Fremdwirken	affecting-the-Other
Gegenstand (and derivatives)	object (and derivatives)
Gegenständlichkeit	objectivity
Geisteswissenschaften	cultural sciences
Gleichzeitigkeit	simultaneity
Handeln	action
Handlung	act
Ich	Ego
Ihrbeziehung	They-relationship (lit., You-relationship)
Kausaladäquanz	causal adequacy

Kundgeben	communication
Mitwelt	world of (mere) contemporaries
natürliche Anschauung	natural intuition or natural perception
Naturwissenschaften	natural sciences
Objekt (and derivatives)	Object
Objektivation	Objectivation
Schema	scheme
Selbstauslegung	self-explication
Selbsthabe	immediate grasp or apprehension of the thing itself
Sinn	meaning (in strict Husserlian terminology: sense)
Sinnadäquanz	meaning-adequacy
Sinndeutung	meaning-interpretation
Sinngebend	meaning-endowing
Sinnhaft	meaningful
Sinnsetzung	meaning-establishment
Sinnzusammenhang	meaning-context
soziale Beziehung	social relationship
soziale Umwelt	world of directly experienced social reality, or world of consociates
Sozialwelt	social world
Um-zu-Motiv	in-order-to motive
umweltliche Beobachtung	direct social observation
umweltliche Situation	face-to-face situation
umweltliche soziale Beziehung	face-to-face relationship
Verhalten	behavior (in Schutz's later English writings: conduct)
Verstehen	understanding
verstehen	to understand
verstehende Soziologie	interpretive sociology
Vorgegebenheit	pregivenness
Vorwelt	world of predecessors
Weil-Motiv	because-motive
Wirbeziehung	We-relationship
Wirkensbeziehung	social interaction
Zeichen	sign
Zeugnis	evidence

The Phenomenology
of the Social World

1 / The Statement of Our Problem: Max Weber's Basic Methodological Concepts

1. Preliminary Survey of the Problem

ONE OF THE MOST REMARKABLE phenomena of the past fifty years of German intellectual history has been the controversy over the scientific character of sociology. The systematic study of the relationship of the individual to society has, from its very beginning, been marked by acrimonious contention over both its proper procedure and its goal. The debate has not been confined, as in other fields, to questions of the truth of this or that theory or the correctness of this or that method. Rather, the whole subject matter of the social sciences as something unique in its own right and having prior existence in prescientific experience has itself been put in question. In one camp, for instance, we find social phenomena treated exactly as if they were natural phenomena, that is, as causally determined physical events. In another camp, however, we find the sharpest contrast drawn between the two classes of phenomena. Social phenomena are here treated as belonging to a world of objective mind,[1] a world which is, to be sure, intelligible, but not under the form of scientific laws. Often enough the attitude of the social scientist toward his subject matter is determined by his own presuppositions, metaphysical, ethical, or political, or by value judgments of whatever kind. These presuppositions may be tacitly assumed or openly stated. As he pursues his research, he finds himself entangled in problems whose solution seems necessary if his work is to have any sense at all. Is social science concerned with the very being of man or only with his different modes of social behavior?

1. [The concept of objective mind (*objektiver Geist*) here referred to is that of Dilthey. It means the totality of the cultural medium considered as having its own inner form and structure. It is the proper object of the *Geisteswissenschaften*, the human or cultural sciences. For a discussion of this concept see the Introduction.]

Is society prior to the individual, so that apart from the social whole the individual does not exist at all? Or should we put it quite the other way and say that the individual alone exists and that social organizations, including society itself, are mere abstractions—"functions" of the behavior of separate individuals? Does man's social being determine his consciousness, or does his consciousness determine his social being? Can the history of man and his culture be reduced to laws such as those of economics? Or, on the contrary, can we not say that so-called economic and sociological "laws" merely express the historical perspectives of the age in which they were formulated? Faced with all these dilemmas, it is hardly surprising that many social scientists try to deal with them prematurely by naïve pseudo-solutions generated from subjective biases which may be temperamental, political, or at best metaphysical.

Now, a priori solutions of this nature are hardly in accord with the basic principle of scientific research, the principle which calls upon us simply to understand and describe the facts before us. To see the world of social facts with an unbiased eye, to classify these facts under concepts in an honest and logical way, and to subject to exact analysis the material thus obtained—this must be the guiding aim of every piece of social research worthy of the name of science.

The acceptance of this aim led to a demand for a theory of the origin of human society. It is the incontestable merit of Simmel that he saw this problem and attempted its solution. To be sure, Simmel's methodology is in many ways confused and unsystematic. As a result, he continually projects into the specific phenomena he is investigating his own theoretical preconceptions about the nature of society. In his specialized studies Simmel has made lasting and valuable contributions, although very few of his basic concepts have survived critical scrutiny, not even his key concept of reciprocal effect (*Wechselwirkung*).[2] However, Simmel's underlying idea has proven fruitful and is still utilized. This is the notion that all concrete social phenomena should be traced back to the modes of individual behavior and that the particular social form of such modes should be understood through detailed description.[3]

2. [Simmel conceives of the drives of individuals—such as hunger and love—as the *content* of social life. On the other hand, reciprocal effects such as competition, domination, cooperation, and solidarity are the *actualizing forms* of social life. See note 3.]

3. "Everything present in the individuals (who are the immediate concrete data of all historical reality) in the form of drive, interest, purpose, inclination, psychic state, movement—everything that is present in them in such a way as to engender or mediate effects upon others or to receive such effects, I designate as the *content*, as the material, as it were, of sociation (*Vergesellschaftung*). . . .

Max Weber's "interpretive sociology" (*verstehende Soziologie*) takes its departure from the same basic idea. This is not to question the originality of Weber's enormous contribution or even to assert his dependence on Simmel. On the contrary, Weber's work, drawing together as it does so many of the currents of his age, is throughout the unique product of an astonishing genius. It was he who gave present-day German sociology its direction insofar as it is a science rather than an ideology, and it was he who gave it the tools it needed for its task. The most important works of contemporary German sociology, for instance those of Scheler, Wiese, Freyer, and Sander, would have been inconceivable had not Weber first laid the foundation.

Now in what does Max Weber's great achievement consist? In the first place, he was one of the first to proclaim that the social sciences must abstain from value judgments. He took up the battle against those political and moral ideologies which all too easily influence the judgment of the social scientist, whether this influence is conscious or not. In the same vein, he defined the task of sociology not as metaphysical speculation but as the simple and accurate description of life in society. "For him sociology is no longer the philosophy of human existence. It is the particular science of human behavior and its consequences." [4]

The logical structure of his sociology [5] corresponds to this basic position. Starting from the concepts of social action and social relationship (*soziale Beziehung*), he derives by means of ever new descriptions and typifications the two categories of "communal relationship" (*Vergemeinschaftung*) and "associative relationship" (*Vergesellschaf-*

Sociation is thus the form (realized in innumerable different ways) in which the individuals grow together into units that satisfy their interests" (Simmel, *Soziologie*, 2d ed. [Munich, 1922]) [English translation by Kurt H. Wolff, *The Sociology of Georg Simmel* (Glencoe, Ill., 1950). Two other chapters of Simmel's work, translated by Albion W. Small, appeared in the *American Journal of Sociology*, XV (1909), 289–320; XVI (1910), 372–91. In the present connection, cf. Simmel (trans. Small), "The Problem of Sociology," *American Journal of Sociology*, XV (1909), 296–97. A more literal if more awkward translation of *Vergesellschaftung* is "societalization." Cf. Theodore Abel, *Systematic Sociology in Germany* (New York, 1929).]

4. Karl Jaspers, *Die geistige Situation der Zeit* (Berlin and Leipzig, 1931), p. 137. [E.T., *Man in the Modern Age*, by Eden and Cedar Paul (London, 1951), p. 151.]

5. Of the works of Max Weber, those which are of chief importance for our purposes are the main work, *Wirtschaft und Gesellschaft*, 1st ed. (Tübingen, 1922), which has unfortunately remained unfinished, and the works contained in the volume *Gesammelte Aufsätze zur Wissenschaftslehre* (Tübingen, 1922). [Part I of Weber's *Wirtschaft und Gesellschaft*, i.e., Vol. I to p. 180, has been translated by A. M. Henderson and Talcott Parsons under the title *The Theory of Social and Economic Organization* (Glencoe, Ill., 1957). This translation (referred to simply as "E.T.") will be used to render Schutz's quotations from Weber.]

tung).[6] Then, by introducing the concept of order, he deduces the particular types of corporate groups and compulsory associations.[7] The way in which Weber makes use of this logical apparatus in order to deal with economy, government, law, and religion as social phenomena cannot be described here in detail. What concerns us is that Weber reduces all kinds of social relationships and structures, all cultural objectifications, all realms of objective mind, to the most elementary forms of individual behavior. To be sure, all the complex phenomena of the social world retain their meaning, but this meaning is precisely that which the individuals involved attach to their own acts. The action of the individual and its intended meaning alone are subject to interpretive understanding. Further, it is only by such understanding of individual action that social science can gain access to the meaning of each social relationship and structure, constituted as these are, in the last analysis, by the action of the individual in the social world.

Never before had the project of reducing the "world of objective mind" to the behavior of individuals been so radically carried out as it was in Max Weber's initial statement of the goal of interpretive sociology. This science is to study social behavior by interpreting its subjective meaning as found in the intentions of individuals. The aim, then, is to interpret the actions of individuals in the social world and the ways in which individuals give meaning to social phenomena. But to attain this aim, it does not suffice either to observe the behavior of a single individual or to collect statistics about the behavior of groups of individuals, as a crude empiricism would have us believe. Rather, the special aim of sociology demands a special method in order to select

6. ["A social relationship will be called *'communal'* if and so far as the orientation of social action . . . is based on a subjective feeling of the parties, whether affectual or traditional, that they belong together. A social relationship will, on the other hand, be called *'associative'* if and so far as the orientation of social action within it rests on a rationally motivated adjustment of interests . . . whether the basis of rational judgment be absolute values or reasons of expediency. It is especially common, though by no means inevitable, for the associative type of relationship to rest on a rational agreement by mutual consent. . . . (Examples of associative relationships) are (a) rational free market exchange, (b) the voluntary association based on self interest, (c) the voluntary association motivated by an adherence to a set of common absolute values, for example the rational sect. (Examples of communal relationships) are a religious brotherhood, an erotic relationship, a relation of personal loyalty, a national community, the esprit de corps of a military unit" (Weber, *Wirtschaft und Gesellschaft*, I, 21–22; E.T., pp. 136–37).]

7. ["A 'voluntary association' (*Verein*) is a corporate group (*Verband*) originating in a voluntary agreement, and in which the established order claims authority over the members only by virtue of a personal act of adherence.

"A 'compulsory association' (*Anstalt*) is a corporate group the established order of which has, within a given specific sphere of activity, been successfully imposed on every individual who conforms with certain specific criteria . . . ; the type case of a compulsory association is the state . . ." (*ibid.*; E.T., p. 151).]

the materials relevant to the peculiar questions it raises. This selection is made possible through the formulation of certain theoretical constructs known as "ideal types." These ideal types are by no means the same thing as statistical averages, for they are selected according to the kind of question being asked at the time, and they are constructed in accordance with the methodological demands of these questions. Neither, however, are the ideal types empty phantoms or mere products of phantasy, for they must be verified by the concrete historical material which comprises the data of the social scientist. By this method of constructing and verifying ideal types, the meaning of particular social phenomena can be interpreted layer by layer as the subjectively intended meaning of human acts. In this way the structure of the social world can be disclosed as a structure of intelligible intentional meanings.

But, imposing as Weber's concept of "interpretive sociology" is, it is based on a series of tacit presuppositions. It is a matter of urgent necessity to identify these presuppositions and to state them clearly, for only a radical analysis of the genuine and basic elements of social action can provide a reliable foundation for the future progress of the social sciences. It was only when this necessity became clear to him, and then with apparent reluctance, that Max Weber concerned himself with the theoretical foundations of sociology, since he greatly preferred to work with concrete problems. He was interested in epistemological problems only insofar as they bore directly on specialized research or provided tools for its pursuit. Once these tools were at his disposal, he lost interest in the more fundamental problems.[8] As significant as were Weber's contributions to methodology, as incorruptible as was his vision of the task of concept formation in the social sciences, as admirable as was his philosophical instinct for the correct critical position on epistemological questions—just as little did the thorough undergirding of his results by a secure over-all philosophical point of view concern him. In fact, he had little interest at all in the clarification of the philosophical presuppositions of even his own primary concepts.

It is at this point that the theoretical limitations of Weber become evident. He breaks off his analysis of the social world when he arrives at what he assumes to be the basic and irreducible elements of social phenomena. But he is wrong in this assumption. His concept of the meaningful act of the individual—the key idea of interpretive sociology—by no means defines a primitive, as he thinks it does. It is, on the contrary, a mere label for a highly complex and ramified area that

8. Cf. Marianne Weber, *Max Weber, ein Lebensbild* (Tübingen, 1926), e.g., p. 322. [2d ed., Heidelberg, 1950.]

calls for much further study. Weber makes no distinction between the *action*, considered as something in progress, and the completed *act*, between the meaning of the producer of a cultural object and the meaning of the object produced, between the meaning of my own action and the meaning of another's action, between my own experience and that of someone else, between my self-understanding and my understanding of another person. He does not ask how an actor's meaning is constituted or what modifications this meaning undergoes for his partners in the social world or for a nonparticipating observer. He does not try to identify the unique and fundamental relation existing between the self and the other self, that relation whose clarification is essential to a precise understanding of what it is to know another person. To be sure, Weber distinguishes between the subjectively intended meaning of an action and its objectively knowable meaning. But he recognizes no further distinctions along this line and pays as little attention to the ways in which an interpreter modifies meaning as he does to the conceptual perspectives in which our fellow human beings are given to us. But, as a matter of fact, there are radical differences in the meaning-structure of my own behavior, the behavior of my consociates,[9] which I immediately experience, and the behavior of those who are merely my *contemporaries* or even my *predecessors*, which is known to me quite indirectly.[10] Far from being homogeneous, the social world is given to us in a complex system of perspectives: my partner and I, for instance, have intimate and rich experience of each other as we talk together, whereas we both appear to a detached observer in an aura of "flatness" and "anonymity." The individual takes these perspectival foreshortenings into account in his acts of meaning-establishment and meaning-interpretation,[11] and they are therefore of direct interest to the social sciences. Here we are not referring to differences between the personal standpoints from which different people look at the world but to the fundamental difference between my interpretation of my own subjective experiences (self-interpretation) and my interpretation of the subjective experiences of someone else. What is given to both the acting self and the interpreting observer is not only the single meaningful act and the context or configuration of meaning to which it belongs but the whole social world in

9. [*Umwelt* (my directly experienced fellow human beings with whom I have a face-to-face relation). Schutz used both "associates" and "consociates" when writing in English.]

10. [The *Mitwelt* (world of my contemporaries) and *Vorwelt* (world of my predecessors) are both known indirectly in contrast to the *Umwelt*. These concepts are developed systematically in Chapter 4.]

11. [See note 26, p. 13.]

fully differentiated perspectives. Only through this insight can one understand how the other self is grasped as an ideal type in the sense we have just discussed.

Without a doubt Weber saw all these problems, but he analyzed them only so far as seemed necessary for his own purposes. He naïvely took for granted the meaningful phenomena of the social world as a matter of *intersubjective agreement* in precisely the same way as we all in daily life assume the existence of a lawful external world conforming to the concepts of our understanding. For in the simple process of living we directly experience our acts as meaningful, and we all take for granted, as part of our natural outlook on the world, that others, too, directly experience their action as meaningful in quite the same sense as we would if we were in their place. We also believe that our interpretations of the meanings of the actions of others are, on the whole, correct. But when common-sense assumptions are uncritically admitted into the apparatus of a science, they have a way of taking their revenge. This may appear through equivocations creeping into its basic concepts and thereby working an adverse effect on research. Or it may occur through a failure to see that apparently diverse phenomena are really of the same type, a failure generated by not having penetrated beyond the appearances to the roots of the phenomena in question. If this danger hangs over every science, its threat to sociology is especially acute. For sociology's task is to make a scientific study of social phenomena. Now, if social phenomena are constituted in part by common-sense concepts, it is clear that it will not do for sociology to abstain from a scientific examination of these "self-evident" ideas.

It is at this point that the complicated relation of the social sciences to their subject matter becomes evident. The structure of the social world is meaningful, not only for those living in that world, but for its scientific interpreters as well. Living in the world, we live with others and for others, orienting our lives to them. In experiencing them as *others*, as contemporaries and fellow creatures, as predecessors and successors, by joining with them in common activity and work, influencing them and being influenced by them in turn—in doing all these things we *understand* the behavior of others and assume that they understand ours. In these acts of establishing or interpreting meanings there is built up for us in varying degrees of anonymity, in greater or lesser intimacy of experience, in manifold intersecting perspectives, the structural meaning of the social world, which is as much our world (strictly speaking, my world) as the world of the others.

Now, this same social world which we immediately experience as meaningful is also meaningful from the standpoint of the social scientist. But the context of meaning in which he interprets this world is that of systematizing scrutiny rather than that of living experience. His data, however, are the already constituted meanings of active participants in the social world. It is to these already meaningful data that his scientific concepts must ultimately refer: to the meaningful acts of individual men and women, to their everyday experience of one another, to their understanding of one another's meanings, and to their initiation of new meaningful behavior of their own. He will be concerned, furthermore, with the concepts people have of the meaning of their own and others' behavior and the concepts they have of the meaning of artifacts of all kinds. So we see that the data of the social sciences have, while still in the prescientific stage, those elements of meaning and intelligible structure which later appear in more or less explicit form with a claim to categorial validity in the interpretive science itself.

Human behavior is thus already meaningful when it takes place, and it is already intelligible at the level of daily life, although, to be sure, in a vague and confused way. The vagueness is cleared up in several stages, at each one of which there takes place a rearrangement of meaning-structure. This is done by taking the meaning-content already clarified and reinterpreting it in terms of its substratum in experience. Two examples of the many levels of meaning-interpretation are, at one end of the scale, the simple "having meaning" of daily life and, at the other, the highly sophisticated understanding of meaning exemplified in the ideal types of interpretive sociology.

It is a matter of urgent necessity at the present time that the theory of the social sciences should clarify the complex relations between the different dimensions of the social world, subject them to an analysis so radical that it goes to their very foundations, and fix the boundaries between their different strata. In fact, the controversy over the proper subject matter and methodology of the social sciences is the result of confusion over precisely these matters. For what is happening at the present time in sociology is that different schools of thought are each choosing one of these levels of interpretation as a starting point. Each school then develops a methodology suitable to that level and initiates a whole new line of research. The level or structure of meaning which was the starting point soon gets defined as the exclusive, or at least the essential, subject matter of sociology.

If one surveys the great systems of contemporary German sociology (following, for example, Freyer's able exposition [12]), one finds that

12. *Soziologie als Wirklichkeitswissenschaft* (Leipzig, 1930).

now the world of objective mind (Dilthey [13]), now the social whole as the content of mind (Spann [14]), or again the formal concept of reciprocal effect (Simmel [15]) is in turn defined as the proper theme of sociology. Now one starts with the fundamental concept of the total unity of culture and proceeds to study the formation of the historically given cultures (Alfred Weber [16]), now one starts with the social relations between individuals and proceeds to describe the nature of the group and social system based upon it (Wiese [17]), or one regards the entire social process as mass movement and develops out of that the idea of progress (Franz Oppenheimer [18]). Still again, one takes as the theme of sociology the development of ideologies during the course of history and the hardening of these ideologies into ways of life (Mannheim [19]). Over against these ventures, Max Scheler's [20] sociology of knowledge occupies a special place in that it represents but one small area of a system of material and cultural sociology planned on a grand scale by its author.

In all these cases certain meaning-structures within the social world are made objects of observation. They are, to be sure, inherently intelligible and as such open to scientific interpretation. But the fact is that each of these meaning-structures is further reducible into certain elements out of which it has been constituted. These elements are nothing else than processes of meaning-establishment and understanding occurring within individuals, processes of interpretation of the behavior of other people, and processes of self-interpretation. But these processes have not as yet received the attention they deserve. Beyond that, the problem of tracing back all the meaning-structures in question to a single basic element has hardly been acknowledged.

To be sure, a few writers have seen the latter problem. They have sought to define the proper subject matter of sociology precisely via a solution of these fundamental problems. This is the case with Litt,[21] who begins with the conscious experience of the individual and then proceeds through the Thou-relationship (*Du-Beziehung*) to the closed culture circle (*Kulturkreis*). The same is true of Freyer,[22] when he

13. "Einleitung in die Geisteswissenschaften: Der Aufbau der geschichtlichen Welt," *Gesammelte Schriften*, Vols. I and IX (Leipzig, 1923————).
14. *Gesellschaftslehre*, 1st ed. (Berlin, 1914); *Kategorienlehre* (Jena, 1924).
15. *Soziologie*.
16. *Ideen zur Staats- und Kultursoziologie* (Karlsruhe, 1917).
17. *Soziologie*, Vols. I and II (Munich, 1924). [English adaptation, *Systematic Sociology*, by Howard Becker (New York, 1932).]
18. *System der Soziologie*, Vol. I (Jena, 1922–23).
19. *Ideologie und Utopie* (Bonn, 1929). [E.T., *Ideology and Utopia*, by Lewis Wirth and Edward A. Shils (New York, 1936).]
20. *Die Wissensformen und die Gesellschaft* (Leipzig, 1926).
21. *Individuum und Gemeinschaft*, 3d ed. (Leipzig, 1926).
22. *Theorie des objektiven Geistes* (Leipzig, 1923).

seeks to derive the world of objective mind from the action of the individual. Above all we must mention in this connection Sander, who, in a profound and very important study,[23] takes as his point of departure Rehmke's [24] philosophy of the momentary consciousness of the solitary Ego and then tries first to deduce communal and associative relationships and finally the state, economy, and law, the deduction being accomplished via an analysis of striving and volition.

The works of these scholars, it is clear, leave unsolved the problem of meaning, a concept which seems to cover so many different things, whether it occurs in the literature of philosophy or that of the social sciences.[25] This concept calls for a radical analysis. To undertake such an analysis, however, requires extensive philosophical preparation. What must be covered includes the entire range of one's own and others' experiences. Moreover, even a superficial examination makes it clear that *the problem of meaning is a time problem*—not a problem of physical time, which is divisible and measurable, but a problem of historical time. The latter is always a passage of time, filled, to be sure, with physcial events yet having the nature of an "internal time conciousness," a consciousness of one's own duration. It is within this duration that the meaning of a person's experience is constituted for him as he lives through the experience. Here and here only, in the deepest stratum of experience that is accessible to reflection, is to be found the ultimate source of the phenomena of "meaning" (*Sinn*) and "understanding" (*Verstehen*). This stratum of experience can only be disclosed in strictly philosophical self-consciousness. Whoever, then, wishes to analyze the basic concepts of the social sciences must be willing to embark on a laborious philosophical journey, for the meaning-structure of the social world can only be deduced from the most primitive and general characteristics of conciousness. Happily, the investigation of these deep strata has now been opened up by the great philosophical discoveries of Bergson and Husserl. The former's philosophy of duration and the latter's transcendental phenomenology have

---

23. *Allgemeine Soziologie* (Jena, 1930).

24. [Cf. Johann Rehmke, *Philosophie als Grundwissenschaft,* 2d ed. (Leipzig, 1929).]

25. Cf. the nine different meanings of "meaning" found by H. Gomperz in examples taken from the more recent literature. Contrast with this the radically different concept of meaning in Heidegger (*Sein und Zeit* [Halle, 1927], esp. pp. 144 f., 147, 151 f. [E.T., *Being and Time*, by J. Macquarrie and E. Robinson (New York, 1962), pp. 183–84, 187–88, 193], or in the very important works of Paul Hofmann ("Das Verstehen von Sinn und seine Allgemeingültigkeit," *Jahrbuch für Charakterologie*, Vol. VI; "Metaphysik oder verstehende Sinn-Wissenschaft," Supplement to *Kant Studien*, 1929).

at last made possible the solution to the riddles of meaning-establishment and meaning-interpretation.[26]

The present study, taking its point of departure from the questions raised by Max Weber, draws freely upon the established conclusions of the two philosophers just mentioned. It seeks to determine the precise nature of the *phenomenon of meaning*, and to do this by an analysis of the constituting function. Only after we have a firm grasp of the concept of meaning as such will we be able to analyze step by step the meaning-structure of the social world. By following this procedure we shall be able to anchor the methodological apparatus of interpretive sociology at a far deeper point than Max Weber was able to do.

We are now clear about both our goal and the way we expect to reach it. The goal is the clarification of Max Weber's basic concept of interpretive sociology. We shall begin by showing the necessity of a further analysis of such concepts as "direct understanding and motivational understanding,"[27] "subjective and objective meaning," and "meaningful action and meaningful behavior." Taking off from this last pair of concepts, we shall deal, in Chapter 2, with the way meaning is constituted in the individual experience of the solitary Ego. In so doing we shall track meaning to its very point of origin in the inner time-consciousness, in the duration of the ego as it actually lives through its experience. Leaning heavily on Bergson's concept of duration and even more on Husserl's analysis of the constitution of subjective experience—starting out with the phenomena of retention and reproduction—we shall describe the nature of discrete experiences, of behavior arising from spontaneous activity, and of action in accordance with a preconceived project. Thus an initial concept of meaning will be laid down on which our further arguments will be based. Our next step will be to call attention to the phenomenon of attentional modification and to analyze the "meaning-context" (*Sinn-zusammenhang*) in the temporal process of synthetically executing a complex act. In this way we will show how the Ego constructs, out of its already lived-through stream of consciousness, a complex world of experience. At the same time we will explain the interpretive schemes within which the Ego organizes its experience in the process of self-

26. [*Sinnsetzung*, "meaning-establishment," is the Act whereby an individual *gives* meaning to a certain piece of behavior, a sign, or a cultural object. *Sinndeutung*, "meaning-interpretation," is the comprehension of what is *meant* by the individual establishing such meaning.]

27. ["Aktuelles und motivationsmässiges Verstehen," *Wirtschaft und Gesellschaft*, pp. 3–4 (E.T., pp. 94–95). If we see a man aiming a gun at someone else, we have a *direct understanding* of *what* he is doing; if we are then told that he is a member of a firing squad, we have acquired a *motivational understanding* of *why* he is doing it.]

interpretation.[28] The last part of Chapter 2 will be given over to the consideration of motivational context, the peculiar and complicated context of meaning that is involved in action.

In Chapter 3 we shall make the transition from self-understanding to the understanding of others. In so doing, we shall make the crucial distinction between understanding *our own experiences of the other person* and understanding *the other person's experiences*. We shall try to trace the relationships between these two types of understanding, paying special attention, as we do, to the theory of sign (*Zeichen*) and indication (*Anzeichen*), of product (*Erzeugnis*) and of evidence (*Zeugnis*). Then the concepts of subjective and objective meaning, which we have already shown in Chapter 1 to be the basic concepts of interpretive sociology, are given precise definition. This is accomplished through an analysis of meaning-establishment and meaning-interpretation. Next, in a brief digression, it will be shown that the corresponding double role of the cultural sciences as sciences of both subjective and objective meaning has its roots in the fundamental nature of human thought itself. Finally, in Chapter 4, we will give an analysis of our knowledge of other persons and, on this basis, will present a general theory of the structure of the social world and thus of the proper subject matter of the social sciences. Once more returning to Weber, we will submit to a thorough examination the concepts of social action and social relationship and determine the total complex of facts denoted by these two terms. It will then be made clear that these phenomena vary in their nature according to whether they occur in the worlds of associates, contemporaries, predecessors, or successors. The remainder of Chapter 4 will mainly be devoted to the changes undergone by meaning-establishment, meaning-interpretation, motivational context, and comprehension-perspective in the worlds or regions just mentioned. This forms the core of the book. The radical contrast we will there draw between the understanding of one's associates and contemporaries, on the one hand, and the construction of ideal types out of these, on the other, throws light on the difference between meaningful life in the social world and meaningful interpretation of that life through the social sciences. In Chapter 4, also, we will show the difference between sociology and history, the former being defined as the science of the world of contemporaries, and the latter as the science of the world of predecessors.

It is only after this achievement of insight into the unique structure of the world of contemporaries, which world is the sole object of

28. [*Sich selbst interpretierend.* Schutz uses the terms "self-interpretation" and "self-understanding" to mean the interpretation or understanding of one's own *experience*.]

the social sciences, that one can take up the methodological problems of the latter. This is especially true of the methodological problems of interpretive sociology. In Chapter 5 the basic concepts of interpretive sociology, especially those of meaning-adequacy and causal adequacy, of subjective and objective probability, and of the rational, are analyzed on the basis of the precise understanding of the method of ideal types already achieved. In this way the mutually confirmatory character of Weber's categories is demonstrated. Then at last we will be able to render the final verdict on the proper subject matter and methodology of interpretive sociology, which was the problem with which we began.

Thus we will have come full circle, and it is hardly accidental, rather quite in the nature of things, that we should end where we began, with the work of the man whose thought has penetrated most deeply into the structure of the social world—Max Weber.

2. Max Weber's Concept of Meaningful Action

ACCORDING TO WEBER, the task of interpretive sociology is to understand and interpret social action. Social action is that action which

> by virtue of the subjective meaning attached to it by the acting individual (or individuals), takes account of the behavior of others, and is thereby oriented in its course. . . . In "action" is included all human behavior when and in so far as the acting individual attaches a subjective meaning to it. Action in this sense may be either overt or purely inward or subjective; it may consist of positive intervention in a situation, or of deliberately refraining from such intervention, or passively acquiescing in the situation.[29]

These basic definitions of Weber's deserve the closest scrutiny.

Let us begin our critique with his definition of action. Action is meaningful for him who acts; this is what distinguishes action from mere behavior. So far, there is no necessary social reference. Every action directed toward an object is *ipso facto* meaningful. When I dip my pen in the ink or turn on my study lamp, I am acting meaningfully. We can now carry over this initial concept of meaning to the social sphere and apply it to social action, which, as we have seen, is action based on the behavior of others.

Let us briefly consider the differentia of social action. First of all, the latter, by its very subjective meaning, must be based on the behavior of another human being. But this means that we are now

29. Weber, *Wirtschaft und Gesellschaft*, p. 1 [E.T., p. 88].

dealing with a different level of meaning. Apart from any social involvement, the individual can already act meaningfully. But the moment he enters into social relationships, his actions take on a further meaning. They are now focused on another—a "Thou." At this new stage his action can only be understood as presupposing the existence of this "Thou." However, in Weber's view, it is not enough for an action to make contact with another person in order for it to qualify as a social action.

> Not every type of contact between human beings has a social charac-
> ter; this is rather confined to cases where the actor's behavior is meaning-
> fully oriented to that of others. For example, a mere collision of two
> cyclists may be compared to a natural event. On the other hand, their
> attempts to avoid hitting each other, or whatever insults, blows, or
> friendly discussion might follow the collision, would constitute social
> "action." [30]

Weber thus requires that the person who is engaged in social action be aware of much more than the mere existence of the other. He must be aware of and interpret the meaning of the other's behavior. But here we reach yet a third level of meaning. It is one thing to have the experience "That is a fellow human being" and quite another to have the experience "That person is behaving in such and such a way, and I am going to act accordingly." These two experiences belong, as a matter of fact, to two different realms of meaning. Weber brings this out when, in the course of explaining the concept of "the Other," he remarks:

> The others may be individual persons and may be known to the actor
> as such, or may constitute an indefinite plurality and may be entirely
> unknown as individuals. Thus "money" is a means of exchange which
> the actor accepts in payment because he orients his action to the expecta-
> tion that a large but unknown number of individuals he is personally
> unacquainted with will be ready to accept it in exchange on some future
> occasion.[31]

In this case the proposition "That is a fellow human being" is not grasped thematically [32] but is taken for granted [33] by the actor on the

30. *Ibid.*, p. 11 [E.T., p. 113].
31. *Ibid.*, p. 11 [E.T., p. 112].
32. ["To grasp something thematically" is to hold it at the center of one's attention. Schutz's usage is here the same as Husserl's. See Husserl's *Ideas*, § 122c, p. 344. (This work of Husserl's, *Ideen zu einer reinen Phänomenologie und phänomenologischen Philosophie*, 3d ed. [Halle, 1928], will be referred to hereafter as "*Ideen*." The English translation by W. R. Boyce Gibson [New York and London, 1931] will be referred to as "*Ideas*.")]
33. This term (*fraglos gegeben*), which we will define more precisely at a later point, was used by Scheler in connection with the development of the

basis of his social experience. Instead, the meaning that is developed thematically in this situation is the reference to the "behavior" of others, who here happen to be anonymous.

A fourth level of meaning is added with the postulate that social action must be *oriented* to the behavior of others. What is meant by this very unclear concept of "being oriented" (and it has been partly misunderstood by one critic [34]) is something whose clarification we must postpone to a later point in our study.[35] All these meaning-structures are *understood* by the social actor, which can only mean that he bases his action on his understanding of the behavior of others. And in Weber's view, the understanding, in turn, of this social behavior, that is, its "interpretation," is the task of sociology. This work of interpretation, however, takes place on yet another, a fifth, level of meaning.

The analysis so far accomplished is still left with three large areas of unsolved problems pertaining to the concept of social action. These are:

1. What does it mean to say that the actor attaches a meaning to his action?
2. In what manner is the other self given to the Ego as something meaningful?
3. In what manner does the Ego understand the behavior of others, (a) in general, (b) in terms of the others' own subjective meaning?

These questions do not as such belong to the social sciences. They refer rather to that substratum of objects of the social sciences which we discussed previously, namely, the level at which the social world is constituted in Acts of everyday life with others—Acts, that is, in which meanings are established and interpreted. As yet we are not prepared for a thorough analysis of these problems but will have to be satisfied with a few imprecise results of merely provisional validity.

Weber takes up repeatedly the question of how meaningful behavior is to be defined and how it is to be distinguished from meaningless

---

"relatively natural world outlook"; cf. his *Wissensformen und Gesellschaft*, p. 59. Felix Kaufmann in turn made use of the concept in the framework of his analysis of value in his book *Die philosophischen Grundprobleme der Lehre von der Strafrechtsschuld* (Leipzig and Vienna, 1929).

34. Sander, who thinks that Weber means by "orientation" that the object of every social act is to cause someone else to behave in a certain way through one's own physical behavior (expressive act). See his "Gegenstand der reinen Gesellschaftslehre," *Archiv für Sozialwissenschaften*, LIV, 329–423, esp. 335.

35. See below, Chap. 2, sec. 17.

behavior. He speaks of the fluctuating boundaries of meaningful behavior and mentions affectual behavior as a borderline case:

> Purely affectual behavior also stands on the borderline of what can be
> considered "meaningfully" oriented, and often it, too, goes over the line.
> It may, for instance, consist in an uncontrolled reaction to some excep-
> tional stimulus. It is a case of sublimation when affectually determined
> action occurs in the form of conscious release of emotional tension.
> When this happens, it is usually, though not always, well on the road to
> rationalization in one or the other or both of the above senses.[36]

With affectual behavior, which is thus meaningless—since it is
beyond the boundaries of "conscious" (N.B.!) behavior—is to be contrasted affectual action. Affectual action shares with action that is
rationally based on a chosen value the fact that its meaning

> does not lie in the achievement of a result ulterior to it, but in carrying
> out the specific type of action for its own sake. Examples of affectual
> action are the satisfaction of a direct impulse to revenge, to sensual
> gratification, to devote oneself to a person or ideal, to contemplative bliss,
> or, finally, toward the working off of emotional tensions. Such impulses
> belong in this category regardless of how sordid or sublime they may be.[37]

Affectual behavior and, to a certain extent, behavior based on the
rational choice of values stand close to the outer limits of the meaningful. But they are not the only types of behavior to be found there.
We also find "certain empirical uniformities . . . certain types, that is,
of action which correspond to a typically appropriate subjective meaning attributable to some actors . . . being frequently repeated by the
same individual or simultaneously performed by many different
ones," [38] such as custom, usage, etc., and likewise "traditional behavior," which Weber regards as

> very close to the borderline of what can justifiably be called meaningfully
> oriented action, and indeed often on the other side. For it is very often a
> matter of almost automatic reaction to habitual stimuli which guide
> behavior in a course which has been repeatedly followed.[39]

The statements we have quoted reveal how vaguely defined is
Weber's concept of action as meaningful behavior. His underlying
motives in formulating the concept as he did are evident. In the first
place, when Weber talks about meaningful behavior, he is thinking
about rational behavior and, what is more, "behavior oriented to a
system of discrete individual ends" (*zweckrational*). This kind of
behavior he thinks of as the archetype of action. As a matter of fact,

36. *Wirtschaft und Gesellschaft*, p. 12 [E.T., p. 116].
37. *Loc. cit.*
38. *Ibid.*, p. 14 [E.T., p. 120].
39. *Ibid.*, p. 12 [E.T., p. 116].

this teleological orientation of action is everywhere in Weber the model for meaningful construction—and with good reason from the standpoint of interpretive sociology.[40]

In the second place, the classification of behavior into different types, such as rationally purposive, rationally value-oriented, emotional, and traditional, itself presupposes that the meaning of an action is identical with the motive of the action. This, as we shall see, leads Weber into many inconsistencies. To be sure, the experiences of everyday life seem to lend support to Weber's thesis. When I review my daily work, the actions I perform all day, whether alone or in the company of others, and ask myself what is the meaning of all these actions, I will no doubt conclude that most of them are automatic. This conclusion seems convincing enough, because I find in many of these actions either no meaning at all or at best a very vague one. However, the meaning of an action is one thing, and the degree of clarity with which we grasp that meaning is quite another. There is one fact which shows that most of my actions do have meaning. This is the fact that, when I isolate them from the flux of experience and consider them attentively, I then do find them to be meaningful in the sense that I am able to find in them an underlying meaning. It is therefore wrong to use the criterion of meaningfulness in order to distinguish action from merely reactive behavior if meaningfulness is thought of in the ordinary broad sense. Even my traditional or affectual behavior has some kind of meaning. As a matter of fact, when I look closely, I find that none of my experiences is entirely devoid of meaning. And so we see that it is useless to say that what distinguishes action from behavior is that the former is subjectively meaningful and the latter meaningless. On the contrary, each is meaningful in its own way. This leads us immediately to the difficult question of the difference between the meaning of action and the meaning of mere behavior. And, of course, just beyond that is the question of what is the nature of action as such. We shall be concerned in a number of ways with all these problems. The mere mention of them, however, is enough to show how deeply we must go if we are to arrive at an adequate analysis of the concept of meaning.

The second problem we mentioned—the way in which the other self is meaningfully given to us—is not dealt with by Weber at all. He presupposes the meaningful existence of the other self as something simply given in all those cases where he speaks of the interpretation of

40. See Chap. 5, sec. 48, below; compare here Walther, "Max Weber als Soziologe," *Jahrbuch für Soziologie,* II (Karlsruhe, 1926), 1–65, esp. 35 f.; also Grab, *Der Begriff des Rationalen in der Soziologie Max Webers* (Karlsruhe, 1927), esp. pp. 25–35.

what I want to know more about

Lay

the behavior of others. Granted his way of conceiving the problem, an exact analysis of the fashion in which the other self is constructed in my consciousness is hardly necessary. Still, the question of how we get to know the other self must be raised as soon as one sets out to study the subjective meaning of the behavior of others.

3. The Pregivenness of the Alter Ego and the Postulate of the Understanding of Subjective Meaning

THE POSTULATE OF INVESTIGATING the subjectively intended meaning behind the actions of others presupposes a theory of the knowability of the other self and therewith a theory of the latter's pregivenness. I am justified in asking what another person means only when I assume (a) that he does mean something and (b) that I can find out what it is, just as I can find out what the meaning of my own behavior is. But we must emphasize, before we even start out on our project, that the subjective meaning of another person's behavior need not be identical with the meaning which his perceived external behavior has for me as an observer. But this point requires proof. Were another person's lived experiences as accessible to me as my own—whether through empathy or, as Scheler thought, through some kind of "inner intuition" [41]—then his experience, that is, the intended meaning of his behavior, would be directly evident [42] to me as I observed it. Even more, his behavior could have for me only the meaning he subjectively attached to it; that it could have another meaning, an objective one, is obviously absurd. Now, of course—and we shall demonstrate this later [43]—this assumption of such a total feeling one's way into the experience of another person is a theory which is inconsistent with the fundamentally lawful character of consciousness. Of a quite different nature is the theory that tells us that "at first" the body of the other

41. Scheler, *Wesen und Formen der Sympathie*, 2d ed. (Bonn, 1923), p. 288 [E.T., *The Nature of Sympathy*, by Peter Heath (New Haven, 1954), p. 249]: "Thus internal perception represents a polarity among acts, such acts being capable of referring both to ourselves *and* to others. *This polarity is intrinsically capable of embracing the inner life of others as well as my own*, just as it embraces myself and my own experience *in general*. . . ." *Ibid.*, pp. 296 f. [E.T., pp. 256 f.]: "Our claim is . . . that so far as concerns the act and its nature and the range of facts appearing within it, everyone can apprehend the experience of his fellow men *just as directly* (*or indirectly*) as he can his own." See also Litt, *Individuum und Gemeinschaft*, pp. 100 f.

42. [*Erfassbar in Selbsthabe*, literally, "comprehensible in the immediate possession of the thing itself." Cf. the use of the term *Selbsthabe* by Husserl, in "Klarheit der Selbsthabe," *Formale und Transzendentale Logik* (Halle, 1929), § 16c.]

43. Cf. Chap. 3, sec. 19, below.

poshlatry inwardness

person and its changes and movements, or, more strictly, the appearances of these, are given to us and that on the basis of such data
we come to postulate his inwardness and his existence as an Other
Self.[44] This line of thinking results ultimately in the conclusion that
we never experience other minds anyway, but only physical objects;
that the concept of the "other mind" is from the standpoint of science
epistemologically superfluous; and that statements about other minds
are scientifically meaningless since they lack empirical content. This
position has been championed by Carnap in some of his writings.[45] It
seems to do justice to the fact that my own actions and behavior are
given to me as *my* experiences but that others' actions and behavior
are not given to me as *their* experiences. Rather, another person's behavior and actions are given to me as sequences of events in the
physical world, as perceived changes in the physical object which I call
his body. However, in order to understand that object as someone else's
body, I must already have presupposed the existence of the other Ego
animating the body in question. Implicit reference to the other's body
generally occurs only insofar as I am directly observing his action and
behavior and have them in view as a sequence of physical events occurring before me. The behavior and action of others are, however, revealed to me, not only through their bodily movements, but also in the
results of these movements, e.g., sound waves, changes in other objects,
and so on. And I can pose the question for myself of what produced these
changes and by what process. Now, I find all these external events
intelligible. They have meaning for me. But the meaning I find in
them need not at all be identical with what the person who produced
them had in mind. For these objectifications of meaning in the external world are mere "indications" (*Anzeichen*) of the intended meaning of the actor or the producer of the object in question. We have
adopted the use of the term "indication" in the technical sense given it
by Husserl in the *Logical Investigations:*[46] We say that we have an
indication in all those cases where

44. Scheler's objections to this theory (*Wesen und Formen der Sympathie*, pp.
281 ff. [E.T., pp. 243 ff.]) are thoroughly justified. It is without doubt quite
impossible to infer the existence of the other self solely from the appearance of its
body and without assuming that the whole psychophysical unity is itself given.
See below, Chap. 3, sec. 19.

45. Rudolf Carnap, *Logischer Aufbau der Welt* (Berlin, 1928), esp. pp. 185 ff.,
and *Scheinprobleme in der Philosophie* (Berlin, 1928), esp. pp. 18 ff. It is possible
to criticize Carnap's concept within his own framework. He appeals to the
evidence of formal logic without realizing that the very intersubjective validity of
the latter presupposes the existence of other minds.

46. Husserl, *Logische Untersuchungen*, 4th ed. (Halle, 1928), II, i, 25.

[Cf. Schutz's discussion of the concept of indication in his "Symbol, Reality
and Society," *Collected Papers of Alfred Schutz*, ed. Maurice Natanson (The
Hague, 1962), I, 310. Cf. also the discussion in Farber, *The Foundation of*

any kind of objects or states of affairs whose existence is known to someone, *indicate* to that person the existence of some other objects or states of affairs in the sense that his belief in the existence of the one is the motive of a belief or suspicion of the existence of the other. The kind of motive we have in mind here is not that of a rational insight into the connection between things.[47]

In what follows, let us, for the sake of simplicity, disregard those products of action which refer back to the action itself and limit ourselves to the consideration of the changes in the body of the other person which render his action visible to the observer. These changes function as indications of the other person's inner life, for his body is no mere physical object, like a stick or a stone, but a *field of expression* for the life-experience of that psychophysical unity we call the other self.

But the term "field of expression" as applied to the body is not precise enough. Husserl himself has, in his *Logical Investigations,* pointed out the ambiguities of the term "expression." [48] It suffices for our purposes to point out that in the sociological [49] literature every action of the other person is at times interpreted as an expression of his experience. However, when used this way, the term "expression" conceals an ambiguity. It may mean (1) that the external behavior of the other person functions as an *indication* of his inner subjective experience or (2) that he "is deliberately seeking to express something" by acting in a certain way. Many things that are expressions in the first sense—reddening with anger, for instance—are hardly expressions in the second. By the same token, a person may be deliberately seeking to express something and fail to "get it across," so that the observer has no true indication of his subjective state.[50]

Phenomenology, 2d ed. (New York, 1962). The term "mark" is used by Farber to mean the same as Schutz's "indication." Schutz uses "mark" in a somewhat different sense. Cf. *Collected Papers,* I, 308.]

47. [It is an "opaque" motive (Schutz, *op. cit.,* I, 311). The relation between indication and what is indicated is that of "reference" (*Hinweis*), not that of "implication." It has its origin in association. Cf. Husserl, *Logische Untersuchungen,* II, i, pp. 25–30.]

48. [*Logische Untersuchungen,* II, 23–105, *passim.* Cf. also Farber, *Foundation of Phenomenology,* Chap. VIII.]

49. See, e.g., Freyer, *Theorie des objektiven Geistes,* pp. 14 ff.; Litt, *op. cit.,* pp. 97 f., 141 f., 182 f.; and, earlier, Sander, "Gegenstand der reinen Gesellschafts-lehre," pp. 338, 354. On the other hand, in his *Allgemeine Soziologie* Sander has, in an acute study, distinguished the many facets of meaning involved in the concept "expression."

50. A further sense of "expression," namely, symbolic expression, as in language, for example, we are reserving for later treatment. Our reason for not dealing with it here is partly the desire to avoid unnecessary complications and partly because every such symbol presupposes a symbolic act, and symbolic acts are just further examples of outward behavior. What we are concerned with here

This distinction is of no small importance. It is permissible to refer to the body as a field of expression to the extent that bodily changes can regularly be interpreted as the subject's inner consciousness "coming to expression" in our first sense.[51] But that merely amounts to saying that his perceived bodily changes are indications of his subjective state. By no means does it imply that these changes are "expressions" in any voluntary sense or that the individual is "expressing an intention." It would be quite incorrect to say that, by the act of chopping, the woodsman is expressing his desire to cut down trees. For every expressed intention is a message, and this presupposes a recipient of the message. One can speak of "expression" in our second sense, therefore, only if that which was expressed was intended as some kind of communication.[52]

What is it, in fact, that is expressed in the other person's field of expression? Is it the other's experience? Is it perhaps his subjectively intended meaning?

Scheler expresses himself quite clearly on this point:

> We certainly believe ourselves to be acquainted with another person's joy in his laughter, with his sorrow and pain in his tears, with his shame in his blushing, with his entreaty in his outstretched hands, with his love in his look of affection, with his rage in the gnashing of his teeth, with his threats in the clenching of his fist, and with the tenor of his thoughts in the sound of his words.[53]

Let us suppose that Scheler is right and that certain contents of the other person's consciousness, such as joy, sorrow, pain, shame, pleading, love, rage, and threats, are given to us directly through acts of inner perception and without any inferential process whatever. Does it follow that the *subjective meaning* of the other person is also given to us in this simple fashion? That we directly perceive the *intention* that lies behind these acts of pleading or menacing? Surely a distinction is called for here. If "subjective meaning" (*gemeinter Sinn*) is a term that denotes merely the surface attitude exhibited by the other person—pleading or begging, for instance—then it is perfectly permissible to say that I directly perceive that attitude. I can even say, if you will, that I intuit it in a single act of "inner perception." But if the

is the general problem of how one infers the subjective experiences of the other person, given his outward behavior.

51. It is only in a limited sense that one can refer to a pathological change in another's body as an indication of his subjective experience: his physical pain, for instance, or his mood. The formulation we have given above is necessarily imprecise and provisional.

52. We are here ignoring the trivial exceptional case in which one "communicates with himself" by taking notes.

53. *Wesen und Formen der Sympathie*, pp. 301 f. [E.T., Heath, pp. 260 f.].

term "subjective meaning" denotes *why* the other person is exhibiting the attitude he does—his intention, for instance, of provoking me to irrational actions by his threats—then it is simply untrue that any such subjective meaning is directly revealed to me. Rather, this bodily movement which I have apprehended as a threat is directly given to me only as an objective state of affairs, as something to be interpreted. Now, when I interpret the shaking of a fist as a threat, I bring in a highly structured context of meaning [54] without noticing it. But even if the awareness of the threat were as direct and immediate as you please, it would still fall far short of intuitive knowledge of the other person's subjective meaning.

When Scheler, in the passage quoted above, speaks of intuiting the experience of the other person, he confines his examples to so-called "expressive movements." But what about other actions or kinds of behavior? When we watch a woodcutter at work, do we directly perceive his subjective experience? If so, which experiences? His experiences of effort as he wields his ax? Or his motive, perhaps, in wielding it? Behind these questions are deep problems with which we shall eventually grapple. For the moment, however, let us make a preliminary survey of the area in which they lie by examining Weber's concepts of observational and motivational understanding.

Weber distinguishes between two types of understanding:

> The first is the direct observational understanding (*aktuelles Verstehen*) of the subjective meaning (*gemeinter Sinn*) [55] of the given act as such, including verbal utterances. We thus understand by direct observation, in this sense, the meaning of the proposition $2 \times 2 = 4$ when we hear or read it. This is a case of the direct rational understanding of ideas. We also understand an outbreak of anger as manifested by facial expression, exclamations or irrational movements. This is direct observational understanding of irrational emotional reactions. We can understand in a similar observational way the action of a woodcutter or of somebody who reaches for the knob to shut a door or who aims a gun at an animal. This is rational observational understanding of actions. Understanding may, however, be of another sort, namely, explanatory un-

54. [*Sinnzusammenhang* is a term used by both Weber and Schutz to refer to "a plurality of elements which form a coherent whole on the level of meaning. There are several possible modes of meaningful relation between such elements, such as logical consistency, the esthetic harmony of a style or the appropriateness of means to an end" (Henderson and Parsons, *op. cit.*, p. 95 n.). "Context" and "complex" of meaning are adequate renderings; Luckmann's "configuration" and "matrix" are probably best when Schutz is speaking more technically. See Luckmann in Schutz, *Collected Papers*, II, 63.]

55. [Henderson and Parsons render *gemeinter Sinn* in two different ways in translating this passage: (1) as "subjective meaning" and (2) as "intended meaning." This fits perfectly the point which Schutz makes at the beginning of sec. 4.]

derstanding (*erklärendes Verstehen*). Thus we understand in terms of motive (*motivationsmässig*) the meaning an actor attaches to the proposition twice two equals four, when he states it or writes it down, in that we understand what makes him do this at precisely this moment and in these circumstances. Understanding in this sense is attained if we know that he is engaged in balancing a ledger or in making a scientific demonstration, or is engaged in some other task of which this particular act would be an appropriate part. This is rational understanding of motivation, which consists in placing the act in an intelligible and more inclusive context of meaning (*Sinnzusammenhang*). Thus we understand the chopping of wood or aiming of a gun in terms of motive in addition to direct observation if we know that the woodchopper is working for a wage or is chopping a supply of firewood for his own use or possibly is doing it for recreation. But he might also be "working off" a fit of rage, an irrational case. . . . In all the above cases the particular act has been placed in an understandable *sequence of motivation* (*Sinnzusammenhang*), the understanding of which can be treated as an *explanation* of the actual course of behavior. Thus for a science which is concerned with the subjective meaning of action, explanation requires a grasp of the complex of meaning (*Sinnzusammenhang*) in which an actual course of understandable action thus interpreted belongs. In all such cases, even where the processes are largely affectual, the subjective meaning (*subjektiver Sinn*) of the action, including that also of the relevant meaning complexes, will be called the "intended" meaning (*gemeinter Sinn*). This involves a departure from ordinary usage, which speaks of intention in this sense only in the case of rationally purposive action.[56]

This very illuminating thesis deserves closer examination.

4. Critique of Max Weber's Concepts of "Observational" and "Motivational" Understanding

FROM THE PRECEDING PASSAGE it ought to be clear that Weber is using the term "intended meaning" in two different senses. First, he is referring to the subjective meaning which the action has for the actor. According to him, this subjective meaning can be understood "observationally," that is, it can be grasped by direct observation. But second, he is referring to the broader framework of meaning in which an action "thus interpreted" (i.e., interpreted according to its subjective meaning) belongs. It is this broader context of meaning which is uncovered by motivational or clarifying understanding.

56. Weber, *Wirtschaft und Gesellschaft*, p. 3 [E.T., pp. 96–98]; cf. also point 3, *ibid.*, as well as Weber's essay "Über einige Kategorien der Verstehenden Soziologie," *Gesammelte Aufsätze zur Wissenschaftslehre*, esp. pp. 408 ff.

Let us look first at *observational understanding*, and, under that heading, first at the observational understanding of "affects" and "thoughts." How can we arrive at an understanding of the subjective meaning of these experiences through direct observation? Whether a given affectual action is meaningful behavior and thus genuine action is very difficult to determine, as Weber himself justly emphasizes.[57] Suppose that I "internally perceive" A's outburst of anger, as Scheler would say. Or, to use Weber's terminology, suppose that in an act of observational understanding I grasp the look on A's face and his gestures as an outburst of anger. But have I thereby determined whether A is merely reacting, whether his behavior is "over the line of what can be considered meaningfully oriented," whether it "consists in an uncontrolled reaction to an exceptional stimulus," or whether A is merely having a tantrum and that the only meaning the outburst has for him is the release of his pent-up feelings? Direct observation gives me no answer to this question. While I know he is angry, I remain in the dark as to what that anger means to him subjectively.

Now this is also true of the "observational understanding" of thoughts, such as the judgment 2 × 2 = 4. Husserl has recently distinguished two different senses of the meaning of a judgment.[58] First, there is the content of the judgment (*Urteilsinhalt*): "that 2 × 2 = 4." Second, there is the epistemic attitude (*subjektiv doxisch Setzungsmodus*) which the person using or uttering the judgment has toward the judgment content. He may, for instance, hold it to be certainly true or only probably true; he may merely suspect that it is true; or he may be simply supposing it true for the sake of argument. Or, finally, he may be denying it. The *judgment content*, it should be noted, remains the same throughout these changes of epistemic attitude. Now, it is this very epistemic attitude which, according to Weber, determines what the utterer of the judgment "means." In other words, what he means when he utters it consists in whether he really believes it, only suspects it may be true, or what not. And yet this epistemic attitude is precisely what *cannot* be determined by direct observation.

We encounter a parallel difficulty when we come to the observational understanding of an *act*. Weber would say that I understand by direct observation the meaning of a man's behavior when I see him performing such acts as chopping wood, grasping a doorknob in order (N.B.!) to shut the door, or aiming a rifle at an animal. These observed movements of the other person's body Weber cites as the substratum of observational understanding. However, it is obvious

57. Weber, *Wirtschaft und Gesellschaft*, p. 12 [E.T., p. 116].
58. *Formale und transzendentale Logik*, pp. 192 f. [The remainder of this paragraph is a paraphrase.]

that they have *already* been understood and interpreted as soon as
they are called "woodchopping," "knob-grasping," or "taking aim."
What if the man wielding the ax is not really chopping wood but
merely appears to be doing so? What if the man holding the doorknob
is not grasping it in order to shut the door but is merely holding it
steady in order to repair it? What if the hunter is not taking aim at all
but is merely watching the animal through the telescopic sight on his
rifle? Observational understanding of the other person's outward behavior is clearly not enough to settle these points. These are questions
of subjective meaning and cannot be answered by merely watching
someone's behavior, as Weber seems to think. On the contrary, we first
observe the bodily behavior and then place it within a larger context of
meaning. One way we may do this is by giving the behavior in
question a name. But this context of meaning need not, in fact cannot,
be identical with the context of meaning in the mind of the actor
himself. Let us call it the *objective* context of meaning as opposed to
the actor's *subjective* context of meaning.

Now let us turn to motivational understanding. Weber says that
this consists in understanding the meaning-context within which an
action belongs, once the action's subjective meaning is itself understood. But in the same place he speaks of this meaning-context as one
of which this action would be, *from our point of view,* an appropriate
part. This is confusing if not downright contradictory, for we have no
means of knowing that the meaning-context which we think appropriate is at all the same as what the actor has in mind. This is a question
to which we shall return later. It suffices at the moment that we have
proved the impossibility of motivational understanding on the basis of
observation alone. Data derived from some other source are essential.
To understand a person's motives it will not do to "size up" his actions
on the basis of a "taking-stock" drawn from the context. Motivational
understanding requires instead a certain amount of knowledge of the
actor's past and future. I look at the two men in Weber's example. One
of them is working on a mathematical equation, the other is cutting
wood. Information about the *past* of the two men that would be
essential might be that the first has embarked on the demonstration of
a point in science and that the second has been employed as a
woodchopper. Information about the *future* of the two men that would
be essential might be that the scientist regards this particular equation
as relevant to his demonstration and that the employer is going to pay
for this particular bit of woodchopping. Knowledge of the two men's
past is necessary if *I* am to find an intelligible meaning-context into
which I can fit their acts. Knowledge of the two men's future is
essential if I am to determine whether their acts *in the subjective*

meaning which those acts have for them fit into the meaning-context I have already recognized.

Motive

In both of these cases I am looking for the "motive." By *motive* Weber understands "a complex of . . . meaning [59] which seems *to the actor himself or to the observer* an adequate (or meaningful) ground for the conduct in question." [60] Weber is here quite logically applying to the meaning-context, which without further elaboration he calls the "motive," the distinction he has already made between the subjective and objective meaning of an action. Now, what is meant by calling the motive "a complex which seems *to the actor* a meaningful ground for his conduct"? Obviously, again two different things. First there appears to me, as the meaningful ground of my behavior, a series of future events whose occurrence I propose to bring about. I am orienting my behavior to this end. But there is a second sense in which I sometimes speak of the meaningful ground of my behavior. Here I refer to those past experiences of mine which have led me to behave as I do. In the first case I regard my behavior as the means of accomplishing some desired goal. If I am trying to find my motive in this sense, I ask myself the following question: "Which of all the future events I expect to happen are distinguished from the rest by the fact that my expectation of their occurrence constitutes or jointly constitutes the meaning of my behavior?" In the second case I regard my present behavior as the result of past experiences, as the effect of preceding "causes." If I am searching for my motive in this sense, then I ask myself a different question: "Which of all my past experiences are distinguished from the rest by the fact that they constitute or jointly constitute the meaning of my behavior?" Note that in both cases the motive being sought after lies outside the time span of the actual behavior.

Weber fails to distinguish between these two quite different questions, and the results of that failure, as we shall see, are far-reaching. Furthermore, he does not answer the question of whether the meaning which the action has for an actor is identical with what appears to the latter to be his motive, i.e., the meaning-complex which he takes to be the meaningful ground of his behavior. In other words, when we have discovered a man's motive, have we discovered the intended meaning of his action? Ordinary usage would seem to say yes. When I have discovered what a man is trying to do and what in his past has led him to try to do it, have I not discovered the meaning of his action? Certainly, if I ask him what he means by acting in such and such a

59. [The word "subjective," occurring only in the English translation, is here omitted.]

60. Weber, *Wirtschaft und Gesellschaft*, p. 5 [E.T., pp. 98–99].

way, he will commonly answer in one of two ways. Either he will say "I am doing it *in order to . . .*" or "I am doing it *because. . . .*" However, we must make clear that these statements are mere abbreviations for highly complex "meaning-experiences" of the actor and that the statement of the "motive" by no means gives an exhaustive account of the whole structure of "intended meaning." On the contrary, the actor takes for granted the meaning of his action: it is self-evident to him in the proper sense of the term. If he asks himself what his motives were, he takes this self-evident meaning as his point of departure and then looks for past experiences which were relevant to his action or for future events toward which his action is conducive. It can, therefore, be said that the actor must already know the intended meaning of his action before he can inquire about its motive. Notice how this applies to Weber's examples. When a man engaged in formulating a scientific demonstration utilizes for that purpose the proposition $2 \times 2 = 4$, this proposition must already be meaningful to him before he selects it as one of the steps toward his conclusion. Likewise the man who seeks employment as a woodcutter must first know what woodcutting is before he concludes that he can make a living at it.

So much for the problem of the person seeking for the subjective context of meaning within which, *from his point of view*, his action belongs. But what about the context of meaning which appears *to the observer* as the meaningful basis of the observed person's behavior? Weber's motivational understanding has as its object the discovery of motives. Now, we have already shown that the motive of an action cannot be understood unless the meaning of that action is first known. But it is the actor who has this knowledge, not the observer. The observer lacks the self-evident starting point which is available to the actor. All he can do is start out with the objective meaning of the act as he sees it, treating this objective meaning as if it were without question the intended meaning of the actor. Weber sees this clearly enough when he says that motivational understanding must search for the context of meaning which is from our point of view appropriate (or which makes sense to us), into which the action, interpreted according to the intended meaning of the actor, fits. However, this so-called "intended" meaning cannot give us any more information in motivational than in observational understanding. In neither case do we advance a step beyond the interpretation of objective meaning.

Indeed, Weber's distinction between observational and motivational understanding is arbitrary and without any logical basis in his own theory. Both types of understanding start out from an objective meaning-context. The understanding of subjective meaning has no place in either. One can treat observational understanding, whenever it concerns itself with subjective meaning, as if it were an inquiry into motives. In such a case one must be willing to take the answer one gets at a convenient cutoff point, since the search for "the" motive always leads to an infinite regress. For instance, the woodcutter is wielding the ax in order to chop the wood to bits. Conversely, one can treat motivational understanding as if it were observational. This is done by dealing with every statement about the motive as if it were a statement of the observer's experiences of the circumstances surrounding the act. These experiences must, of course, be arranged in a continuous series and cover a sufficient span. Such a series might consist of the observation of the signing of the wage contract, of the wielding of the ax, of the splitting of the wood, and of the collection of the wages. All of these observations would then be lumped together as one unified act of the subject under observation: "working for a lumber company."

Nevertheless, there is a valid epistemological point underlying the distinction between observational and motivational understanding. In everyday life we directly experience the acts of another. We interpret those external events which we call "another's act" as indications of a stream of consciousness lying outside our own. To the extent that we do these things, we can "understand" the events in question, reading the indications as they occur, and thus directly witness the action as it unfolds, witness it "in the mode of actuality." Observational understanding is then focused on the action as it takes place, and we, as beings living alongside the actor and sharing his present, participate experientially in the very course of his action. In essence, therefore, observational or direct understanding is simply the understanding we exercise in daily life in our direct relations with other people. Precisely for that reason, however, the inference from the overt behavior to the intended meaning lying behind it is anything but a cut-and-dried matter.[61]

Motivational understanding, on the other hand, is not tied to the world of directly experienced social reality (*Umwelt*). It can take as its object any action of the more distant worlds of contemporaries (*Mitwelt*), or predecessors (*Vorwelt*), or even to a certain extent of successors (*Folgewelt*).[62] For this kind of understanding does not take as its starting point an *ongoing* action. Rather, as we will later demonstrate, its object is the *accomplished act*. This may be considered as something really completed in the past or as something whose future completed form is now being envisaged. It may be regarded as motive in terms of origin or motive in terms of goal, as we said above. Furthermore it should be noted that motivational understanding starts

61. Husserl, *Logische Untersuchungen*, II, 25.
62. These terms will be defined precisely in Chap. 4.

out on the basis of an established objective meaning as merely an indication of the existence of a subjective meaning. This is all the more reason why a higher degree of scientific clarity and exactitude is attainable in motivational understanding. From this we must in turn conclude that the "interpretive understanding" which is definitive of interpretive sociology cannot be observational understanding. Rather, the scientific method of establishing subjective meaning is motivational understanding, whereas the kind of understanding proper to everyday life is observational in character.

But this is by no means the end of our problems. We have seen that the intended meaning eludes the grasp not only of the simple everyday act of "getting the meaning" but of the two kinds of understanding as well. We have seen, further, that external behavior is merely an "indication" of the existence of subjective meaning and that all meaning-contexts are given to us only objectively. Inasmuch as we have drawn a sharp distinction between subjective and objective meaning, a closer analysis of these two concepts is in order before we proceed any further.

5. Subjective and Objective Meaning

So FAR WE HAVE BEEN USING the term "objective meaning" in a merely negative sense, that is, to refer to a meaning *other* than the subjective one in the mind of the actor. It is time that we stated in detail the positive meaning that we assign to the term.

Let M^1 be the meaning which a given action A has for a given actor X. Let the action A manifest itself by some bodily movement of X. Let A be observed by his friend F and by a sociologist S. Suppose, further, that the action A makes sense to both observers. Both of them will then connect the external course of the action A, which they take as an indication of X's subjective experiences, with a meaning. However, we have already demonstrated that the intended meaning M^1 which X gives to his action cannot be discovered either by observational or motivational understanding. What will happen, then, is that F will, on the basis of his practical experience, interpret the external action A as having the meaning M^2, and S will, on the basis of the ideal-typical constructs of interpretive sociology, assign to the action yet a third meaning, M^3. Whereas in Weber's terminology M^1 would be the subjective or intended meaning which A attributed to his own act, M^2 and M^3 would constitute the objective meaning of this act. But after all, M^2 is only the objective meaning relative to F, and M^3 is only the objective meaning relative to S. Therefore, to call M^2 and M^3 objective meaning-contents is merely to say that they are different from M^1. As a matter of fact, since M^1 can only be inferred from the evidence of A's external behavior, the intended meaning must be regarded as a limiting concept with which M^2 and M^3 would never coincide even under optimum conditions of interpretation.

Let us first try to clear up the concept of objective meaning as exemplified in M^2 and M^3. One interpretation should be ruled out at once. This is that M^2 is the subjective meaning which F gives to X's act A and that M^3 is the subjective meaning which S gives to it. Such a reading would entirely miss what Weber has in mind when he uses the term "subjective or intended meaning." For it is obvious that an action has only one subjective meaning: that of the actor himself. It is X who gives subjective meaning to his action, and the only subjective meanings being given by F and S in this situation are the subjective meanings they are giving to their own actions, namely, their actions of observing X. It is obvious that there are so many riddles surrounding the problem of subjective meaning that at this early stage of the discussion we can hardly expect to achieve a clear understanding of its nature.

F and S, of course, see X's action A as an event of the external world. As they live in that world, they seek to understand it. They not only live *in* their subjective experiences, they reflect *on* them. They not only have direct experience of the world, but they think and speak of their experiences, using concepts and judgments. They thus explain their experiences of the world, understanding them by means of interpretive schemes. The world and their experience of the world make sense for them just as it does for you and for me and for every rational being. This usage of "sense" or "meaning" signifies no more than that a rational being takes up a certain attitude toward any object he may confront. Since F and S witness the course of the act as an event of their world, experience it pre-predicatively, and proceed to explain it, they "interpret" this, their experience; and its meaning for them is merely an explanation of one item of their own experience.

But the phenomena of the external world have meaning not only for you and me, for F and S, but for everyone living in it. There is only one external world, the public world, and it is given equally to all of us. Therefore, every act of mine through which I endow the world with meaning refers back to some meaning-endowing act (*Sinngebung*) [63] of yours with respect to the same world. Meaning is thus constituted as an intersubjective phenomenon. The problem of how the intersubjectiv-

---

63. [Husserl, *Logische Untersuchungen*, II, 37. Cf. also Farber, *The Foundation of Phenomenology*, pp. 227 and 232–36.]

ity of all knowledge and thought can be transcendentally deduced is something beyond the scope of the present study, even though its analysis would completely clarify the concept of objective meaning. This most difficult and basic problem of every phenomenology of knowledge was stated in Husserl's *Formal and Transcendental Logic* [64] but by no means solved.

When we speak of objective meaning, we refer not only to those broad contexts of meaning we have just discussed. We intend to attribute objective meaning also to certain ideal objectivities (*idealen Gegenständlichkeiten*), such as signs and expressions. In so doing, we mean to say that these ideal objectivities are meaningful and intelligible in their own right—in their, so to speak, anonymous nature— regardless of whether anyone is thinking of them, regardless of whether anyone is using them. For instance, the expression $2 \times 2 = 4$ has an objective meaning regardless of what is in the minds of any or all of its users. A linguistic expression can be understood as an objective complex of meaning without reference to the speakers of the language. A theme from the *Ninth Symphony* is meaningful in itself wholly apart from the question of what Beethoven meant to express by it. Here the term "objective meaning" signifies a unit of meaning considered as an ideal object. But only insofar as an expression can be considered in terms of *what it means* (*Bedeutung*) can it be regarded as truly objective. In his *Logical Investigations* Husserl taught us to distinguish between "meaning" (*Bedeuten*) as an act and "that which is meant" (*Bedeutung*), the latter being an ideal unity in contrast to the multiplicity of all possible acts of meaning. Husserl's distinction between "essentially subjective and occasional" expressions, on the one hand, and "objective" expressions, on the other, is only a special case of this general and fundamental insight.[65] "An expression is *objective* if it binds its meaning merely by its appearance-content of sound and can be understood without regard to the person uttering it or the circumstances of its utterance." On the other hand, an expression is *essentially subjective and occasional* when it is "such that its occasional and actual meaning must be oriented with respect to the speaking person and his condition." [66]

64. Esp. § 96, pp. 210 ff. Cf. also Husserl, *Méditations cartésiennes*, Meditation V. [E.T., from the German text, *Cartesian Meditations*, by Dorion Cairns (The Hague, 1960).]

65. [The reader is referred to the concise summary of Husserl's views on these matters in Farber, *The Foundation of Phenomenology*, pp. 237 ff.; cf. also pp. 231–32.]

66. *Logische Untersuchungen*, II, 80. [The English rendition of Husserl's words is Farber's (Farber, *op. cit.*, p. 237).]

Now the question is whether this sense of the term "objective meaning" is the same as what we had in mind when we identified the objective meaning of the action A with the two meaning-interpretations M^2 and M^3 given that action by F and S. This is obviously not the case, not even if X's action is the utterance of an expression with objective meaning, such as a sentence. For, in the last analysis, F and S are not interested in what X has to say, that is, the content of his statement considered as an ideal objectivity. Rather, any observer of the social world is interested in interpreting *the phenomenon of X's utterance* of this statement here, now, and in such and such a manner. (By utterance we mean lip movements, sound waves, word meanings, and sentence meaning.) This interpretation consists in taking the utterance as a sign that A is undergoing certain conscious experiences, of which the having of an intention would be one example. From this point of view, the precise content of the utterance is of only indirect interest. What F and S want to know is whether A said it and why. In the terminology we have established thus far, it would be proper to say that the utterance of the statement here and now by A is objectively meaningful.

Now, to be sure, the ideal objectivities (*ideale Gegenständlichkeiten*) which form the meaning-content of expressions and of the great systems of language, art, science, myth, etc., of which they are inseparable parts, play their own specific role in everyone's interpretation of the behavior of other persons. All such interpretations presuppose the use of such *interpretive schemata*. This holds also for the account of the objective meaning observable by F and S as action D takes place. The interpretation of such courses of action takes place regularly according to schemata that are on hand to begin with, even though they are selected by F and S and are therefore relative to them.

Our analysis, so far cursory and superficial, must now proceed to a deeper level. The two concepts of subjective and objective meaning [67] will in the process undergo extensive modification, and only at the end of Chapter 3 will we be in a position to give each of them a satisfactory definition. At this point we shall be content to add a few preliminary remarks on the direction of our investigations.

From our treatment of the different senses of the term "objective meaning," it is clear that we call the real and ideal objectifications of the world surrounding us "meaningful" as soon as we focus our atten-

67. Lest there be any confusion with a concept to be found in a number of contemporary authors, it should be noted that our use of the term "objective meaning" is without axiological implications. The fact that objective meaning may occasionally presuppose objective values (*objektive Werte*) and the fact that ideal objectivities (*Gegenständlichkeiten*) are constituted out of objective values are both matters that lie beyond the scope of this study.

tion upon them.[68] We have known ever since Husserl's *Ideas* [69] that meaning-endowment is the act wherein pure sense experiences ("hyletic data") are "animated." What in a cursory glance we see as meaningful has already been constituted as such by a previous intentional operation of our consciousness. The most profound treatment given by Husserl to this question is to be found in his *Formal and Transcendental Logic*, although there he is concerned with the sphere of logical objectivities. He explains the process by which meaning originates and notes that intentionality is really a synthesis of different operations,

> which are included in the intentional unity existing at a given time, and in their manner of being given on each occasion, as *a sedimented series of strata [sedimentierte Geschichte]*, a series of strata which, however, in each case *can be laid bare by a rigorous method of investigation.*[70]

> Every meaning structure can be analyzed in terms of the *meaning stratification that is essential to it.* . . . All intentional unities have an intentional origin, are "constituted" unities, and in every case one can subject the "completed" unities to an analysis in terms of their over-all origin and of course their essential form, which is to be grasped eidetically.[71]

> Whereas "static analysis" is governed by the unity of the intended object [*Gegenstand*] and in that way, by the unclear mode of givenness, following its reference as intentional modification, resists clarification, on the other hand, genetic intentional analysis is directed upon the entire concrete context in which every consciousness and its intentional object as such stand.[72]

This phenomenon of constitution can be studied in genetic-intentionality analysis, and, from an understanding of this intentionality, the genesis of meaning can be traced. Conversely, every objectivity which can be regarded as an already given and constituted meaning-content can be analyzed in terms of its meaning-stratification. The *solitary Ego* can assume either point of view. *On the one hand,* I can look

---

68. ["*Sobald wir sie in spezifischen Zuwendungen unseres Bewusstseins auffassen.*" The term *Zuwendung* is used by Husserl to mean a "turning toward" or "glancing toward" the intentional object, which is thereby "known in a general way." It is *present in* every act of apprehension, valuation, fancy, etc., but it is "not itself a proper act." It is "perceptive in perception, fanciful in fancy, approving in approval, volitional in will and so forth" (*Ideas*, § 37; E.T., pp. 121–22).]

69. *Ideen*, pp. 172 ff. [E.T., pp. 247 ff.].

70. *Formale und Transzendentale Logik*, p. 217.

71. *Ibid.*, pp. 184–85.

72. *Ibid.*, p. 277.

upon the world presenting itself to me as one that is completed, constituted, and to be taken for granted. When I do this, I leave out of my awareness the intentional operations of my consciousness within which their meanings have already been constituted. At such times I have before me a world of real and ideal objects, and I can assert that this world is meaningful not only for me but for you, for us, and for everyone. This is precisely because I am attending not to those acts of consciousness which once gave them meaning but because I already presuppose, as given without question, a series of highly complex meaning-contents. The meaning-structure thus abstracted from its genesis is something that I can regard as having an objective meaning, as being meaningful in itself, just as the proposition $2 \times 2 = 4$ is meaningful regardless of where, when, or by whom it is asserted. On the other hand, I can turn my glance toward the intentional operations of my consciousness which originally conferred the meanings. Then I no longer have before me a complete and constituted world but one which only now is being constituted and which is ever being constituted anew in the stream of my enduring Ego: not a world of being, but a world that is at every moment one of becoming and passing away—or better, an emerging world. As such, it is meaningful for me in virtue of those meaning-endowing intentional acts of which I become aware by a reflexive glance. And as a world that is being constituted, never completed, but always in the process of formation, it points back to the most basic fact of my conscious life, to my awareness of the actual ongoing or passage of my life, to my duration; in Bergson's words, to my durée,[73] or, in Husserl's terminology, to my internal time-consciousness.[74] In everyday life, occupying as I do the position of the natural attitude (or standpoint),[75] I live within the meaning-endowing acts themselves and am aware only of the objectivity constituted in them, i.e., objective meaning. It is only after I, "by a painful effort," as Bergson says, turn away from the world of objects (Gegenstände) and direct my gaze at my inner stream of conscious-

73. Essai sur les données immédiates de la conscience (Paris, 1889) [E.T., Time and Free Will, by F. L. Pogson (New York, 1912; also 1960)]; Matière et mémoirs (Paris, 1896) [E.T., Matter and Memory, by N. M. Paul and W. Scott Palmer (New York, 1959)]; L'Evolution créatrice (Paris, 1907) [E.T., Creative Evolution, by Arthur Mitchell (New York, 1911)]; L'Energie spirituelle (Paris, 1920) [E.T., Mind Energy, by H. Wildon Carr (New York, 1920)]; Introduction à la métaphysique (Paris, 1903) [E.T., Introduction to Metaphysics, by T. E. Hulme (1955)]; and finally, Durée et simultanéité (Paris, 1922).

74. Vorlesungen zur Phänomenologie des inneren Zeitbewusstseins (ed. Heidegger), Suppl. VIII, Jahrbuch für Philosophie und phänomenologische Forschung, Vol. IX (Halle, 1928). [E.T., The Phenomenology of Internal Time Consciousness, by James S. Churchill (Bloomington, Ind., 1964).] This subject will be treated in detail in the following chapter.

75. [Cf. Husserl's Ideas, § 1; E.T., p. 51.]

ness, it is only after I "bracket" [76] the natural world and attend only to my conscious experiences within the phenomenological reduction, it is only after I have done these things that I become aware of this process of constitution. To the solitary Ego occupying the natural attitude, the problem of objective and subjective meaning is quite unknown. It only comes to light after the carrying-out of the phenomenological reduction; and insofar as it concerns the realm of logical objects and the corresponding antithesis of "formal" and "transcendental" logic, it has been stated with incomparable mastery by Husserl.

The distinction between the two ways of looking at the meaningful which we have just pointed out is, however, not the same as the distinction between objective and subjective meaning. We encountered the latter problem in the course of an analysis of the meaningful interpretation of the *social* world. "Meaning" was for us not the generic "predicate" of my intentional consciousness but had a specific social connotation. When we make the transition to the social sphere, there accrues, in fact, to the pair of concepts "objective and subjective meaning" a new and sociologically relevant significance. I can, on the one hand, attend to and interpret in themselves the phenomena of the external world which present themselves to me as indications of the consciousness of other people. When I do this, I say of them that they have objective meaning. But I can, on the other hand, look over and through these external indications into the constituting process within the living consciousness of another rational being. What I am then concerned with is subjective meaning. What we call the world of objective meaning is, therefore, abstracted in the social sphere from the constituting processes of a meaning-endowing consciousness, be this one's own or another's. This results in the anonymous character of the meaning-content predicated of it and also its invariance with respect to every consciousness which has given it meaning through its own intentionality. In contrast to this, when we speak of subjective meaning in the social world, we are referring to the constituting processes in the consciousness of the person who produced that which is objectively meaningful. We are therefore referring to his "intended meaning," whether he himself is aware of these constituting processes or not. The world of subjective meaning is therefore never anonymous, for it is essentially only something dependent upon and still within the operating intentionality of an Ego-consciousness, my own or someone else's. Now in the social world the question can in principle be posed—and this by means of a special technique yet to be described—as to what the subjective meaning is of any datum of objec-

76. [*Ibid.*, §§ 31–32; E.T., pp. 107–11.]

tive meaning-content which we attribute to another mind. Further-more, it can be asserted that it is possible to comprehend the meaning-content with a maximum degree of clarity. We can fulfill this claim if, by "subjective meaning," we mean nothing more than the referral of constituted objectivities (*Gegenständlichkeiten*) to the consciousness of others.[77] On the other hand, we shall be unsuccessful if, by "subjective meaning," we mean the "intended meaning" of other persons. The latter remains a limiting concept even under optimum conditions of interpretation. We shall show this later.[78] All of this calls for a thorough study, which we shall carry out in Chapter 3. Here let it suffice to state emphatically that the maximum possible grasp of subjective meaning in the social world cannot be expected on the common-sense level. In ordinary life we call a halt to the process of interpreting other people's meanings when we have found out enough to answer our practical questions; in short, we stop at the point that has direct relevance to the response we shall make ourselves. The search for the other person's subjective meaning will very likely be abandoned if his action becomes evident to us as objective content in a manner that relieves us of any further trouble. This is, perhaps, most obviously true of strictly "rational" action,[79] so-called, on the part of the person being observed. In such cases the overt meaning is sufficient for us to respond appropriately; we do not therefore try to interpret the other person's behavior beyond a rela-tively superficial level. Otherwise, if we have any doubts about the objective meaning of a person's conduct, we ask ourselves, "What is the fellow up to?" and so on. To this extent we can say of every meaning-interpretation of the social world that it is "pragmatically determined."

6. Transition to the Analysis of the Constituting Process. Clarification of the Concept of "Attaching Meaning to an Act"

IN ORDER TO GET CLEAR as to the essence of interpretive sociology, we took as our starting point Weber's definition of social action. Our first step was to analyze the statement, "The actor attaches a meaning to his action." We carried out part of this analysis in section 2 but found it necessary to make a digression in order to clarify

77. Or, in the sphere of the solitary Ego, to the "intended meaning" consti-tuted each time in its own consciousness.
78. See Chapter 3, sec. 19, below.
79. [Cf. Weber, *Wirtschaft und Gesellschaft*, E.T., p. 92.]

the concepts of objective and subjective meaning. We can now get back onto the main track of our argument.

First of all, we must point out an ambiguity in the term "action." This word can, first of all, mean the already constituted act (*Handlung*) considered as a completed unit, a finished product, an Objectivity. But second, it can mean the action in the very course of being constituted, and, as such, a flow, an ongoing sequence of events, a process of bringing something forth, an accomplishing. Every action, whether it be my own or that of another person, can appear to me under both these aspects. My *action as it takes place* presents itself to me as a series of *existing* and *present* experiences, experiences that are coming to be and passing away. My *intended* (*intendiertes*) *action* presents itself to me as a series of *future* experiences. My *terminated, completed act* (which is my expired action) presents itself to me as a series of *terminated* experiences which I contemplate in memory. The meaning of my action consists not only in the experiences of consciousness I have while the action is in progress but also in those future experiences which are my intended action and in those past experiences which are my completed action. We can at this point utilize the distinction we made at the end of the preceding paragraph between meaning-contents that are already constituted and meaning-contents still in the process of constitution. The distinction can now be applied specifically to action in such a way as to differentiate between the action in progress (*actio*) and the already finished and constituted act (*actum*) which has been produced by the former.

Likewise we should distinguish between the action of the other person and his act. The other person's conscious experiences in which his action is constituted present themselves to me as events of the external world. These may be his bodily movements or they may be changes in the external world brought about by such bodily movements. At any rate, we interpret these movements or changes as indications of another person's conscious experiences. Now we can regard these indications either as the other person's *actio* or as his *actum*, depending on whether our attention is focused on his conduct as it transpires before our eyes or on the act-objectivity (*Handlungsge-genständlichkeit*) produced and constituted by that conduct.

An act is therefore always something enacted (*ein Gehandelt-worden-sein*) and can be considered independently of the acting subject and of his experiences. Every act presupposes an action, but this by no means implies that reference to the action must enter into discussion of the act. In contrast to the act, the action is *subject-bound*. Whereas the act is, so to speak, performed anonymously, the action is a series of experiences being formed in the concrete and individual consciousness of some actor, be it myself or someone else.

We have already seen that it is only by studying the structure of the meaning-configuration in the stream of an Ego-consciousness that we can ever come to an understanding of the deep-seated difference between objective and subjective meaning. Meaning harks back to the internal time-consciousness, to the *durée* in which it was constituted originally and in its most generic sense. We see this point borne out in our analysis of the concepts of action and act. All action takes place in time, or more precisely in the internal time-consciousness, in the *durée*. It is duration-immanent enactment. Act, on the other hand, is duration-transcendent enactedness.

Having cleared up this point, we can now return to the question of what is meant by Weber's statement that the actor attaches meaning to his action. Does the actor give meaning to his action or to his act in the sense that we have defined these terms? In other words, is it the conscious processes which are being constituted in his *durée* which he endows with meaning, or is it the completed and constituted deed?

Before we answer this question, we must point out that we are speaking metaphorically when we say that a meaning is "attached" to an act. This is also true of Max Weber. For although Weber's concept of action, like that of Sander,[80] contains a number of ambiguities, one thing about it is certain. This is that he did not mean by "action" the physical event or bodily movement on the part of the actor. Nor did he think of the meaning as something which the individual in question "attached" to his bodily movement in the sense of sending it along a parallel track in a kind of pre-established harmony. Weber's definition of action, in fact, includes also a person's inner behavior [81] or activity to the extent that these can properly be regarded as meaningful. We have already demonstrated that this thesis must not be understood to assert that all behavior that is not action is therefore meaningless. Obviously, what he means is that action, as opposed to behavior in general, has a specific kind of meaning.

The first characteristic that suggests itself as a possible way of differentiating between action and behavior is the *voluntary* nature of action as opposed to the automatic nature of behavior. If this were

80. Sander, "Der Gegenstand der reinen Gesellschaftslehre," pp. 367 ff.

81. [*Innerliches Verhalten*. In his later writings Schutz distinguishes between "behavior" and "conduct." He notes that the former term "includes in present use also subjectively non-meaningful manifestations of spontaneity such as reflexes" (*Collected Papers*, I, 211.) Where subjective meaning is present, Schutz prefers the term "conduct." However, as Schutz is in the present work analyzing Weber's concept of *Verhalten*, we have decided to use the preferred translation "behavior," even where we have to speak of "inner behavior," especially since "inner conduct" would be even more awkward.]

what Weber had in mind when he defined action as meaningful behavior, then meaning would consist in choice, in decision, in the freedom to behave in a certain way while not being forced to act in that way. However, that would take care of only one of the two meanings of "free choice." The term "free choice" covers highly complex conscious events, and these need systematic study. The phenomenon of "will" should by no means be left unanalyzed as a vague label used to describe a metaphysical position. Rather, the analysis of voluntary behavior must be carried out without reference to metaphysical problems.

A second superficial difference distinguishes action as behavior which is *conscious* from unconscious or reactive behavior. In that case, the meaning "attached" to behavior would consist precisely in the consciousness of that behavior. However, what is "known" in this consciousness is evidently the truth about the behavior as it is disclosed to him whose behavior it is. How difficult is the disclosure of this truth Husserl has shown in his *Formal and Transcendental Logic*. It is, for example, a complicated problem whether a person's behavior is known to him simply in one particular mode of givenness or, rather, whether there are different modes or tenses of givennesss for one's past, present, and future (i.e., intended) behavior. This problem must be cleared up by any analysis of meaningful behavior.

This brief survey ought to be enough to show that an analysis of the constituting process (*Konstitutionsanalyse*) is necessary if we are going to understand the concept of meaningful action. In short, we must examine the formation and structure of those lived experiences which give meaning to an action. This investigation must, however, proceed to a still deeper level. For even what we call behavior is already meaningful in a more primitive sense of the term. Behavior as a lived experience is different from all other lived experiences in that it presupposes an activity of the Ego. Its meaning is therefore established in Acts wherein the Ego takes up one attitude or position after another. However, I can also attribute meaning to those of my experiences which do not involve activity (*Aktivität*). Even the fact that I become aware of the meaning of an experience presupposes that I notice it and "select it out" from all my other experiences. In each moment of its duration the Ego is conscious of its bodily state, its sensations, its perceptions, its attitude-taking Acts, and its emotional state. All these components constitute the "thus" or "whatness" (*So*) of each Now (*Jetzt*) of the Ego's conscious life. If I call one of these experiences meaningful it is only because, in taking heed of it, I have "selected it out" of and distinguished it from the abundance of experiences coexisting with it, preceding it, and following it. Let us call an experience that has been "selected out" in this way a "discrete" (*wohlumgrenztes*) experience and say that we "attach a meaning to it." We have now defined the first and most primitive sense of the word "meaning."

Notice, however, that we have ourselves just used the phrase "attach a meaning to," a metaphor to which we had previously taken exception. The later course of our investigations will fully justify our negative attitude toward this metaphor. By no means is the meaning of an experience a new, additional, and secondary experience which is somehow "attached" to the first. By no means, either, is meaning a *predicate* of an individual experience—a conclusion suggested by such usages as "having meaning," "meaning-bearing," and "meaningful." To anticipate ourselves, we will say that *meaning is a certain way of directing one's gaze at an item of one's own experience.* This item is thus "selected out" and rendered discrete by a reflexive Act. Meaning indicates, therefore, a peculiar attitude on the part of the Ego toward the flow of its own duration. This holds true of all stages and levels of meaning. Thus that theory is completely wrong which maintains that one's behavior is distinct from one's conscious experience of that behavior and that meaning belongs only to the latter. The difficulty lies chiefly in language, which, for certain deep-seated reasons, hypostatizes as behavior certain experiences of which we become aware and afterward predicates of this behavior as its meaning the very way of directing the gaze upon these experiences which made them into behavior in the first place. In just the same way, action is only a linguistic hypostatization of experiences of which we have become heedful and whose meaning (supposedly attached to them) is nothing more than the particular manner or "how" (*Wie*) of this heeding (*Zuwendung*).

Our analysis of meaningful action has thus led us back to the problem of how the meaning of an experience is constituted in internal time-consciousness. No science which aspires to give a radical description of the phenomenon of meaning, including an account of its origin, can shrink from studying this difficult problem. The investigations upon which we are about to embark will provide us with the answers to a series of hitherto unsolved questions: the question of what meaning is, generically; what specific kind of meaning pertains to behavior and to action; whether meaning pertains to the action in progress or to the completed act; how the objective meaning is constituted out of the "intended meaning," and so forth. These investigations will serve as preparatory studies to a precise understanding of Weber's concept of "the subjective meaning of the behavior of the other self." At the same time, it will be shown of what fundamental importance this concept is for the interpretive Acts of everyday life as well as for the methods of the social sciences. The achievement of Weber is all the more inspired in that he who in so many ways took over in philosophy the teachings of the Southwest German school nevertheless recognized quite independently the significance of the problem of intended meaning as the fundamental and basic principle of knowledge of the social world. Our further purpose in the considerations to follow will be to give to interpretive sociology the philosophical foundation which it has hitherto lacked and to establish its basic position securely on the assured conclusions of modern philosophy.

In this process we will be touching upon the work of two philosophers who have made the problem of the inner meaning of time the central point of their studies. The first is Bergson, whose *Essai sur les données immédiates de la conscience* (*Time and Free Will*), appearing as long ago as 1888, in a very impressive way made the phenomenon of inner duration the focal point of a whole philosophical system. The second is Husserl, who already in his *Vorlesungen über die Phänomenologie des inneren Zeitbewusstseins* (*Phenomenology of Internal Time Consciousness*), which was presented in part in a series of lectures in 1904 and was finally published by Heidegger in 1928, and also in his later works [82] gave systematic phenomenological descriptions of the genesis of meaning.

APPENDED NOTE

In order to be clear about the status of the following investigations from the point of view of phenomenology, it should be stated that:

Our studies of the constituting process in internal time-consciousness will be carried out within the "phenomenological reduction." Therefore they presuppose the bracketing (disconnection) [83] of the natural world and therewith the carrying into effect of a complete change of attitude (the *epoché*) toward the thesis of the "world given-to-me-as-being there (*als daseiende gibt*)." Husserl's description of this change of attitude is to be found in the first chapter of the second section of his *Ideas*. [84] However, our analysis will be carried out within the phenomenological reduction only so far as this is necessary for acquiring a clear understanding of the internal time-consciousness.

---

82. Husserl's *Méditations cartésiennes* (Paris, 1931) became available to me only after I had completed the present work, and I could not therefore rely upon it in my presentation of Husserl's views.

83. See above, sec. 5.

84. Pp. 48–57 [E.T., pp. 101–11].

The purpose of this work, which is to analyze the phenomenon of meaning in ordinary (*mundanen*) social life, does not require the achievement of a transcendental knowledge that goes beyond that sphere or a further sojourn within the area of the transcendental-phenomenological reduction. In ordinary social life we are no longer concerned with the constituting phenomena as these are studied within the sphere of the phenomenological reduction. We are concerned only with the phenomena corresponding to them within the natural attitude. Once we have understood by eidetic description the "problem of the inner development (*Zeitigung*) of the immanent time sphere," [85] we can apply our conclusions without risk of error to the phenomena of the natural attitude. With one proviso, however: that we now as "phenomenological psychologists" remain "on the ground of inner appearance as the appearance of that which is peculiar to the psychic." [86] Even then we do not set as our goal a science of the facts of this inner sphere of appearance, but a science of essence (*Wesenswissenschaft*).[87] What we are thus seeking is the invariant, unique, a priori structure of the mind, in particular of a society composed of living minds.[88] However, since all analyses carried out within the phenomenological reduction hold true essentially also in psychological introspection, and thus within the sphere of the natural attitude, we shall have to make no revisions whatsoever in our conclusions concerning the internal time-consciousness when we come to apply them to the realm of ordinary social life. Leaving aside all problems of transcendental subjectivity and intersubjectivity, which in fact emerge only after the phenomenological reduction, we shall—above all in Chapters 3 and 4—be carrying on "as constitutive phenomenology of the natural standpoint" [89] that phenomenological psychology which, according to Husserl, is, in the final analysis, nothing other than a psychology of pure intersubjectivity.

85. Husserl, "Nachwort zu meinen 'Ideen,'" *Jahrbuch für Philosophie und phänomenologische Forschung*, XI (Halle, 1930), 549–70, esp. 553.

86. *Ibid.*, p. 554.

87. [A descriptive study of the appearances as such, not as exemplifications of psychological laws.]

88. *Ibid.*, p. 555.

89. *Ibid.*, p. 567.

2 / The Constitution of Meaningful Lived Experience in the Constitutor's Own Stream of Consciousness

7. The Phenomenon of Inner Duration. Retention and Reproduction

LET US BEGIN BY CONSIDERING Bergson's distinction between living within the stream of experience and living within the world of space and time. Bergson contrasts the inner stream of duration, the *durée*—a continuous coming-to-be and passing-away of heterogeneous qualities—with homogeneous time, which has been spatialized, quantified, and rendered discontinuous. In "pure duration" there is no "side-by-sideness," no mutual externality of parts, and no divisibility, but only a continuous flux, a stream of conscious states. However, the term "conscious states" is misleading, as it reminds one of the phenomena of the spatial world with its fixed entities, such as images, percepts, and physical objects. What we, in fact, experience in duration is not a being that is discrete and well-defined but a constant transition from a now-thus to a new now-thus. The stream of consciousness by its very nature has not yet been caught up in the net of reflection. Reflection, being a function of the intellect, belongs essentially in the spatiotemporal world of everyday life. The structure of our experience will vary according to whether we surrender ourselves to the flow of duration or stop to reflect upon it, trying to classify it into spatiotemporal concepts. We can, for example, experience motion as a continuously changing manifold—in other words, as a phenomenon of our inner life; we can, on the other hand, conceive this same motion as a divisible event in homogeneous space. In the latter case, however, we have not really grasped the essence of that motion which is ever coming to be and passing away. Rather, we have grasped motion that is no longer motion, motion that has run its course, in short, not the motion itself, but merely the space traversed. Now, we can look at

[45]

enduring or frozen (margin note)

human acts under the same double aspect. We can look at them as enduring conscious processes or as frozen, spatialized, already completed acts. This double aspect appears not merely in transcendent "temporal Objects," [1] but throughout experience in general. Its deeper basis has been established and set forth by Husserl in his study of the internal time-consciousness.

Husserl refers explicitly to the double intentionality of the stream of consciousness:

> Either we consider the content of the flux with its flux-form—we consider then the series of primal lived experience, which is a series of intentional lived experiences, consciousness of . . . ; or we direct our regard to intentional unities, to that of which we are intentionally conscious as homogeneous in the streaming of the flux. In this case there is present to us an Objectivity in Objective time, the authentic temporal field as opposed to the temporal field of the stream of lived experience.[2]

Cool (margin note)

In another place Husserl calls these two types of intentionality, respectively, "longitudinal intentionality" (*Längs-intentionalität*) and "transverse intentionality" (*Quer-intentionalität*):

> By means of the one [transverse intentionality] immanent time is constituted, i.e., an Objective time, an authentic time in which there is duration [3] and alteration of that which endures. In the other [longitudinal intentionality] is constituted the quasi-temporal disposition of the phases of the flux which ever and necessarily has the flowing now-point, the phase of actuality, and the series of pre-actual and post-actual (of the not yet actual) phases. This pre-phenomenal, pre-immanent temporality is constituted intentionally as the form of temporally constitutive consciousness and in the latter itself.[4]

Now how are the individual experiences within the stream of consciousness constituted into intentional unities? If we take as our starting point Bergson's concept of the *durée*, then it becomes clear

1. [A transcendent temporal Object is a thing or event, with a temporal beginning, middle, and end, which lies outside the individual's consciousness but which he can perceive, think of, etc. An immanent temporal Object is a conscious content (such as a sound in the sense of auditory sense datum) whose duration is wholly within the individual's stream of consciousness. See Husserl's *Vorlesungen zur Phänomenologie des inneren Zeitbewusstseins* (hereafter cited as "*Zeitbewusstsein*"), *passim* (E.T., *The Phenomenology of Internal Time Consciousness*, by James S. Churchill; hereafter cited simply as "E.T."). For Husserl's general discussion of the concepts of transcendence and immanence see Husserl's *Ideas*, §§ 39–46 (the English translation of Husserl's *Ideen*, by W. R. Boyce Gibson, hereafter referred to simply as "E.T.").]

2. Husserl, *Zeitbewusstsein*, p. 469 [E.T., p. 157].

3. Husserl is here using the term "duration" (*Dauer*) in the German colloquial sense. He understands by the term the constancy of an object in space-time. This is the opposite of Bergson's usage; however, Bergson's German translator renders *durée* by *Dauer*.

4. *Zeitbewusstsein*, p. 436 [E.T., p. 109].

that the difference between the flowing experiences in pure duration and the discrete discontinuous images in the space-time world is a difference between two levels of consciousness. In everyday life the Ego, as it acts and thinks, lives on the level of consciousness of the space-time world. Its "attention to life" (*attention à la vie*) [5] prevents it from becoming submerged in the intuition of pure duration. However, if the "psychic tension" for any reason relaxes, the Ego will discover that what formerly seemed to be separate and sharply defined items are now dissolved into continuous transitions, that fixed images have become supplanted by a coming-to-be and passing-away that has no contours, no boundaries, and no differentiations. And so Bergson concludes that all distinctions, all attempts to "separate out" individual experiences from the one unity of duration, are artificial, i.e., alien to the pure *durée*, and all attempts to analyze process are merely cases of carrying over spatiotemporal modes of representation to the radically different *durée*.

Indeed, when I immerse myself in my stream of consciousness, in my duration, I do not find any clearly differentiated experiences at all. At one moment an experience waxes, then it wanes. Meanwhile something new grows out of what was something old and then gives place to something still newer. I cannot distinguish between the Now and the Earlier, between the later Now and the Now that has just been, except that I know that what has just been is different from what now is. For I experience my duration as a uni-directional, irreversible stream and find that between a moment ago and just now I *have grown older*. But I cannot become aware of this while still immersed in the stream. As long as my whole consciousness remains temporally uni-directional and irreversible, I am unaware either of my own growing older or of any difference between present and past. The very awareness of the stream of duration presupposes a turning-back against the stream, a special kind of attitude toward that stream, a "reflection," as we will call it. For only the fact that an earlier phase preceded this Now and Thus makes the Now to be Thus, and that earlier phase which constitutes the Now is given to me in this Now in the mode of remembrance (*Erinnerung*). The awareness of the experience in the pure stream of duration is changed at every moment into *remembered* having-just-been-thus; it is the remembering which lifts the experience out of the irreversible stream of duration and thus modifies the awareness, making it a remembrance.

Husserl has given us a precise description of this process.[6] He

5. [See Bergson, *Matter and Memory*, trans. N. M. Paul and W. Scott Palmer (New York, 1959), pp. 220–32.]

6. *Zeitbewusstsein*, pp. 382–427 [E.T., pp. 40–97]; *Ideen*, pp. 77 ff., pp. 144 f.

distinguishes between primary remembrance, or *retention,* as the af-
ter-consciousness of the primal impression, and secondary remembrance, recollection or *reproduction.* "To the 'impression,'" says
Husserl, "'primary remembrance' [*primäre Erinnerung*], or, as we say,
retention is joined. . . ."

> In the case of the perception of a temporal Object (it makes no
> difference to the present observation whether we take an immanent or
> transcendent Object), the perception always terminates in a now-
> apprehension, in a perception in the sense of a positing-as-now. During
> the perception of motion there takes place moment by moment, a "com-
> prehension-as-now"; constituted therein is the now actual phase of the
> motion itself. But this now-apprehension is, as it were, the nucleus of a
> comet's tail of retentions, referring to the earlier now-points of the
> motion. If perception no longer occurs . . . no new phase is joined to the
> last phase; rather we have a mere phase of fresh memory, to this is again
> joined another such and so on. There continually takes place, thereby, a
> shoving back [*Zurückschiebung*] into the past. The same complex contin-
> uously undergoes a modification until it disappears, for hand in hand
> with the modification goes a diminution which finally ends in imphercepti-
> bility.[7]

> *Secondary remembrance or recollection* is completely different from
> this. After primary remembrance is past, a new memory of this motion
> . . . can emerge.[8]

> We accomplish it either by simply laying hold of what is recollected
> . . . or we accomplish it in a real, re-productive, recapitulative memory
> in which the temporal object is again completely built up in a continuum
> of presentifications, so that we seem to perceive it again, but only
> seemingly, as-if.[9]

Retentional modification conforms directly to a primal impression
in the sense that it is a continuum retaining throughout the same
basic outline: it therefore starts out in perfect clarity and gradually
fades away, running off into the past.[10] Its degree of evidence is that of
absolute certainty, for the intentionality of the primal impression is
retained in retentional modification, although, to be sure, in altered
form. The feature of the identical basic outline carrying over from
impression to retention is missing in secondary remembrance or reproduction. On the contrary, there is a sharp discontinuity between repro-

7. *Zeitbewusstsein,* p. 391 [E.T., pp. 51–52].
8. *Ibid.,* p. 395 [italics ours; E.T., p. 57].
9. *Ibid.,* p. 397 [E.T., p. 59].
10. [Cf. *ibid.* (E.T., pp. 44–50) for a detailed description of the "running-off phenomenon."]

duction and impression. Presentification is a free running-through:
"We can carry out the presentification 'more quickly' or 'more slowly,'
clearly and explicitly or in a confused manner, quick as lightning at a
stroke or in articulated steps, and so on." [11] Reproduction, unlike
retention, is not originary consciousness and is therefore always unclear in comparison with it. It is by no means absolutely indubitable in
its degree of evidence.

To be sure, retention makes it possible for the regard (*Blick*) to
light upon the enduring, flowing, ever changing character of experience, but retention is not that regard itself:

> Retention itself is not an act [in our terminology: Act] of looking back
> which makes an object of the phase which has expired. Because I have
> the phase which has expired in hand, I live through [*durchlebe*] the one
> actually present, take it—thanks to retention—"in addition to" and am
> directed to what is coming. . . . But because I have this phase in hand, I
> can turn my regard toward it in a new act which—depending on whether
> the living experience which has expired is being generated in a new
> primal datum (therefore, is an impression), or whether, already com-
> pleted, it moves as a whole "into the past"—we call a reflection (imma-
> nent perception) or recollection. These acts stand to retention in the
> relation of fulfillment.[12]

It is, therefore, by virtue of retention that the multiplicity of the
running-off of duration is constituted: the present Now differs from
the earlier Now if only because retention, as the being-still-conscious
of the just-having-been, is carried out in a Now in whose constitution
it partakes. On the other hand, the identity of the object and objective
time itself is constituted in recollection (reproduction):

> Only in recollection can I have repeated an identical temporal object.
> I can also verify in recollection that what is perceived is the same as that
> which is subsequently recollected. This takes place in the simple re-
> membrance, "I have perceived that," and in the recollection of the second
> level, "I have a memory of that." [13]

The reproduction of a temporal object—and even experience in its
running-off is an immanent temporal object—can, as we noted before,
be accomplished either as a recapitulative ordering, in which the
temporal object is completely reconstructed, or in a simple laying-hold,
"as when a recollection 'emerges' and we look at what is remembered
with a glancing ray [*Blickstrahl*] wherein what is remembered is

11. *Ibid.*, p. 406 [E.T., p. 71].
12. *Ibid.*, p. 472 [E.T., p. 161].
13. *Ibid.*, p. 459 [E.T., p. 143].

indeterminate, perhaps a favored momentary phase intuitively brought forth, but not a recapitulative memory." [14] This form of reproduction exhibits all the characteristics of reflection in the previously described sense. Simple looking or apprehending

> is an act which, developed in successive stages, also in stages of spontaneity, e.g., the spontaneity of thought, is possible for everyone. . . . It appears, therefore, we can say that objectivities which are built up originally in temporal processes, being constituted member by member or phase by phase (as correlates of continuous, multiformed, cohesive and homogeneous acts), may be apprehended in a backward glance as if they were objects complete in a temporal point. But then this givenness certainly refers back to another "primordial" one. [15]

All this implies a distinction within the concept of "lived experience" (*Erlebnis*) which is of major significance for our topic:

> Even an experience is not, and never is, perceived in its completeness, it cannot be grasped adequately in its full unity. It is essentially something that flows, and starting from the present moment we can swim after it, our gaze reflectively turned towards it, whilst the stretches we leave in our wake are lost to perception. Only in the form of retention or in the form of retrospective . . . [recollection] have we any consciousness of what has immediately flowed past us. [16]

> We must, therefore, distinguish between the pre-empirical being of the lived experiences, their being prior to the reflective glance of attention directed toward them, and their being as phenomena. Through the attending directed glance of attention and comprehension, the lived experience acquires a new mode of being. It comes to be "differentiated," "thrown into relief," and this act of differentiation is nothing other than the act of comprehension, and the differentiation nothing other than being comprehended, being the object of the directed glance of attention. However, the matter is not to be thought of as if the difference consisted merely in this, that the same lived experience just united with the directed glance of attention is a new lived experience, that of directing-oneself-thither-to; as if, therefore, a mere complication occurs. Certainly when a directed glance of attention occurs, it is evident that we distinguish between the object of the directed glance of attention (the experience A) and the directed glance of attention itself. And certainly we have reason to say that our glance of attention was previously directed toward another, that the directed glance of attention toward A then took place, and that A "was already there" before this act. [17]

This insight is crucial to the question we previously raised about the nature of *discrete* experiences and therewith about the first and most

14. *Ibid.*, p. 397 [E.T., p. 59].
15. *Ibid.*, p. 397 [E.T., pp. 59–60].
16. *Ideen*, p. 82 [E.T., p. 140].
17. *Zeitbewusstsein*, p. 484 [E.T., pp. 178–79].

primitive sense of the term "meaning of an experience." Let us outline the critical stages, following Husserl.

If we simply live immersed in the flow of duration, we encounter only undifferentiated experiences that melt into one another in a flowing continuum. Each Now differs essentially from its predecessor in that within the Now the predecessor is contained in retentional modification. However, I know nothing of this while I am simply living in the flow of duration, because it is only by an Act of reflective attention that I catch sight of the retentional modification and therewith of the earlier phase. Within the flow of duration there is only a living from moment to moment, which sometimes also contains in itself the retentional modifications of the previous phase. Then, as Husserl says, I live *in* my Acts, whose living intentionality carries me over from one Now to the next. But this Now should not be construed as a punctiform instant, as a break in the stream of duration, as a cutting-in-two of the latter. For in order to effect such an artificial division within duration, I should have to get outside the flow itself. From the point of view of a being immersed in duration, the "Now" is a phase rather than a point, and therefore the different phases melt into one another along a continuum. The simple experience of living in the flow of duration goes forward in a uni-directional, irreversible movement, proceeding from manifold to manifold in a constant running-off process. Each phase of experience melts into the next without any sharp boundaries as it is being lived through; but each phase is distinct in its thusness, or quality, from the next insofar as it is held in the gaze of attention.

However, when, by my act of reflection, I turn my attention to my living experience, I am no longer taking up my position within the stream of pure duration, I am no longer simply living within that flow. The experiences are apprehended, distinguished, brought into relief, marked out from one another; the experiences which were constituted as phases within the flow of duration now become objects of attention as constituted experiences. What had first been constituted as a phase now stands out as a full-blown experience, no matter whether the Act of attention is one of reflection or of reproduction (in simple apprehension). For *the Act of attention*—and this is of major importance for the study of meaning—presupposes an elapsed, passed-away experience—in short, one that is already in the past, regardless of whether the attention in question is reflective or reproductive.[18]

Therefore we must contrast those experiences which in their running-off are undifferentiated and shade into one another, on the one

18. "Reflection has this remarkable peculiarity, that that which is thus apprehended through perception is, in principle, characterized as something which not

hand, with those that are discrete, already past, and elapsed, on the other. The latter we apprehend not by living through them but by an act of attention. This is crucial for the topic we are pursuing: Because the concept of meaningful experience always presupposes that the experience of which meaning is predicated is a discrete one, it now becomes quite clear that only a past experience can be called meaningful, that is, one that is present to the retrospective glance as already finished and done with.

Only from the point of view of the retrospective glance do there exist discrete experiences. Only the already experienced is meaningful, not that which is being experienced. For meaning is merely an operation of intentionality, which, however, only becomes visible to the reflective glance. From the point of view of passing experience, the predication of meaning is necessarily trivial, since meaning here can only be understood as the attentive gaze directed not at passing, but at already passed, experience.

Is, however, the distinction just made between discrete and nondiscrete experience really justified? Is it not at least possible that the attentive glance can light upon each item of experience which has passed by, can "throw it into relief" and "distinguish" it from other items? We believe that the answer must be in the negative. There are, as a matter of fact, experiences which are experiences when they are present but which either cannot be reflected upon at all or can be reflected upon only through an extremely vague apprehension and whose reproduction, apart from the purely empty notion of "having experienced something"—in other words, in a clear way—is quite impossible.[19] We will call this group "essentially actual" experiences because they are by their very nature limited to a definite temporal position within the inner stream of consciousness. They are known by their attachment or closeness to that innermost core of the Ego which Scheler in a happy turn of phrase called the "absolute personal privacy" (absolut intime Person) of an individual.[20] About the absolute personal privacy of a person we know both that it must necessarily be there and that it remains absolutely closed to any sharing of its experience with others. But also in self-knowledge there is a sphere of

only is and endures within the gaze of perception, but already was before this gaze was directed to it" (Husserl, Ideen, p. 83 [E.T., p. 141]). Further: "We can now raise the question: what about the beginning phase of a self-constitutive lived experience? . . . . It can be said that the beginning phase can become an Object only after its running off in the way indicated, through retention and reflection (or reproduction)" (Husserl, Zeitbewusstsein, p. 472 [The italics are Husserl's; E.T., p. 162]).

19. Cf. sec. 16, below.

20. Sympathiegefühle, p. 77. [E.T., Heath, p. 66. Schutz is here referring to the first edition of Scheler's Wesen und Formen der Sympathie. See Bibliography.]

absolute intimacy whose "being there" (*Dasein*)[21] is just as indubitable as it is closed to our inspection. The experiences peculiar to this
sphere are simply inaccessible to memory, and this fact pertains to
their mode of being: memory catches only the "that" of these experiences. For the confirmation of this thesis (which can only be stated
here and not fully proved), an observation which can be performed
immediately furnishes support, namely, that the reproduction becomes
all the less adequate to the experience the nearer it comes to the
intimate core of the person. This diminishing adequacy has in consequence an ever greater vagueness of reproduced content. Concomi-
tantly, the capacity for recapitulative reproduction diminishes, that is,
the capacity for the complete reconstruction of the course of the
experience. As far as reproduction is possible at all, it can only be
accomplished by a simple act of apprehension. The "How" of the
experience can, however, be reproduced only in recapitulative reconstruction. The recollection of an experience of the external world is
relatively clear; an external course of events, a movement perhaps,
can be recollected in free reproduction, that is, at arbitrary points of
the duration. Incomparably more difficult is the reproduction of experiences of internal perception; those internal perceptions that lie close to
the absolute private core of the person are irrecoverable as far as their
How is concerned, and their That can be laid hold of only in a simple
act of apprehension. Here belong, first of all, not only all experiences
of the corporeality of the Ego, in other words, of the Vital Ego (muscular tensings and relaxings as correlates of the movements of the body,
"physical" pain, sexual sensations, and so on), but also those psychic
phenomena classified together under the vague heading of "moods," as
well as "feelings" and "affects" (joy, sorrow, disgust, etc.). The limits
of recall coincide exactly with the limits of "rationalizability," provided
that one uses this equivocal word—as Max Weber does at times—in
the broadest sense, that is, in the sense of "capable of giving a meaning." Recoverability to memory is, in fact, the first prerequisite of all
rational construction. That which is irrecoverable—and this is in
principle always something ineffable—can only be lived but never
"thought": it is in principle incapable of being verbalized.

8. Husserl's Meaning-endowing Experiences and the Concept of Behavior

WE MUST NOW ANSWER the question, "How am I to distinguish my behavior from the rest of my experiences?" The answer is

21. [As Schutz explains at a later point, his use of this term of Heidegger's
does not necessarily involve the full range of meaning attributed to it by
Heidegger. Cf. sec. 9, below.]

supplied by ordinary usage. A pain, for instance, is not generally called behavior. Nor would I be said to be behaving if someone else lifted my arm and then let it drop. But the *attitudes* I assume in either of these cases *are* called behavior. I may fight the pain, suppress it, or abandon myself to it. I may submit or resist when someone manipulates my arm. So what we have here are two different types of lived experiences that are fundamentally related. Experiences of the first type are merely "undergone" or "suffered." They are characterized by a basic passivity. Experiences of the second type consist of the attitudes taken toward experiences of the first type. To put it in Husserl's words, behavior is a "meaning-endowing experience of consciousness." When he studied the "important and difficult problem of the defining characteristics of thought," Husserl showed that not all experiences are meaning-endowing by nature. "Experiences of primordial passivity, associations, those experiences in which the original time-consciousness, the constitution of immanent temporality takes place, and other experiences of this kind, are all incapable of it" (that is, of conferring meaning). A meaning-endowing experience must rather be an "Ego-Act (attitudinal Act) or some modification of such an Act (secondary passivity, or perhaps a passively emerging judgment that suddenly 'occurs to me')." [22]

One can, if one wishes, define attitude-taking Acts as Acts of primary engendering activity,[23] provided that, with Husserl,[24] one includes here feelings and the constitution of values by feelings, whether these values be regarded as ends or means. Husserl uses the term "meaning-endowing conscious experiences" (*sinngebende Bewusstseinserlebnisse*) to cover all experiences given in intentionality in the form of spontaneous activity or in one of the secondary modifications thereof. Now, what are these modifications? The two principle ones are retention and reproduction. Husserl describes them as follows:

> With every Act of spontaneity something new emerges. This Act functions, so to speak, in every moment of its flux as a primal sensation which undergoes its shading-off according to the fundamental law of consciousness. The spontaneity which sets about its work in steps in the

22. Husserl, *Formale und Transzendentale Logik*, p. 22 [hereafter referred to as "*Logik*"]. With respect to the theme of passivity and activity, cf. also Reiner's excellent detailed study, *Freiheit, Wollen und Aktivität* (Halle, 1927), which did not come to my attention until after the completion of the present work. I am in agreement with Reiner on all essential points.

23. Or, as it is characteristically stated in *Ideen*, "The fulfilled Act, or [since they are] . . . processes, *the Acts in process of fulfillment* compose what *in the broadest sense* we term 'attitudes' " (*Ideen*, I, p. 236 [E.T., p. 323]).

24. *Logik*, p. 281.

flux of consciousness constitutes a temporal Object, namely an Object of becoming, a process, essentially only a process, and not an enduring Object. And this process sinks back into the past.[25]

Whenever there is an original constitution of an objectivity of consciousness by means of an Activity, the *original Action* is changed in retentional constancy into a *secondary form* which is no longer Activity, but is a passive form, the form of a *"secondary sensuousness,"* as we call it. By virtue of the constant synthesis of identity, the passive consciousness is consciousness of the very same thing which was constituted a moment before in active originality.[26]

All this is true of judgment, which is a type of action, but an action which "from the beginning and throughout all the forms which it takes on at every stage, is concerned exclusively with the irreal." [27] Even the ideal objectivities

are conceivable goals, ends and means, they are what they are only because they have been engendered by consciousness. But this does not mean that they are what they are only *in* and *during* the primary originating *production*. They are "in" the primary engendering production in the sense of being known in it as a certain intentionality of the form of *spontaneous Activity*, and in the mode of the original self. This mode of givenness out of such primordial Activity is nothing other than its own peculiar mode of perception.[28]

Let us now try to restate these concepts of Husserl in such a way as to apply them to our own problems. We define "behavior" as an experience of consciousness that bestows meaning through sponta-

behavior
defined

25. *Zeitbewusstsein,* p. 487 [E.T., p. 184].

26. *Logik,* p. 281.

27. *Logik,* p. 149.

28. *Logik,* p. 150. Cf. Husserl's views on the thesis as Act of free spontaneity and activity, *Ideen,* p. 253 [E.T., p. 342]. Recently in his *Cartesian Meditations* (Meditation IV) Husserl drew a radical distinction between active and passive genesis as two fundamental forms of conscious life. He says (pp. 65 f., § 38): "Let us ask what are the universal principles of constitutive genesis which are important from the point of view of the relation of the subject to the world. These principles are of two basic types: principles of active genesis and principles of passive genesis. In the first case the Ego actively engenders, creates and constitutes. . . . Here the essential thing is that the acts of the Ego, already internally related to one another, join together in complex syntheses and on the basis of objects already given, proceed to constitute new objects in an original manner. These objects then appear to consciousness as products. . . . But all such cases of active construction presuppose on a lower level a floor of passive awareness. We never fail to find this floor of passive constitution when we analyze an actively constituted object." [This passage has been freely translated from the French edition cited by Schutz; cf. also *Cartesian Meditations,* translated from the German by Dorion Cairns (The Hague, 1960), pp. 77–78.]

neous Activity. Action and behavior [*in the narrower sense of conduct*—Trans.] form a subclass within behavior so conceived; we shall discuss them at length later. What distinguishes the objectivity of consciousness, which is constituted in original Activity and is therefore a case of behavior, from all other experiences of consciousness, and makes it "meaning-endowing" in Husserl's sense, becomes intelligible only under one condition, namely, that one apply the distinctions explained above between the constituting Act and the constituted objectivity also to the sphere of spontaneous Activity. If one does so, one will distinguish between the spontaneous Act itself and the object constituted within it. In the direction of the occurrence or running-off of the behavior, the spontaneous Act is nothing more than the mode of intentionality in which the constituting objectivity is given. In other words, behavior as it occurs is "perceived" in a unique way as primordial activity.

This perception functions as a primal impression, which of course undergoes the usual "shading" in the retentional process, just as all other impressions do. Activity is an experience which is constituted in phases in the transition from one Now to the next. The beam of reflection can only be directed at it from a later vantage point. This necessarily involves either retention or recollection. The latter may consist in a simple Act of apprehension or may involve reconstruction in phases. In any case the original intentionality of spontaneous Activity is preserved in intentional modification.

Applied to the theory of behavior, this means that one's own behavior, while it is actually taking place, is a *prephenomenal* experience. Only when it has already taken place (or if it occurs in successive phases, only when the initial phases have taken place) does it stand out as a discrete item from the background of one's other experiences. Phenomenal experience is, therefore, never of oneself behaving, only of having behaved. Yet the original experience in another sense remains the same in memory as it was when it occurred. My past behavior is, after all, *my* behavior; it consists of *my* Act wherein *I* take up some attitude or other, even if I see it only "in profile" as something past. And it is precisely this attitudinal character which distinguishes it from all the rest of my experience. My elapsed experience is still mine, since it is I who once lived through it; this is simply another way of asserting that duration's elapse or "running-off" is continuous, that there is a fundamental unity in the time-constituting stream of consciousness. Even experiences of primordial passivity are grasped retrospectively as *my* experiences. My behavior is distinguished from these by the fact that it refers back to my primal impression of spontaneous Activity.

Behavior, then, consists of a series of experiences which are distinguished from all other experiences by a primordial intentionality of spontaneous Activity which remains the same in all intentional modifications. Now it becomes clear what we meant when we said that behavior is merely experiences looked at in a certain light, that is, referred back to the Activity which originally produced them. The "meaning" of experiences is nothing more, then, than that frame of interpretation which sees them as behavior. So in the case of behavior, also, it turns out that only what is already over and done with has meaning. The prephenomenal experience of activity is, therefore, not meaningful. Only that experience which is reflectively perceived in the form of spontaneous Activity has meaning.

[margin note: Only what is over has meaning]

Let us now proceed a step further and seek to define the concept of action within the category of behavior.

9. The Concept of Action. Project and Protention

IN COMMON USAGE WE TEND to distinguish action from behavior by simply saying that the former is "conscious" or "voluntary," while the latter is "reactive" in character and includes such things as reflexes. We must now look into the deeper reasons for this apparently superficial distinction.[29]

First of all, every action is a spontaneous activity oriented toward the future. This orientation toward the future is by no means peculiar to behavior. It is, on the contrary, a property of all primary constituting processes, whether these arise from spontaneous activity or not. Each such process contains within itself intentionalities of lived experience that are directed toward the future. It is to Husserl that we owe the clarification of this point.[30]

"Reflection" in the broader sense is not confined to retention and reproduction, according to Husserl. Protentions into the future are a part of every memory, and in the natural standpoint they are merged with retentions. "Every primordially constitutive process is animated by protentions, which . . . constitute and intercept what is coming, as such, in order to bring it to fulfillment" (*Zeitbewusstsein*, p. 410 [E.T., p. 76]). To be distinguished from immediate protention is anticipation (*Vorerinnerung*) or foreseeing expectation. This "represents" where

[margin note: protention]

29. We trust we have by now demonstrated the inadequacy of Weber's distinction between action and behavior.

30. *Ideen*, pp. 145, 149, 164 [E.T., pp. 216, 220, 238]; *Zeitbewusstsein*, pp. 396, 410 [E.T., pp. 58, 76].

protention only "presents." It is reproductive in nature, being the future-directed counterpart of recollection.

> Here the intuitively expected whereof, thanks to the reflection possible "in" anticipation, we are aware through prevision as "presently coming," has at the same time the meaning of *what will be perceived,* just as the recalled has the meaning of what has been perceived. Thus we can reflect in anticipation also, and bring to consciousness experiences of ours for the enjoyment whereof the anticipation itself did not offer the proper standpoint, as none the less belonging to the anticipated as such: as we do each time we say that we *shall see* what is coming, when in so saying, the reflecting glance has turned toward the "coming" perceptual experience.[31]

The fact that every action necessarily involves anticipation of the future in the sense that it is "future-directed" has been stated with great clarity by Husserl:

> In every action we know the goal in advance in the form of an anticipation that is "empty," in the sense of vague, and lacking its proper "filling-in," which will come with fulfillment. Nevertheless we strive toward such a goal and seek by our action to bring it step by step to concrete realization.[32]

From the foregoing it would seem that action could be defined as a type of behavior which anticipates the future in the form of an empty protention. The future would in this case be that which is to be realized through the action, in short, the act (*Handlung*). But this definition would be incomplete. It is not only in the case of action that we find anticipation of the future via *empty* protention. We find empty protention as well in all attitude-assuming Acts (*Akten*). But then the protentions appear as *empty* and *unfulfilled* only in the constitutive process of unreflected-upon action, in the gradual unrolling of experiences in spontaneous Activity. But as soon as the intentional glance lights upon the action, the situation becomes different. Then the action is contemplated as if it were already over and done with, fully constituted. If only one phase of the action has been thus fixed by the reflective glance, it is that phase which appears as completed. But in such reflective attention (above all, in remembering), protentions are never expectations which are still empty, determinable, and yet to be filled in. Rather they bear the marks of fulfillment. In the primordial Now to which they first belonged they were, to be sure, empty. But later, due to the transformation of this Now into a Has Been, this Has

31. *Ideen*, I, p. 145 [E.T., pp. 216–17].
32. *Logik*, pp. 149 f.

Been is now looked back at from a new vantage point. So the peculiar function of protention becomes clear only in memory.

> Every Act of memory contains intentions of expectation whose fulfill-ment leads to the present. . . . The recollective process not only renews these protentions in a manner appropriate to memory. These protentions were not only present as intercepting, they have also intercepted, they have been fulfilled, and we are aware of them in recollection. Fulfillment in recollective consciousness is refulfillment (precisely in the modifica-tion of the positing of memory), and if the primordial protention of the perception of the event was undetermined, and the question of being-other or not-being was left open, then in the recollection we have a pre-directed expectation which does not leave all that open. It is then in the form of an incomplete recollection whose structure is other than that of the undetermined primordial protention. And yet this is also included in the recollection.[33]

Therefore, what was empty expectation for the actor is either fulfilled or unfulfilled expectation for him who remembers. That which, for the actor, points from the present into the future, for him who is remem-bering points from the past to the present moment, while still retain-ing the temporal character of the future.[34] The intentional glance, then, is concerned only with the act (*Handlung*), not with the action (*Handeln*); and acts are always fulfilled, never empty, protentions.

Now let us turn to "anticipation," that reflexive looking-forward-to which corresponds to reproduction, and ask what is meant by saying that the aims of an action are always known in advance by means of this faculty. The analysis of action shows that it is always carried out in accordance with a plan more or less implicitly preconceived. Or, to use a term of Heidegger's, an action always has "the nature of a project" (*Entwurfcharakter*).[35] But the projection of an action is in principle carried out independently of all real action. Every projection of action is rather a phantasying of action,[36] that is, a phantasying of spontaneous activity, but not the activity itself. It is an intuitive advance picturing which may or may not include belief, and, if it does, can believe positively or negatively or with any degree of certainty.[37]

33. *Zeitbewusstsein*, p. 410 [E.T., p. 76].
34. [Recollection's horizon is "oriented on the future, that is, the future of the recollected" (*ibid.*).]
35. *Sein und Zeit*, p. 245 [E.T., *Being and Time*, by Macquarrie and Robinson (New York, 1962), p. 185]. We are here borrowing Heidegger's term without committing ourselves to the explicit meaning he gives it. The term is also used by Pfänder in his excellent study, "Motiv und Motivation," *Festschrift für Lipps* (Leipzig, 1930).
36. We are, contrary to Husserl's usage, using the term "phantasy" to include anticipation. Cf., below, sec. 11.
37. *Zeitbewusstsein*, p. 453 [E.T., p. 134].

These phantasies differ from protentions in that protentions (unless they actually intercept the future experience) are *empty* representations, whereas phantasies are intuitive representations. This does not mean that they are filled-in or very specific; indeed, all anticipation of future action is quite vague and indeterminate compared to the real thing when it finally occurs, and this is as true of rational action as any other.

We spoke in the preceding paragraph of a phantasy of *action*. However, it is a question whether this way of speaking can be maintained in view of our distinction between the action and the act. The difficulty is the following. Is it the action or the act that is thus projected and phantasied?

The answer is not hard to find. What is projected is the act, which is the goal of the action and which is brought into being by the action. Indeed, this follows from the nature of projection. The action itself could hardly be projected were not the completed act projected with it. Indeed, only the completed act can be pictured in phantasy. For if the act is the goal of the action, and if the act were not projected, then the picturing of the action would be necessarily abstract. It would be an empty protention without any specific content, without any intuitive "filling-in." To be sure, it is proper to speak in ordinary language of my imagining my own action. But what is it which is really imagined here? Suppose I imagine myself getting up out of my chair and going over to the window. What I really picture to myself is not a series of muscle contractions and relaxations, not a series of specific steps—one, two, three—from chair to window. No, the picture that I have in mind is a picture of the completed act of having gone over to the window. To this might be raised the objection that this is an illusion and that if we pictured our trip to the window with proper attentiveness we would count the steps and picture them. But to this objection there is a ready answer. If we do concentrate on each step or on each stretching of the leg, it will then turn out that what we are picturing is in each case a completed act: the act of having taken step one, the act of having taken step two, and so on. And the same will hold true of the parts of these steps in case we carry our analytic inclinations any further.

The separate motions which constitute the execution of an action cannot therefore be pictured apart from the intended act which is constituted in the action. What is true in the case of memory is true in the case of anticipation. In both cases what is visible to the mind is the completed act, not the ongoing process that constitutes it. It is the act, therefore, that is projected, not the action.

It must be stressed that projection is given only to reflective thought, not to immediate experience or to spontaneous Activity. To be sure, immediate experience is surrounded by its aura of expectations, but these are empty protentions. Sometimes these protentions may seem to be "filled-in": for instance, in performing an act we may experience quite definite immediate expectations. But these expectations have actually been influenced by the plan or project we have in mind. The project is carried over from moment to moment and renders each momentary expectation quite concrete, even though the concreteness is a derived one and is the result of the "feeding" of the project into this particular moment.

Now we are in a position to state that what distinguishes action from behavior is that *action is the execution of a projected act*. And we can immediately proceed to our next step: *the meaning of any action is its corresponding projected act*. In saying this we are giving clarity to Max Weber's vague concept of the "orientation of an action." An action, we submit, is oriented toward its corresponding projected act.

Now let us look at *rational* or *purposive* action, that is, action which has a goal of optimum clarity. How does a person acting rationally proceed? The plan or projection of his action begins with choosing a goal. Next he realizes that, if he is to achieve his goal, he must adopt certain means. This is merely a recognition on his part of a certain causal regularity existing between the events which he calls his means and the end event which he calls his goal. Now, of course, if he chooses M_1, M_2, and M_3 as his means, he is also projecting them as intermediate goals. *Rational action can therefore be defined as an action with known intermediate goals*. At the same time, it is essential that the person acting rationally make a judgment of this kind: "Goal G is to be reached through means M_1, M_2, and M_3. Therefore, given M_1, M_2, and M_3, G will result." We can see, therefore, even at this stage of rational action, that the project is directed at the act as being fulfilled in the future, for only if the fulfillment of the future act is thus assumed or posited can the means be selected. To put it another way: the actor projects his action as if it were already over and done with and lying in the past. It is a full-blown, actualized event, which the actor pictures and assigns to its place in the order of experiences given to him at the moment of projection. Strangely enough, therefore, because it is pictured as completed, *the planned act bears the temporal character of pastness*. Of course, once the action begins, the goal is *wished for* and *protended*. The fact that it is thus pictured as if it were simultaneously past and future can be taken care of by saying that it is thought of in the future perfect tense (*modo futuri exacti*). Indeed, not only projection but any expectation may be regarded as picturing its object in the future perfect tense, provided that the picture is clear and well defined.

To illustrate the point we have just made, let us recall that Tiresias in *Oedipus Rex* was able to see his dire predictions as already having come true, able to see them with all the vividness of remembered events. Yet do not forget that he also saw them as future events. If he had not been able to foresee the events as completed, he would have been merely forecasting from known tendencies and would then have been no true prophet. But if he had not seen them as being yet in the future, he would have been no prophet but a mere historian.[38]

Our definition of action as projected behavior has an additional advantage: it solves the problem of the *unity of an action*. This problem is of crucial importance for interpretive sociology, yet up to the present it has gone unsolved. When an interpretive sociologist examines an action, he assumes that it has unity and that this can be defined. Yet in practice, when he comes to relate observational and motivational understanding, he defines the concrete action arbitrarily, without reference to the intended meaning of the actor. The analysis of rational action leads to the same result. If the goal is given, the means follows, and each means then becomes an intermediate goal which must be accomplished by still other means. The total act thus divides into component acts, and an external observer who is "objectively" watching such a series of "component" acts is in no position to say whether the goal has yet been reached or whether there is more to come. Each component stage can be regarded as a new unity. It is up to the observer, be he the actor's partner or a sociologist, to decide arbitrarily where the total act begins and ends. The paradox is insoluble. Of what use is it to talk about the intended meaning of an action if one ignores that phase of the action which is relevant to the actor and substitutes for it as the interpretation an arbitrarily chosen segment of the observed performance—"the facts"? When one is watching a woodcutter it will make a great deal of difference whether we try to analyze "objectively" the individual blows of the ax or whether we simply ask the man what he is doing and find that he is working for a lumber company.

We have traced back the analysis of the action to the projection of the act in the future perfect tense. From this can be deduced with complete necessity the concept of the unity of the action. The unity of the action is constituted by the fact that the act already exists "in project," which will be realized step by step through the action. *The unity of the act is a function of the span or breadth of the project.* The

38. *Zeitbewusstsein*, p. 413 [E.T., p. 79].

[handwritten margin note: speaks to impulion ce of understanding intention]

unity of the action is, then, *subjective,* and the problem of inserting the subjective meaning into a piece of behavior which supposedly already has *objective* unity turns out to be a pseudo-problem.[39] It must now be clear that an action is meaningless as action apart from the project which defines it. This is only the proof of what we asserted in section 6: a meaning is not really *attached* to an action. If we say it is, we should understand that statement as a metaphorical way of saying that we direct our attention upon our experiences in such a way as to constitute out of them a unified action.

10. Conscious Action and Its Evidence

WE MUST NOW ASK what is meant by calling an action "conscious" in contrast to "unconscious" behavior.[40] Our thesis is this: An action is conscious in the sense that, before we carry it out, we have a picture in our mind of what we are going to do. This is the "projected act." Then, as we do proceed to action, we are either continuously holding the picture before our inner eye (retention), or we are from time to time recalling it to mind (reproduction). The total experience of action is a very complex one, consisting of experiences of the activity as it occurs, various kinds of attention to that activity, retention of the projected act, reproduction of the projected act, and so on. This "map-consulting" is what we are referring to when we call the action conscious. Behavior without the map or picture is unconscious. To forestall confusion, let us mention that there are several other senses in which human experiences are distinguished as "conscious" versus "unconscious." Some are legitimate and others are not. For instance, there is the theory which alleges the existence of experiences totally alien to, and having no effect on, consciousness. We ourselves reject this concept as self-contradictory, since in our view experience implies consciousness. Then, of course, there is the very different sense in which one might call those experiences "unconscious" which have not yet been reflected upon. Regardless of the problems involved in such a usage,[41] the dichotomy we are drawing is a quite different one. Our actions are conscious if we have previously mapped them out "in the future perfect" tense."

[handwritten margin note: Conscious vs Unconscious]

39. We cannot here go into the obvious consequences for ethics and jurisprudence, especially criminal law.

40. The reader is referred to Moritz Geiger's excellent study of this topic, "Fragment über das Unbewusste," *Jahrbuch für Phänomenologie,* IV (1921), 1–136. Our own terminology differs, of course, from Geiger's. [This first paragraph of sec. 10 is a paraphrase rather than a translation of Schutz's original.]

41. *Zeitbewusstsein,* p. 473 [E.T., pp. 161–63].

Our next question concerns the mode of our knowledge of conscious action. What is the "evidence" [42] with which it presents itself, that is, how do we "encounter" the action in our experience? The answer is that the evidence or mode of presentation differs according to whether (1) the act is still in the "pure project" stage, (2) the action as such has begun and the act is on its way to fulfillment, or (3) the act has been executed and is being looked back on as a *fait accompli*.

Let us look at the first situation. What kind of knowledge can we have of our project? As a matter of fact, it can be of any degree of clarity, from one of total vagueness to one of maximum detail. However, it must be remembered that our knowledge here is of the *project of the act*, not of the *act itself*. Naturally, the first is what its name implies, a mere sketch with many empty places and variables in it. These empty places are filled in, and the variables are given values as the action progresses step by step. At any moment we can compare our blueprint with what we are actually doing. Now we know each of these two items differently. We remember our blueprint or project, whereas we directly experience what we are doing. Naturally, memory-evidence is weaker and has less claim on us than direct, present experience. And the closer it is to the latter, the stronger it is.[43] The various degrees of evidence in which experiences are presented to us in relation to their temporal positions have been developed at length by Husserl. We need concern ourselves with this diversity here only to the extent of noting that it exists and that it is very complex. To cite a frequent example: we may start out with a clear plan of action, then get rather confused while we are executing it, and in the end not be able to explain what we have done.

The number of possible variations is unlimited. However, we are *conscious* of an action only if we contemplate it as already over and done with, in short, as an *act*. This is true even of projects, for we project the intended action as an act in the future perfect tense.

When we were previously considering the thesis that conscious behavior is behavior with meaning attached to it,[44] we said that "the meaning 'attached' to the behavior would consist precisely in the consciousness of the behavior." We now see in how many different ways this can be interpreted. But our main point remains unaffected: that the meaning of an action is the corresponding act. This follows

42. "Evidence" (*Evidenz*) is used here in Husserl's sense as the specific experience of this "being conscious of." Cf. *Logik*, pp. 437 ff., esp. p. 144.

43. *Ideen*, pp. 293–94 [E.T., pp. 392–93].

44. In sec. 6, p. 41, above.

strictly from our definition of action as behavior oriented to a previously made plan or project.

Beyond this, our analysis in terms of time has illuminated the radical difference between action before its execution, on the one hand, and the completed act, on the other. From this it follows that the question of what is the intended meaning of an act already performed requires one answer, whereas the question of the meaning of the concrete action first intended requires another.

What is this important difference? It is that while the action has yet to take place it is phantasied as that which will have taken place, that is, in the future perfect tense as something already performed. Thus what occurs is a reflective Act of attention to an action phantasied as over and done with. This Act of attention, of course, temporally precedes the action itself. Then as the action takes place and proceeds to its termination, the actor's experience is enlarged—he "grows older." What was inside the illuminated circle of consciousness during the moment of projection now falls back into the darkness and is replaced by later lived experiences which had been merely expected or protended. Let us imagine a person who projects a rational action that had been planned a long time before and whose goals, both final and intermediate, had, therefore, been clearly anticipated. It cannot be doubted that this person's attitude toward his plan will necessarily differ from his attitude toward the finished deed. This will be true even if the action proceeded according to plan. "Things look different the morning after." This has been a problem of the social sciences. It has been emphasized in every historical interpretation which has pointed out the discrepancies between what was intended and what actually resulted. Within interpretive sociology the problem crops up in the distinction between subjective and objective likelihood or probability, between interpretive adequacy on the causal level and interpretive adequacy on the level of meaning.[45] We shall concern ourselves in detail with these questions at a later point.[46] These examples could be enlarged upon considerably. They all serve to illustrate the point that the meaning of an action is different depending on the point in time from which it is observed. One cannot, therefore, speak simply of the intended meaning attached to an action. The concept "intended meaning" is an incomplete function; to become fully meaningful, it requires a date index specifying the moment of the meaning-interpretation. This point never occurs to Weber. When he speaks of the intended

45. [Weber, *Wirtschaft und Gesellschaft*, E.T., Henderson and Parsons, p. 99.]
46. Cf. below, Chap. 5, sec. 47.

meaning of an action, he is thinking simultaneously of the reason-why of the project, on the one hand, and the causal determinants of the executed act, on the other. He also includes under the concept "intended meaning" both a reference to the actor in the process of action and a reference to the actor after the completion of the act. Both of these are lumped together in his interpretation of the actor's project.

11. Voluntary Action and the Problem of Choice

ONCE WE STRIP AWAY from the concept of will the metaphysical speculations and antinomies which have historically surrounded it, we are left with the simple experience of spontaneous Activity based on a previously formulated project. This experience lends itself readily to sober description. In the last few paragraphs we have made clear what this experience is—what, in detail, a project is and what the "evidence" is with which we know the project and the spontaneous activity which is based on it. We shall discuss how the project itself is constituted when we take up the concept of motive. An analysis of the phenomenal experience of will, the peculiar "fiat," as James calls it, by which the project is carried over into action, is not essential for our purposes and will, therefore, be dispensed with. However, the point should be made in passing that in any phenomenology of the will [47] Husserl's distinction between reflective and nonreflective experiences is of major importance.

Let us turn, then, to the second class of topics included under the heading "voluntary action": the problems of choice, decision, and freedom. If it is maintained that voluntary action is the criterion of meaningful behavior, then the "meaning" of this behavior consists only in the choice—in the freedom to behave one way rather than another. This would mean not only that the action is "free" but that the aims of the act are known at the moment of decision; in short, that a free choice exists between at least two goals. It is the indisputable merit of Bergson that in his Time and Free Will,[48] published as long ago as 1888, he succeeded in clearing up the basic problem of determinism. In what follows, we will briefly summarize his arguments.

What does a choice between two possible acts X and Y mean? Both the determinists and the indeterminists tend to conceive X and Y as points in space: the deciding Ego stands at the crossroads O and can

47. Cf. the previously cited works of Geiger, Pfänder, and Reiner.
48. Cf. especially Chapter III, "The Organization of Conscious States; Free Will." [We are referring to the English translation by F. L. Pogson (New York, 1912).]

decide freely whether to go to X or to Y. But this very way of thinking is fallacious. The problem should not be conceived in terms of spatial goals, of pregiven pathways, of the coexistence of acts X and Y before one of them is performed. These goals do not exist at all before the choice, nor do the paths to them exist until and unless they are traversed. However, if the act—let us say X—has been performed, then the claim that, back at point O, Y could equally well have been chosen is necessarily meaningless. Equally meaningless is the assertion that, since the determining cause of X was already in existence back at O, only X could have been chosen. Both determinism and indeterminism read back "the deed already done" (*l'action accomplie*) to point O, seeking to attribute all its characteristics to the deed in the doing (*l'action s'accomplissante*). Behind both of these doctrines lurks the fallacious assumption that spatial modes of thought can be applied to duration, that duration can be explained through space, and succession through simultaneity. But the real way in which choice occurs is the following: The Ego imaginatively runs through a series of psychic states in each of which it expands, grows richer, and changes (*grossit, s'enrichit et change*), until "the free act detaches itself from it like an overripe fruit." The two "possibilities," "directions," or "tendencies" which we read back into the successive conscious states do not really exist there at all before the act is performed; what does exist is only an Ego, which, together with its motives, comprises an unbroken becoming. Both determinism and indeterminism treat this oscillation as if it were a spatial seesawing. The arguments of determinism are based one and all on the formula, "The deed once done is done" (*l'acte une fois accompli, est accompli*). The arguments of indeterminism, on the other hand, are based on the formula, "The deed was not done until it was done" (*l'acte avant d'être accompli, ne l'était pas encore*). So much for Bergson.

What do we conclude from all this as far as our own argument is concerned? Let us bring together Bergson's thesis and the points we have previously made. We have seen that the project anticipates not the action itself but the act, and this in the future perfect tense. We have studied further the peculiar structural linkage between the project, the ongoing action, and the act which is seen in reflection either to fulfill or fail to fulfill the project. The project itself is a phantasy; it is only the shadow of an action, an anticipative reproduction, or, in Husserl's terminology, a "neutralizing representation." [49]

On the other hand, the phantasy is a real lived experience which in

49. *Ideen*, pp. 223 and 234. [E.T., pp. 307 and 321. The preceding paragraph has been abridged in translation.]

turn can be reflected upon in all its modifications. How, then, does the "choice" take place? Apparently in this way: First of all, an act X is projected in the future perfect tense. *Thereupon* the actor becomes self-consciously aware of his phantasying the intentional Act and of its content. *Next* the act Y is projected; *then* the process of its projection becomes an object of the actor's reflective attention. These are retained, reproduced, compared reflectively in innumerable further intentional Acts following and lying over one another in an enormously complicated network of relationships. So far they are all neutralizing, noncommittal, ineffectual shadow actions. But these are not merely the "psychical states" of Bergson, for the latter are immersed in duration and are not reflective in nature.[50] Indeed, and this is the crux of Bergson's argument, if these psychic states of his were reflective in character, they would be concerned with the deed already done rather than with the deed in the doing.

Our analysis, aided as it is by Husserl, goes a considerable distance beyond Bergson's thesis. In our view the process of choice between successively pictured projects, plus the action itself right up to its completion, comprises a synthetic intentional Act (*Akt*) of a higher order, an Act that is inwardly differentiated into other Acts. Such an Act Husserl calls a *polythetic Act.*[51]

Husserl distinguishes between intentional Acts which are continuous syntheses and intentional Acts which are discontinuous syntheses. For instance, an Act of consciousness which constituted the "thinghood" of a thing in space is a continuous synthesis. Discontinuous syntheses, on the other hand, are *bindings-together* of other discrete Acts. The unity formed is an *articulated* unity and is a unity of a higher order. This higher Act (which he calls a *polythetic* Act) is both polythetic and synthetic. It is polythetic because within it several different "theses" are posited. It is synthetic because they are posited together. As every constituent Act within the total Act has its object, so the total Act has its total object. But something distinctive happens in the constitution of this total object. It might be explained like this: The object of each constituent Act has a single shaft of attention or ray (*Strahl*) of awareness directed toward it. The synthetic Act which ensues is necessarily *many-rayed,* since it is to start with a synthetic *collection.* But it is not satisfied in being a *plural consciousness.* It transforms itself into a *single consciousness,* its complex collection of objects becoming the object of one ray, a "one-rayed object."

50. For the Ego immersed in duration there is no choice, but only impulse, as Reiner has shown (*op. cit.,* p. 22).

51. [The next three paragraphs are an adaptation rather than a direct translation.]

Now let us apply this to the Act (*Akt*) of choice. Originally, alternatives X and Y were projected. Each of these projective Acts directed a single ray of attention upon its object (the alternative in question). However, once the wavering between alternatives is resolved, once the choice is made, this choice appears to the reflective glance as a unified Act of projection or phantasy. The individual phantasy Acts or projections meanwhile drop out of view. Nevertheless, the total object of the new synthetic Act still has a projected status, a mere quasi-being; it is, in Husserl's terminology, "neutral" rather than "positional"; it is concerned, not with what *is*, but with what the actor has decided *will be*. On the other hand, once the deed (*Handlung*) is completed, the whole thing can be looked upon "positionally" as something actually existent. In any case the deed is now grasped in a monothetic intentional Act and is referred backward to the moment of choice, when there were originally only polythetic Acts. This is an illusion, as Bergson pointed out, but it is indulged in equally by determinists and indeterminists. The error is to suppose that the conscious state (*état psychique*), which only exists after the deed is done, lies back at some "point of duration" before the actual choice.

But this transformation from multiplicity to unity is of great importance from our point of view. For it means that the action, once completed, is a unity from original project to execution, regardless of the multiplicity and complexity of its component phases. This is the way in which the action presents itself to the Ego as long as the latter remains in the natural or naïve attitude.

12. Summary: The Essence of Meaning in Its Primordial Sense

WE ARE NOW FAR ENOUGH ALONG in our investigation to define the concept of meaning in its first and primordial sense. However, in so doing we will—as throughout the present chapter—be limiting ourselves to the meaning each of us gives to his own action. The problem of intersubjectivity we are leaving until later.

Let us recall the tension we have pointed out between thought and life. Thought is focused on the objects of the spatiotemporal world; life pertains to duration. The tension between the two is of the essence of the "meaningfulness" of experience. It is misleading to say that experiences *have* meaning. Meaning does not lie *in* the experience. Rather, those experiences are meaningful which are grasped reflectively. The meaning is the *way* in which the Ego regards its experience. The meaning lies in the attitude of the Ego toward that part of its stream of consciousness which has already flowed by, toward its "elapsed duration." Let us try to be more precise. We said that the Ego looks at its experience and thereby renders it meaningful. Do we here mean a discrete and well-defined experience? If so, the two statements "Experience E is meaningful" and "Experience E is being looked at" are convertible. Are all my experiences, then, meaningful? Not at all. Many of my experiences are never reflected upon and remain prephenomenal. As long as I have durée, as long as I have internal time-consciousness, I will have experiences whether these ever become the objects of reflection or not. These experiences are the essentially actual and prephenomenal experiences and are the sum total of my lived experiences, even if I never reflect on them. For the constituting of the "mineness" (Je-Meinigheit) [52] of all my lived experiences, there suffices merely the inner time-form of the Ego, the durée, or, as Husserl calls it, the internal time-consciousness, all of these being no more than expressions for the correlativity of the constituting of the enduring Ego and of the constituting of the mineness of all my lived experiences. It is, then, incorrect to say that my lived experiences are meaningful merely in virtue of their being experienced or lived through. Such a view would eliminate the tension between living experience within the flow of duration and reflection on the experience thus lived through, in other words, the tension between life and thought. But this is the very tension that is presupposed in all talk about meaning. Let us, then, reject the position that meaningfulness pertains either to the noematic structure [53] (i.e., lived experience itself) or to the mere fact of belonging to the stream of duration. We shall say rather that each Act of attention to one's own stream of duration may be compared to a cone of light. This cone illuminates already elapsed individual phases of that stream, rendering them bright and sharply defined [and, as such, meaningful].

We conclude, then, that the concept of meaning and its problematic have no application to life considered as duration. It would be trivial at the very least to say that the unreflected-upon Here and Now is meaningful. The Acts of the cogito in which the Ego lives, the living present in which the Ego is borne along from each Here and Now to the next—these are never caught in the cone of light. They fall, therefore, outside the sphere of the meaningful. On the contrary (and this also emerges from our argument): the actual Here and Now of the living Ego is the very source of the light, the apex from which emanate the rays spreading out conelike over the already elapsed and receding phases of the stream of duration, illuminating them and marking them off from the rest of the stream.

52. [Cf. Heidegger, Sein und Zeit, p. 42; E.T., p. 68].
53. [Cf. Husserl's Ideas, § 3, ch. 3.]

We have now achieved a preliminary concept of meaningful lived experience. The reflective glance singles out an elapsed lived experience and constitutes it as meaningful. If afterward there occurs an intentional backward reference to the spontaneous Activity which engendered the experience as discrete unity, then it is by and through this Act of attention that meaningful behavior is constituted. If the reflective glance goes beyond this, too, and lights upon the project, then it constitutes meaningful action as well. It is clear that turning the attention to behavior and action are species of turning the attention to experience in general, which of course thereby becomes discrete.[54] From this it follows that behavior and action are always being constituted from polythetically organized series of lived experiences which can be looked at in two ways: either as a rerun of the stages in which the action was performed or as a total unified view of *what* was thus brought to fruition; in short, either as behavior or as deed.

Now so far we have been talking about meaning in general. But we must also remember that every action has its own specific meaning, which distinguishes it from every other action. It is with this specific meaning that Max Weber was concerned when he formulated the concept of "intended meaning." How is the specific meaning constituted within the stream of consciousness, and how is the concept of specific meaning derivable from the general concept of meaning which we have just stated? How, above all, does it happen that the meaning of one and the same experience can change as it recedes into the past?

We have spoken of the Act of attention, which brings experiences which would otherwise be simply lived through into the intentional gaze. This Act of attention itself admits of various modifications that are difficult to separate out and distinguish from one another. We shall, following Husserl, call them "transformations of attention" or "attentional modifications." It is they which are the different modes of attention, and it is they, therefore, that constitute the specific meaning of experiences.

13. Amplification of the First Concept of Meaning: The Attentional Modification of Meaning

HUSSERL describes the nature of attentional modifications:

Our concern here is with a series of transformations . . . which already presupposes a noetic [55] nucleus and certain characterizing phases

54. Cf. Reiner, *op. cit.*, pp. 24 ff., for a study of the fundamental correlation between activity and passivity.
55. The crucial distinction between *noesis* and *noema* is stated by Husserl in the following words: "We have to distinguish the parts and phases which we find

of a different order which necessarily belong to it, transformations which do not . . . [alter the noematic side of the experiences] and yet exhibit modifications of the *whole* experience on its noetic as well as on its noematic side.[56]

Let us fix in idea and in respect of its noematic content some thing of which we are perceptively aware or some occurrence connected with it. . . . Then the fixing also of the beam of attention in its own *appointed* circuit belongs to this idea. For the beam also is a phase of experience. It is then evident that modes of alteration of the fixed experience are possible which we indicate by the rubric "alterations in the distribution of attention and its modes." [57]

It is clear that these modifications are not only those of the experience itself in its noetic aspect, but that they also cover its *noemata*, that, on the noematic side—without prejudice to the identical noematic nucleus—they exhibit a new class of characterizations. . . . It is obvious, moreover, that the modifications in the noema are not of such a kind that they simply annex to something that remains the same throughout some merely external addition; on the contrary, the concrete noemata are changed through and through, what is of prime importance here being the necessary modes of givenness of that which is identical with itself.[58]

All types of experiences admit of attentional modifications: experiences of the perceptual world, of the world of memory, of the world of

through a *real* analysis of the experience, in which we treat the experience as an object like any other. . . . But on the other hand the intentional experience is the consciousness of something, and is so in the form its essence prescribes: as memory, for instance, or as judgment, or as will, etc., and so we can ask what can be said on essential lines concerning this 'of something' " (*Ideen*, I, p. 181 [E.T., p. 257]).

The first kind of inquiry is noetic, the second is noematic. Noetic phases are, for instance, "the directing of the glance of the pure Ego upon the object intended by it in virtue of its gift of meaning, upon that which 'it has in mind as something meant,' further the apprehension of this object, the steady grasp of it whilst the glance has shifted to other objects which have entered into the circle of 'conjecture'; likewise the effects of bringing out, relating, apprehending synoptically, and taking up the various attitudes of belief, presumption, valuation, etc." (*ibid.*, p. 181 [E.T., pp. 257–58]). "Corresponding at all points to the manifold data of the real, noetic content, there is a variety of data displayable in really pure intuition, and in a correlative '*noematic content*,' or briefly, '*noema.*' . . . Perception, for instance, has its *noema*, and at the base of this its perceptual meaning, that is the *perceived as such*. Similarly, recollection . . . has as its [*noema*] *the remembered as such*, precisely as it is 'meant' and 'consciously known' in it; judging has as its [*noema*] the *judged as such*; pleasure *the pleasing as such*, and so forth" (*ibid.*, p. 181 [E.T., p. 258]).

56. *Ideen*, p. 190 [E.T., p. 267]. Concerning the problem of attention, cf. also *Logische Untersuchungen*, II, i, 160 ff., *Zeitbewusstsein*, pp. 484 f. [E.T., pp. 178–79 f.].

57. *Ideen*, loc. cit.

58. *Ideen*, p. 191. [E.T., p. 269. We have departed to some degree from the Boyce Gibson translation.]

pure phantasy and consequently of projects.[59] As we have known since Husserl pointed it out, changes of attention can affect whether we take up a neutral or a positing attitude toward some content of consciousness.[60] The attentional modifications themselves show again all sorts of shadings: from actual comprehending to merely noting to hardly noticing to leaving completely unobserved.[61]

> The attentional formations, in their modes of actuality, possess in a very special sense the *character of subjectivity*, and all the functions which are modalized through these modes, or presuppose them, as species their genera, gain thereby this character also. The attending ray . . . is not separate from the Ego, but itself is and remains personal.[62]

The fact that the shaft of attention remains personal, that is, an "Ego-ray," signifies that it accompanies the changes of the Ego within the stream of duration, in other words, that it participates in the constitution of the actual Here-Now-and-Thus, because the Here and Now would be no "Thus," that is, it would lack determinate quality of its own were the Ego not directing its attention toward it. Conversely one can say that the actual Here-Now-and-Thus is the basis of attentional modification, for it is from the point of view of the present moment that the shaft of attention is directed backward on the elapsed phases.

This point requires some clarification. From moment to moment the Ego shows, toward the objects of its attention, attitudes which vary in degree and kind. Its consciousness manifests, for instance, different degrees of tension depending on whether it is directed in lively activity on the world of space and time or whether it is submerged in its inner stream of consciousness. And, all together, there are many different fundamental attitudes that the Ego can assume toward life, attitudes similar to the "moods" of which Heidegger speaks under the heading of "the existentialia of *Dasein*."[63] Now the attitude of the Ego toward life—its *attention à la vie*—determines in turn its attitude toward the past.

The last point is equivalent to the statement that the *meaning* of a lived experience undergoes modifications depending on the particular kind of attention the Ego gives to that lived experience. This also implies that the meaning of a lived experience is different depending

59. See above, p. 59, n. 36.
60. *Ideen*, pp. 228 ff. [E.T., pp. 314 ff.].
61. *Ideen*, p. 192 [E.T., p. 270].
62. *Ideen*, p. 192 [E.T., p. 270].
63. [The existentialia are *"Dasein's* characters of Being," the elements of *Dasein's* structure. Care (*Sorge*) is one such structural element (cf. *Sein und Zeit*, p. 44; E.T., p. 70). *Moods* are fundamental existentialia (*Sein und Zeit*, p. 134; E.T., pp. 172–73.]

on *the moment from which* the Ego is observing it. For instance, its meaning is different depending upon the *temporal distance* from which it is remembered and looked back upon. Likewise, the reflective glance will penetrate more or less deeply into lived experience depending on its point of view. Some points of view may not, for instance, require very deep penetration. We noted this when we were discussing Weber's concept of intended meaning. We saw that there are many cases of meaning-interpretation in everyday life where it is not worth the trouble to seek a person's deeper meaning because knowledge of his surface meaning is quite enough for us to orient ourselves to his behavior. Thus, meaning-establishment and meaning-interpretation are both pragmatically determined in the intersubjective sphere. But this is not the end of the matter. Even the deepest level of the stream of consciousness of the solitary Ego to which the reflective glance can penetrate is pragmatically determined.

We have up to this point repeatedly made use of the concept of the taken-for-granted. Now, thanks to our analysis of attentional modification, we can give it a very precise meaning. The taken-for-granted (*das Fraglos-gegeben*) is always that particular level of experience which presents itself as not in need of further analysis. Whether a level of experience is thus taken for granted depends on the pragmatic interest of the reflective glance which is directed upon it and thereby upon the particular Here and Now from which that glance is operating. To say that some content of consciousness is thus taken for granted still leaves it open as to whether any kind of existence or reality is credited to that content, i.e., whether it is given in acts of *positional* or of *neutral* consciousness. Nevertheless, a change of attention can transform something that is taken for granted into something problematical.

The present section has merely suggested the starting point for a phenomenological analysis of attention, and the detailed execution of the latter is not called for within the limits of the present essay. It is enough that we have discovered in attentional modification a point of departure for a theory of the constitution of the specific meaning of particular experiences. But understanding the nature of attentional modification affords us only a starting point, and we must now proceed to examine a further class of problems.

14. Further Amplification: Configurations of Lived Experiences. Context of Meaning and Context of Experience

LET US TRY TO GET TO the root of the problem of intended meaning. In doing this, the important step is to recognize the existence of configurations within our conscious life. We have already exposed the fallacy that intended meaning is an isolated lived experience (*Erlebnis*).[64] As long as consciousness remains a pure stream of duration, there are no discrete lived experiences. The latter appear only when the reflective glance of attention begins to operate. Within the stream, then, instead of discrete experiences, we have everywhere continuity, with horizons opening equally into the past and the future. However diverse the lived experiences may be, they are bound together by the fact that they are *mine*. To this primal unity there is added another unity at the next-higher level. This is the unity conferred by the reflective glance, the unity of *meaning*. The reflective glance is the Act (*Akt*)[65] which raises the content of consciousness from prephenomenal to phenomenal status.

But there is yet a higher stage of unity within experience. This stage consists in the gathering of separate Acts into a higher synthesis. This synthesis then becomes an "object" within consciousness. What was polythetic and many-rayed has now become monothetic and one-rayed. We now have a *configuration of meaning* or meaning-context. Let us define meaning-context formally: We say that our lived experiences $E_1, E_2, \ldots, E_n$ stand in a meaning-context if and only if, once they have been lived through in separate steps, they are then constituted into a synthesis of a higher order, becoming thereby unified objects of monothetic attention.

Meanwhile we will keep very clearly in mind the distinction between configurations of meaning and lower-order configurations such as that of simple attention to experiences and that of duration itself, the configuration which makes my experiences "mine."[66] Configurations *of* meaning, let us remember, consist of meanings already created in more elementary acts of attention.

First a project is sketched out in an *intentional Act*. Then the project is brought to fulfillment by *action*. The result is an *act* or completed deed. This act is itself a *meaning-context*, for it gives unity to all the intentional Acts and all the actions involved in its perform-

---

64. [*Erlebnis* has, especially for Husserl, the connotation of a lived-through conscious state. We have translated it as "lived experience." On the other hand, *Erfahrung* means essentially a cognitive encounter with some datum or other. We have translated it simply as "experience." In cases where the meaning is clear from the context and where awkwardness would otherwise result, *Erlebnis* also is rendered simply as "experience."]

65. [We have translated *Akt* as "Act." It is to be contrasted with *Handlung*, which we have translated as "act" and which has the sense of completed deed, and with *Handeln*, which we have translated as "action," in accordance with Schutz's later English usage (cf. *Collected Papers*, I, 19 f. and *passim*).]

66. *Ideen*, p. 246 [E.T., pp. 334–35].

ance. Higher and more complex meaning-contexts can then be constructed out of individual acts.

This can be applied on the most general scale. Our whole experience (*Erfahrung*) [67] of the world as such is built up in polythetic Acts. We can synthesize these Acts and then think of the resultant synthesis as the experienced (*das Erfahrene*), this becoming the unified object of monothetic attention. This holds true of Acts of both external and internal experience. Along with the constitution of "the experienced" out of separate experience, the object of experience (*Erfahrungsgegenstand*) is constituted.

> The object of experience by its very nature is built up before our eyes in continuous and discrete syntheses of manifold experiences and in the shifting appearance of ever new sides and phases that are peculiar to it as an individual. Out of this building-up process, which is always sketching out beforehand and hinting what it will be like when it is finished, both the separate appearances and the object itself derive their meaning. The meaning of the object, however, is always that of an object which is changing in this manner, as the identical unity of possible self-manifestations that can be actualized over and over again. [68]

It is self-evident that such syntheses can be apprehended together with other syntheses and, by means of polythetic Acts, brought into some kind of higher order with them. Husserl has worked this process out to its last detail in his *Ideas*. Keeping this in mind, one can define the context of experience (*Erfahrungszusammenhang*) as (a) the content of the totality of meaning-configurations brought together within one moment or (b) as a meaning-context of a higher order. For, as I look back upon my elapsed experience, I see it monothetically, even though it has come into existence in phases and through many intentional Acts. [69] The total content of all my experience, or of all my perceptions of the world in the broadest sense, is, then, brought together and coordinated in the total context of my experience. This

67. Our concept of experience (*Erfahrung*) should be distinguished from the unclear concept to be found in empiricistic naturalism (sensationalism). Rather, we are using the term in the broader sense Husserl gave it in the *Formal and Transcendental Logic*, namely, the apprehension and possession of the thing itself (*Selbsterfassung und Selbsthabe*), the thing being an individual datum, even of a nonexistent object (*eines irrealen Gegenstandes*).

68. *Logik*, p. 147.

69. It should be understood clearly that experience (*Erfahrung*), even in its final coherent state, is completely lacking in any hint as to *how* it was constituted in consciousness. Experience *can* be constituted in a series of positing Acts which together can be turned into a unified object of monothetic attention. But within the total context of experience there are to be found not only such positional Acts but also all contents of neutralizing consciousness, whether they always remain such or are at some time brought into positionality.

total context grows larger with every new lived experience. At every moment there is thus a growing core of accumulated experience. This growing core consists of both *real* and *ideal* objects of experience (*Erfahrungsgegenständlichkeiten*), which of course had once been produced in polysynthetic intentional Acts. But the objects in this reserve supply are always taken for granted. We pay no attention to the fact that they are products of previous conscious activity, that they have gone through a complex process of constitution. (We can, of course, pay such attention if we choose.) This constitution is carried out, layer by layer, at lower levels of consciousness no longer penetrated by the ray of attention. The total context of experience at any given moment thus itself consists of objects of a higher order which are apprehended monothetically and taken for granted without reverting to the question of how or in what polythetic Acts they were constructed.

This reserve stock of knowledge is preserved in the form of mere passive content. However, some of that content now in passive form was once produced by intentional Activity. Any such content which is now an object of monothetic attention can be reactivated, changed back into the active mode, so to speak, and then re-enacted step by step, as Husserl demonstrated at length in his *Formal and Transcendental Logic*. Completed judgments are therefore present within our consciousness not as ongoing judgings but as ideal objectivities, as essences,[70] always capable, however, of being "unfrozen" and brought back to their original active state. "Whenever we light upon the passive contents of consciousness, upon the 'essence' side of meaning, a process of free creativity occurs, in which there spring forth in our minds new categorial structures of meaning in agreement with corresponding signs or words." [71] This is true of all judgments, but also generally of all products of categorial Activity,[72] including behavior and action, judgment itself being a kind of action. It is in fact a characteristic of all products of spontaneous Activity that they can be reconstituted as Acts that are in principle repeatable (*in einer Idealität des Immer Wieder*).[73] However, if I can identify the product of my reiterated Act

---

70. Husserl speaks also in this connection of the "repeatable and revivifiable nature" of the categorial structures ingredient in the judgment (*Logik*, p. 104).

71. *Logik*, p. 285.

72. *Logik*, p. 282.

73. This is especially true of judgments. Because their basic form is of the indefinitely iterable type "I can do it again," * they can, whenever encountered, be transformed back into active judgings. There is an unsolved problem here, and it only further obscures the situation to bring in the concept of "knowing," which we have up to now avoided. For "knowing" (cf. Scheler and Sander) can mean two quite different things: (a) the merely passive "possession" of knowledge, that

with one from an earlier Here and Now, this identification is itself a new context of meaning; in Husserl's terminology, it is a *Synthesis of Recognition*.[74] This again is a case of "experiencing Act and no longer experiencing present-at-hand—at least not present-at-hand in the Here and Now of the reactivation."

Let us therefore limit the term "stock of knowledge at hand" to the store of already constituted objectivities of experience in the actual Here and Now, in other words, to the passive "possession" of experiences, to the exclusion of their reconstitution.

What thus re-emerges in apperceptive consciousness, or is even reconstituted, depends on the Act of attention of the Ego to its own stock of knowledge. It is therefore pragmatically determined in the sense we discussed previously. We can now define the total context of experience as the content of all the Acts of attention which the Ego as a free being can direct at any given moment of its conscious life toward those of its elapsed lived experiences that have been constituted in step-by-step syntheses. This would, of course, include all attentional modifications of such Acts. The specific meaning of a lived experience, and therefore the particular mode of the Act of attention to it, consists in the ordering of this lived experience within the total context of experience that is present-at-hand. We can also put the point in a way which is somewhat different but which will give us a precise definition of "intended meaning": The intended meaning of a lived experience is nothing more nor less than a self-interpretation of that lived experience from the point of view of a new lived experience.

Our next step is to discover what this self-interpretation is and how it takes place. In so doing, we shall be content with a rough concept, since we are seeking phenomenological insight not as an end in itself but as a means to the proper formulation of a sociological problem.

15. The Construction of the World of Experience and Its Ordering under Schemes

LET US TRY TO UNRAVEL the complicated structural contexts that are involved in the constitution of an external object. The object is constituted out of appearances as we encounter them in our

---

is, the presence in one's mind of prefabricated judgments as ideal objectivities, and (b) the explicit reiteration or rejudging of these judgments.

*["The assumption that I may under typically similar circumstances act in the typically similar way that I did before in order to bring about a typically similar state of affairs" (Schutz, *Collected Papers*, I, 20; cf. also Natanson's remarks in his Introduction to the same volume, p. xxxvii).]

74. *Logik*, p. 143.

stream of consciousness. Such appearances hang together in a context of meaning. As they follow one another in regular sequence, our experience of the object is built up. We can by means of a monothetic glance look upon the whole sequence as a unity in itself—the object of outer experience, the thing of the external world. The fact that the individual lived experiences of the individual appearances are linked together in the experience of the object is itself experienced (*erfahren*).[75] We thus experience within the living present the actual constitution of objects. This stage of analysis is complicated enough, but, if we look more deeply, we will find greater complexity yet. Every lived experience which enters into the constitution of the total object experience is surrounded by a halo of retentions and of protentions. It pertains to the essence of the synthesis that the different phases are linked up in this way. The linkage occurs in the following manner: the later lived experience occurs within a Here and Now whose intrinsic quality is partially determined by the retention of the earlier lived experiences. And below this level, of course, there lies the still more basic configuration which constitutes the "mineness" [76] of all my lived experiences.

If, starting from an object of experience, say a table, we can dig downward into ever deeper levels of the process by which it was constituted, we can also go in the opposite direction. Starting from the table itself, we can proceed upward into the levels of symbolism, from the table to talk about "the table." Here, if we wished, we could get involved in the basic problems of the relation of a word to a thing. No doubt the judgment "This is a table" (and a judgment is implied in every act of name-giving) refers back to one's previous experience of other tables.[77]

It should be remembered that this concept is the lowest level of that "syntax" on which the world of language and logic must interpret all phases of formalization and generalization in terms of their history, which means in terms of the living experiences of the ego cogitans.

75. In a "subjective a priori" sense prior to all experience in the empirical sense. The latter is based on and presupposes the former.

76. [Cf. Heidegger, *Sein und Zeit*, p. 42; E.T., p. 67.]

77. The eidetic domain, i.e., the pure world of essence, can be left out of account in considering the constitution of the world of experience. For the disclosure of an essence is itself experience in our sense of "experience." One must remember that we are using the terms "experience" and "configuration of experience" not in the narrow empiricistic sense of these words but in the phenomenological sense. Phenomenology allows phantasy a role in the building-up of the Ego's configuration of experience in the Here, Now, and Thus in addition to the part played by the encounter with external objects. In Husserl's terminology, we are concerned with the intentional states of affairs among essences within the realm of experience, but not with empirical facts (*Logik*, p. 279).

These we call "the phenomena of the constituting process" or simply "constituting phenomena." For—again we emphasize—the actual *occurrences* of such processes as formalization and generalization are parts of the ego's experience as we are using the word "experience."

We have been using the construction of an experience of an external object only as an example of the implications contained in the concept of experience that is present-at-hand. Our analysis can, however, be applied to every area of lived experience, first of all, to all doxic syntheses having a "collective function," [78] in the pure logical sense—in other words, to the constitution of one judgment out of another—and then also to all practical and axiological syntheses of every kind, [79] for these are based on the former, purely logical syntheses. But these also are experienced in the sense of being part of a present supply of experience already at hand as the uppermost configuration of meaning in the ego cogitans' Here and Now.

In view of the highly complex structure of the meaning-configurations which are ready at hand for the ordering of experience, it is necessary to define what is meant by the interpretation of one's own lived experience, in other words, by specific intended meaning. We have already indicated our answer when we were discussing how the level to which the reflective glance penetrates is pragmatically determined. We can now develop this point further.

Suppose some lived experience of ours catches our attention. We can ask how this lived experience came to be, and carry our analysis of its origin right down to the rock-bottom level of its constitution in the inner time-form of pure duration. However, our stock of knowledge (*Erfahrung*) does not by any means refer back directly to the inner time-form as its source and origin. Rather, the meaning-configuration of past experience is a higher-level configuration which has other configurations as its elements, and these in turn were constituted out of still lower-level complexes of meaning. The lower strata of what has been already experienced are, however, taken for granted, i.e., they lie at so deep a level that the reflective glance does not reach them. All of this is true relative to the actual Here and Now: The demarcation of the layer of that which is taken for granted depends on the modifications of the Act of attention directed upon it, and this in turn is dependent on the *attention à la vie* that actually exists in the individual's Here and Now. Certainly, given a suitable act of attention, all

78. [An example of a "collective doxic synthesis" would be the forming of a conjunctive judgment out of two others by inserting an "and" between them. Cf. *Ideas* (E.T., pp. 335 and 339).]

79. ["For example, the mother who gazes lovingly at her little flock and embraces each child singly and all together in one act of love" (*ibid.*, p. 340).]

polythetic syntheses can be traced back to the original constitution of lived experience in pure duration. We have just seen how this was possible in the case of an experiential object of the external world. However, this calls for an Act of strictly philosophical reflection, which in its turn also presupposes a particular kind of *attention à la vie.*

Our next task is to carry through a meaning-analysis of the Ego in the natural attitude.[80] The ordinary man in every moment of his lived experience lights upon past experiences in the storehouse of his consciousness. He knows about the world and he knows what to expect. With every moment of conscious life a new item is filed away in this vast storehouse. At a minimum this is due to the fact that, with the arrival of a new moment, things are seen in a slightly different light. All of this is involved in the conception of a duration that is manifold, continuous, and irreversible in direction. It can, however, be demonstrated not only deductively but by examination of one's own consciousness as one lives in the natural standpoint, grows older, and accumulates knowledge. Now, to the natural man all his past experiences are present as *ordered,* as knowledge or as awareness of what to expect, just as the whole external world is present to him as ordered. Ordinarily, and unless he is forced to solve a special kind of problem, he does not ask questions about how this ordered world was constituted. The particular patterns of order we are now considering are synthetic meaning-configurations of already encountered lived experiences.

Let us give a few examples of these patterns of syntheses of past experiences. First of all, there are experiences of the external world and its objects, animate and inanimate. The man in the natural attitude "has," therefore, a stock of knowledge of physical things and fellow creatures, of social collectives and of artifacts, including cultural objects. He likewise "has" syntheses of inner experience. Among these are to be found judgment contents (or propositional contents) which are the result of his previous acts of judgment. Here also are to be found all products of the activity of the mind and will. All these experiences, whether internal or external, enter into meaning-contexts of a higher order for the man in the natural standpoint, and of these, too, he has experience. Within his Here and Now, therefore, belong all his experience of the ordering procedures of both theoretical and applied science and the very rules governing these, such as the rules of formal logic. To these we should add his experience of all sorts of practical and ethical rules.

Let us call these patterns the schemes of our experience (*Sche-*

80. Cf. the Appended Note to Chap. I, p. 43, above.

mata unserer Erfahrung).[81] A scheme of our experience is a meaning-context which is a configuration of our past experiences embracing conceptually the experiential objects to be found in the latter but not the process by which they were constituted. The constituting process itself is entirely ignored, while the objectivity constituted by it is taken for granted.[82]

By defining the schemes of experience as contexts of meaning, we have given them both a formal and a material definition. We have given them a formal definition by identifying the mode of their constitution as a synthesis of a higher stage out of polythetic Acts of once-lived-through experiences. We have given them a material definition by referring to the total object which comes into view when such syntheses are viewed monothetically. We speak of all the component once-lived-through experiences as having coherence (*Einstimmigkeit*) with one another. By this we mean (a) their mutual conditioning of one another, (b) their synthetic construction into higher-level patterns, and finally (c) the meaning-configuration of these patterns themselves, namely, the "total configuration of our experience in the actual Here and Now." This we previously referred to as the "uppermost meaning-configuration of our once-lived-through experiences." Therefore, in every Here and Now there is a total coherence of our experience. This means merely that the total configuration of our experience is a synthesis of our already-lived-through experiences brought about by a step-by-step construction. To this synthesis there corresponds a total object, namely, the content of our knowledge in the Here and Now. Of course, within this total coherence of experience, contradictory experiences can occur without impairing the over-all unity.

> *Prior* to all judgments, there is a universal ground of experience. It is continuously presupposed *as the coherent unity of possible experience.* Within this coherent unity all facts hang together and are congruent with one another. Yet there can be discord in this unity in the sense that *two discordant elements have an essential community,* and the essential community remains unimpaired in spite of or even because of its oppos-

81. It is evident that our concept of the "scheme" has nothing to do with the Kantian *schema* which is "a synthesis of imagination" (cf. *Critique of Pure Reason,* B 185). [Because of this difference of meaning and in accordance with Schutz's own English usage, "schema" and "schemata" are, when referring to his own concept, rendered by us as "scheme" and "schemes."]

82. Cf. as an example of this what Husserl has to say about science. "Science" is possible only when the results of thought can be preserved in the form of knowledge and remain available for further thinking as a system of propositions distinctly stated in accordance with logical requirements but lacking the clear support of presentations, and so, understood without insight, or else actualized after the manner of a judgment (*Ideen,* p. 124 [E.T., p. 192]).

ing elements. And so every *primordial judging in its content,* and every succeeding judgment that is correlated with it, has *configuration after configuration of objects in the synthetic unity of the experience* on which it is grounded.[83]

The unity of experience into which all these schemes enter as constituted objects must, however, not be construed as if its presentational availability in the Here and Now were structurally homogeneous, as if somehow all these existing schemes were equally clear and distinct, as if all objects within consciousness were "on an equal plane with respect to our consciousness of them." [84] Rather, the schemes have their horizons and perspectives, their lights and their shadows, depending upon the degree of attention which the Ego bestows upon them.

16. The Schemes of Experience as Interpretive Schemes. Self-Explication and Interpretation. Problem and Interest

THE SCHEMES OF EXPERIENCE have a special task in connection with the constitution of the specific meaning of a lived experience, once the latter is brought within the glance of attention. They are essential, therefore, to the Ego as it explicates what it has already lived through from the point of view of a later Here and Now. We have defined the Act of endowing with specific meaning as *self-explication,* i.e., as the ordering of a lived experience within the total configuration of experience. This ordering is accomplished in a synthesis of recognition. The synthesis of recognition takes the lived experience that is to be classified, refers it back to the schemes on hand, and fixes its specific essence. The lived experience is thus brought back to an objectification already on hand within the store of experience and identified with this objectification. By no means does this imply that the subsumption under this objectification is a separate intentional Act from the glance of attention. What we have here is rather one Act whose intentional reference is in two opposite directions. This double directionality can be demonstrated by an analysis of the constitution of any intentional Act which encounters a datum; for instance, a perception. On the other hand, when looked back upon, attention and subsumption, perception and recognition, seem to take place in one step.

83. Husserl, *Logik,* p. 194.
84. *Ibid.,* p. 254.

It is obvious from what has been said earlier that the ordering we are speaking of can be carried out in many different ways. It can take place in any one of the different stages of logical formulation right up to the simple apprehension which occurs within the Here and Now. It can take place in the activities of the reason, the emotions, or the will. It can take place in a flash or in problem-solving operations that proceed step by step. It can take place in vague Acts of habitual recognition or, on the other hand, with complete clarity. There are different types of scheme for each of these different types of ordering, and each of the different types of scheme can be known with different degrees of clarity.

We shall call the process of ordering lived experience under schemes by means of synthetic recognition "the interpretation of the lived experience," and we shall include under this term the connection of a sign with that which it signifies. Interpretation, then, is the referral of the unknown to the known, of that which is apprehended in the glance of attention to the schemes of experience. These schemes, therefore, have a special function in the process of interpreting one's own lived experiences. They are the completed meaning-configurations that are present at hand each time in the form of "what one knows" or "what one already knew." They consist of material that has already been organized under categories. To these schemes the lived experiences are referred for interpretation as they occur. In this sense, schemes of experience are interpretive schemes, and from now on let us call them such. The interpretation of a sign through reference to a sign system is only a special case of what we have in mind; we are therefore using the term for the genus instead of the species.

The picture of self-explication we have just drawn seems to be at variance with the fact that there are lived experiences which are unique and *sui generis*. We have already pointed out [85] that there are lived experiences which because of the degree of their intimacy cannot be comprehended by the glance of attention—at least insofar as their intrinsic quality is concerned. We must now add that it is impossible to order these experiences and thereby to endow them with a specific meaning. This stems from their intimacy and their essential confinement to a single moment of the stream of consciousness, which prevent us from identifying in any one of them any essence or "nucleus" and thus recognizing it as belonging to a class. On the other hand, we do sometimes recognize that a lived experience is novel, that it is a "first" for us. This presupposes a reference back to the schemes we have on hand, followed by a "failure to connect." This in turn throws

85. In sec. 7, above.

the validity of the scheme into question. Whenever a phenomenon turns out to be unexplainable, it means that something is wrong with our scheme.

Our next task is to explain the criterion by which one interpretive scheme is chosen out of the many that are available when the moment comes to explicate a given lived experience. For the choice is by no means prescribed from the start as either obvious or exclusive; as a matter of fact, no lived experience can be exhausted by a single interpretive scheme. Rather, every lived experience is open to numerous interpretations (noeses) without in any way detracting from the identity of its noematic nucleus. The schemes which are drawn upon for such interpretations always bear the mark of a particular Here and Now, since this is true of the syntheses of recognition and the acts of reflective awareness which underlie them. The clarification of this complex process would require a very detailed study. For our purposes it is enough to say that the selection of the requisite schemes is dependent upon the particular attentional modification that happens to be operative at the time. The Ego will of course always undergo different modifications of attention both toward the lived experience which presents itself for ordering and toward the whole stock of its past experience. Paradoxically it could be said that the lived experience itself decides the scheme into which it is to be ordered, and thus the problem chosen proposes its own solution.

But isn't that just pushing the question further back? How does that help toward the solution of our problem? How is the lived experience which becomes the focus of attention selected in the first place? To this one can only reply that the Act of attention itself is a free Act of the Ego which singles out the lived experience and chooses it as its problem. Of course, once the choice of problem is made, one can ask the reasons for that choice, specifically, what "interest" prompted it. We shall deal with this problem at a later point.[86]

But isn't this a fatal begging of the question? How can the interpretive scheme be in part constituted through that which is to be interpreted? The circularity is only apparent. The appearance of circularity is caused by the fact that two fundamentally different modes of observation are confused and by the way in which the problem set up in one sphere is confronted by its mirror image in another.

The two spheres to which we refer are formal and transcendental logic. When we think of the interpretive scheme as something ready to be applied to some datum of lived experience, then we are thinking of it as an already constituted "logical objectification," an ideal object of

86. In sec. 18, below.

formal logic. On the other hand, when we think of the interpretive scheme as itself something dependent upon a particular Here and Now, then we are thinking of it in terms of its genesis, in terms of its constitution, and so we are dealing with it in terms of transcendental logic. If we keep this distinction clearly and rigorously in mind, then the equivocation contained in the term "scheme of interpretation" is harmless. However, the equivocation itself is only another illustration of the fundamental opposition we have already pointed out between the constitution of the lived experience in pure duration, on the one hand, and the being of the constituted objectification of the spatiotemporal world, on the other, between the modes of awareness proper to becoming and being, life, and thought.

So far we have merely given a general sketch of a theory of how the Ego interprets its experiences. Later we shall be able to enlarge upon this theory and to make it more exact. This can only be done through an analysis of the processes of meaning-establishment and meaning-interpretation in the intersubjective world. Before we proceed to this task, however, let us first give our attention to an important preliminary. This is the analysis of the meaning-context proper to *projects*, in other words, *motivational context.*

17. Motivational Context as Meaning-Context. (A) The "In-Order-To" Motive

IN OUR INTRODUCTION to Chapter 1 we examined Weber's theory of motivation. According to Weber, motive is a configuration or context of meaning which appears either to the actor or to an observer as a meaningful ground of a given piece of behavior. Let us summarize our criticisms of that view.

1. Under the concept of "motive" Weber lumps together two quite different things. These are (a) that context of meaning which the *actor subjectively feels* is the ground of his behavior and (b) that context of meaning which the *observer supposes* is the ground of the actor's behavior. This is a peculiar error for Weber to make, since, from the standpoint of a theory of intended meaning, the two are quite incommensurable. As we have already noted, the consequences of this confusion for Weber's theory of our knowledge of other selves are disastrous. Later we shall examine this matter in detail. For the time being, we shall be concerned only with the "motive" which seems *to the actor himself* the "meaningful ground of his behavior." The following analysis, like the whole of this chapter, will confine itself to the sphere of the solitary Ego.

2. "Behavior" or "action" is for Weber a discrete unified datum with which one can operate immediately, without further inquiry as to the principle of its unity. Our study of internal time-consciousness showed us how the action is constituted from the preceding project of the corresponding act and how the action derived its unity from the range or scope of this project. We thus established that the unity of action is subjective in its very foundation and dependent on the Here and Now in which the project is formulated. Therefore, the "meaningful ground" of an action that is apprehended as a unity is always merely relative to a particular Here and Now of the actor and is therefore necessarily in need of supplementation.

3. Weber fails to discuss either the nature of the meaning-context or its dependence on the meaning of a particular concrete actor. For that reason he assimilates the so-called "clarifying" or "motivational" understanding to observational understanding and leaves it unclear whether the "intended" meaning of an action is identical with its motive or not. We have already clarified the concept of meaning-context. Our next two questions will be whether the motivational context is in fact a meaning-context for the actor (which we shall answer in the affirmative), and what particular structure it involves.

4. When Weber uses the term "motive" he means sometimes (a) the "in-order-to" of the action—in other words, the orientation of the action to a future event—but at other times (b) the "because" of the action, that is, its relation to a past lived experience. He does not in any way justify this ambiguous way of speaking. Let us now look closely at these two different senses of "motive."

We explained the first, or "future-directed," sense of motive when we were analyzing meaningful action in terms of internal time-consciousness. We saw that every action is carried out according to a project and is oriented to an act phantasied in the future perfect tense as already executed. The unity of the action is constituted exclusively by this project, whose span may be very different depending on how explicitly it is planned, as was shown in the example of rational action with known intermediate goals. Suppose, for instance, that I want to talk to a friend of mine who lives just around the corner. To do this I must get up out of my chair, a process involving all sorts of muscular tensions and relaxations; I must go through the next room into the vestibule of my apartment, then down the steps and around the corner to my friend's house. Now if anyone I meet on the way should ask me about the "rational basis" or "meaning" of my trip out of the house, I shall answer that I am going to look in on *A*, who lives around the corner, and see if he is at home. The "motive" of all the successive acts just described is the project of my visit to *A*, because the final aim of my action is to talk to him; all the other acts are intermediate aims oriented to the final one. However, since I have devised the plan to call on *A*, in other words, since I have phantasied in the future perfect tense that we were talking together, the action which leads up to this goal exists within a meaning-context for me.

Interpreting the actor's "motive" as his *expectations*, we can say that the motivational context is by definition the meaning-context within which a particular action stands in virtue of its status as the project of an act for a given actor. In other words, the act thus projected in the future perfect tense and in terms of which the action receives its orientation is the "in-order-to motive" (*Um-zu-Motiv*) for the actor.

This definition still stands if (as was not the case in the example we just used) elements other than the activity of the agent are included in the project. One example of such elements would be physical events. Suppose, for instance, I call up my friend on the telephone. In this case I assume that my dialing will trip off a chain of electronic events leading straight to my goal. The laws of physics and their application to the situation are, of course, taken for granted. No doubt it is correct in a sense to say that I am expecting this whole process to spring into operation. But the process is something that I take into account only by implication; that is, if I really thought about it, I would see that all this is involved in ringing up my friend. In order to plan the telephone call, I do not have to plan the electronic process or even give it a thought. All I have to do is to project a picture of the call as "something I will have done in a few minutes"—in short, project it in the future perfect tense—and then proceed to dial. Only a few people out of the millions who use the telephone know anything about the physical processes involved when they "put in a call." The result is all the average caller cares about, and he takes everything else for granted. He remembers that dialing causes the ringing of a bell in someone else's apartment. He "knows" about this causal link; it is part of the baggage of experience that he carries around with him. Nevertheless, it is he who sets in motion this particular "run" of the causal series in question. Now, of course, this whole situation will vary according to the particular use that is being made of the telephone and who the user is. For instance, a telephone repair man will have as his "in-order-to motive," his final goal, not a call to a friend but the restoration of the regular state of the electronic events as something that can be relied on. In order to restore the regularity of these events, he must find his own means, e.g., the use of certain tools. Once he reaches his final goal, then I can use his goal—the repaired telephone—as my means.

All that has been said in the preceding paragraph about the use of physical processes as means can be applied to the social sphere as well. In this case we use as means for our ends the actions of other people. This point will be of special interest to us later on.

If, therefore, I give as the motive of my action that it is in-order-to-such-and-such, what I really mean is the following: The action itself is only a means within the meaning-context of a project, within which the completed act is pictured as something to be brought to fulfillment by my action. Therefore, when asked about my motive, I always answer in terms of "in-order-to" if the completed act is still in the future. What is presupposed in such a case is that the act is only being phantasied (or fancied) [87] in the mode of anticipation. Since the concrete action and its accompanying lived experiences have not yet occurred, so that we can say that they have succeeded or failed in carrying out the act, what we have on our hands is a project not yet actualized and made concrete. It is still characterized by "empty protentions" waiting upon the future. The goal of an action can only be chosen as such by the actor himself, and he must be about to act in a rational manner. Furthermore, he must survey the total action in one glance. This is, of course, a reproductive operation. But he must, at the same time, survey the component actions, no matter at what stage of completion they may be. This latter survey can be of either a reproductive or retentive character.

When we say that the final goal of action always has the temporal character of futurity, this does not mean that it must be literally *in* the future. Suppose that I have just come back from a visit to my friend, and you ask me why I went out. Even though my visit to my friend is now literally *in* the past, I can still reply, "I went out in order to see *A*." The time contained within, or expressed by, the phrase "in order to see *A*" is *future*. Yet, from the point of view of the moment of the utterance, the actual seeing of *A* is past, so that what I am actually referring to in the in-order-to phrase is the project with its still empty protentions. Now, ordinary language fudges this distinction and allows the translation of every "in-order-to" statement into a "because" statement. "Because I wanted to talk to *A*, I went out" or "I'm going out because I want to talk to *A*." Let us call any because-statement which is logically equivalent to an in-order-to statement a "pseudo because-statement." The interesting feature of this double mode of expression is that the in-order-to statement pictures the goal as future, while the pseudo because-statement pictures it as a project which occurred in

87. [This is the English rendering Schutz preferred for "phantasiert" and will be used by us as an alternative translation.]

the past. This is only another example of the double relational *sense* of the action, which comprises both a backward reference to the past and an orientation toward the future.

We need to explain in greater detail the configuration of meaning within which are mutually correlated the projected act and the actions necessary to bring it about. If we are to have a meaning-configuration at all, there must occur a monothetic apprehension of actions in themselves consisting of steps but pictured as completely constituted, i.e., over and done with. But how can this be done in the *project,* when the actions which serve as means are not yet established? The explanation is that the project itself necessarily refers back to past acts analogous [88] to the projected one. These past acts are now reproduced in the consciousness of the person formulating the new project.

In order to project an act, I must know how acts of the same kind have been carried out in the past. The more cases there are of such acts and the better their rational principles understood, the more are they "taken for granted." This explains why practice and exercise increase efficiency. The more a given action—a technical accomplishment, for instance—is exercised, the less noticeable to the actor are its separate steps, although in the beginning he had to proceed in one-two-three fashion.

From this it is easy to see that how broad the span of the project is depends precisely on how "accomplished" the actor is. Therefore, generally speaking, the more commonplace the project, the greater its breadth, for we will be more likely to have an automatic "knowledge" of how to run through the component steps. Here we see another example of the pragmatically conditioned character of the self-interpretation of one's own lived experience. For every project "interprets" the meaning being constituted in the projected action by referring it back to analogous acts. This is done by a synthesis of recognition and is seldom explicit. The in-order-to motivation is therefore a context of meaning which is built on the context of experience available in the moment of projecting. The means-end sequence itself is in fact a context of past experiences, experiences involving the successful realization of certain ends by the use of certain means. Every in-order-to motivation presupposes such a stock of experience which has been elevated to an "I-can-do-it-again" status.

How far back into the past this meaning-structure can be pursued is determined by the span of the project and is therefore pragmatically

88. What we mean is that there is an identical nucleus of meaning (in the phenomenological sense) between the two acts that are being compared.

conditioned.[89] And so both the project and goal of action can be taken for granted and as such ignored until some special circumstance, such as the questions of another person, can force one to take account of it. On such an occasion the actor will always answer the question "Why?" with either an in-order-to statement or a pseudo because-statement, all depending on whether he is thinking of his goal or his having previously projected that goal.

18. Motivational Context as Meaning-Context.
(B) The Genuine Because-Motive

IN THE PREVIOUS SECTION we dealt with what we called "pseudo because-statements." These we now wish to contrast with genuine because-statements. The difference between them lies in the fact that the latter cannot be translated into in-order-to statements. Let us look at an example. Suppose I say that a murderer perpetrated his crime for money. This is an in-order-to statement. But suppose I say that the man became a murderer because of the influence of bad companions. This statement is of an order quite different from the first. The whole complicated structure of projection in the future perfect tense is inapplicable here. What our second statement does is to take a past event—namely, the murder—and connect this with an event still further back in the past, namely, the influence of bad companions. Now, this is a *different* kind of meaning-context. This we are very likely to call an "explanation of the deed." But obviously what is being said in such an explanation is only that certain past experiences of the murderer have created a disposition on the part of the murderer to achieve his goals by violence rather than by honest labor. The difference, then, between the two kinds of motive as expressed in our two statements is that the in-order-to motive explains the act in terms of the project, while the genuine because-motive explains the project in terms of the actor's past experiences.

Let us use another example. Suppose I say, "I open my umbrella because it is raining." First of all, let us note that my statement expresses a pseudo because-motive. This, translated into the language of "in-order-to," gives us the following: "I open my umbrella in order to keep from getting wet." The project expressed here takes for granted that it would be unpleasant to have soggy clothes. But this considera-

89. Weber's so-called "traditional action" is a special case in that the reference to the past is vague and confused and that not only the "precedents" appealed to, but also the goals of action, are taken for granted.

tion does not itself belong to the in-order-to series. The in-order-to series starts out with the project, which in turn has taken for granted that it is not pleasant to get wet. I therefore project an act in order to prevent an unpleasant situation. The ensuing action is oriented to the project which was posited in the future perfect tense, perhaps in the judgment, "If I open my umbrella, I shall avoid the displeasure of getting my clothes wet." Therefore, the action with its step-by-step structure is to be understood within the meaning-context of the project, which sees the whole act monothetically as a unity. As we have just shown, this project itself is based on a meaning-context of the type, "Putting up one's umbrella keeps one dry when it is raining." I have already experienced the truth of this statement, and I now take it for granted in performing the action. So much for the in-order-to motive and its corresponding pseudo because-motive.

However, in the statement, "I open my umbrella because it is raining," there lies concealed a genuine because-motive. It can be described alternatively as follows: first I see that it is raining, then I remember that I could get wet in the rain and that that would be unpleasant. I am then ready to plan any appropriate preventive step, whether this be running for shelter or spreading my umbrella. This, then, explains the constitution of the project of opening my umbrella. It is motivated by the genuine because-motive. Once this is done, the in-order-to motive motivates the act which is itself being constituted on that occasion, using the project as its basis. In the in-order-to relation, the already existent project is the motivating factor; it motivates the action and is the reason why it is performed. But in the genuine because-relation, a lived experience temporally prior to the project is the motivating factor; it motivates the project which is being constituted at that time. This, then, is the essential difference between the two relations.

Let us state the point in greater detail. In the in-order-to relation, the motivated lived experience (i.e., the action) is anticipated in the motivating lived experience (i.e., the project), being pictured there in the future perfect tense. A similar relation of anticipation is not to be found in the genuine because-situation. The difference is the following: The project of opening the umbrella is not the cause of that action but only a fancied anticipation. Conversely, the action either "fulfills" or "fails to fulfill" the project. In contrast to this situation, the perception of the rain is itself no project of any kind. It does not have any "connection" with the judgment, "If I expose myself to the rain, my clothes will get wet; that is not desirable; therefore I must do something to prevent it." The connection or linkage is brought into being through an intentional act of mine whereby I turn to the total complex of my past experience. Within this total complex, of course, will be found the judgment in question as an abstract logical object. But even though this judgment is part of the store of my experience, it may never be "connected up" to the perception of the rain at all. Thus, if I perceive the rain from my window, I may not reactivate the judgment at all or proceed to any project. In that case the judgment will retain its status as a purely hypothetical maxim for me.

Now we can describe in somewhat greater generality the meaning-context of the genuine because-motivation: in every genuine because-motivation both the motivating and motivated lived experiences have the temporal character of pastness. The formulation of a genuine why-question is generally possible only after the motivated experience has occurred and when one looks back on it as something whole and complete in itself. The motivating experience in turn is past once again in relation to the motivated one, and we can therefore designate our intentional reference to it as *thinking in the pluperfect tense*. Only by using the pluperfect tense can I say anything about the true "because" of a lived experience. For if I am to do this, I must refer to the motivated experience, in our case the project, and this must be already over and done with either in reality or in phantasy in the future perfect tense. The meaning-context of the true because-motive is thus always an explanation after the event.

Applied to our example, the whole process would run as follows. The perceiving of the rain, as long as it remains a mere observation, has no connection with the opening of the umbrella. But the perceiving of the rain does cause an Act of attention to the total complex of my past experience, and the latter, since it is pragmatically conditioned, lights upon the judgment, "If I expose myself unprotected to the rain I will get wet and soon it will become unpleasant. The way to stop this is to open my umbrella, and that is just what I will do." As yet there is given no meaning-context wherein the perception of rain and the opening of an umbrella are connected elements. If, however, I have projected the action of spreading the umbrella in this way, or if I have already performed the action, and now ask myself how this project was constituted, then I shall grasp the whole process from the perception of the rain to the spreading of the umbrella in one glance as a unity. If a companion should ask me why I am spreading the umbrella, I should reply, "Because it is raining." In so doing, I should be expressing a genuine because-motive of which I am aware. Were I answering in terms of the in-order-to relation, I should say, "In order not to get wet." The meaning-context in which the genuine because-motive stands to my action is clearly constituted only in a backward glance. This backward glance sees both the motivated action and its motivating experience, the latter in the pluperfect tense. Precisely for that reason the meaning-context itself is also a different one each time I look back upon the two experiences from a new Here and Now.

Now we can see the significance of the distinction we drew in Chapter 1 between the motive and the subjective meaning of an action. We found the meaning of an action in the attention focused upon the preceding project. This project anticipates the action in the future perfect tense and makes it the particular kind of action it is. If "action" refers to a constituted unity within the span of the project, then the project is the in-order-to motive of the action and also the meaning of the action as it is carried out. However, if by "action" we mean only a component action within the larger context of an act—as we often do—then the meaning and the in-order-to motive of the action no longer coincide. In this case, the goal pictured in the project is detachable from the "meaning" of the component action, which can be treated as something quite distinct. This is true whether the action in question is merely intended, still in progress, or already carried out. *But the case is different with the genuine because-motive.* The latter consists of those past lived experiences of the actor to which he gives his attention after the act (or at least its initial phases) has been carried out. Those lived experiences are then pictured by him in the pluperfect tense and in a meaning-context which he can contemplate monothetically. Within this meaning-context he can visualize in a synthesis of component phases both the motivating and the motivated experiences. Our equation of the motivated experience with the completed action, or its completed phases, calls for one correction. One can, as a matter of fact, contemplate the genuine because-motive even from the point of view of the project. But it pertains to the nature of a project to anticipate its projected action in the future perfect tense as something already carried out. A merely projected action appears to the monothetic glance always merely as a phantasy of an executed act. Admittedly as a phantasy, as a causally inefficacious shadow—yet necessarily as the shadow of an act bearing within itself the intrinsic temporal character of the past.

These considerations supply a broader foundation for the points we made in Chapter 1.[90] The meaning of an action—that is, its relation to the project—is, we maintain, taken for granted by the actor and is quite independent of the genuine because-motive. What appears to the actor as the meaning of his action is its relation to the project. It is *not* the process by which the act was constituted from the genuine because-motives. In order to comprehend the genuine because-motives of

90. See sec. 4, p. 28.

his action, the actor must carry out a new Act of attention *of a special kind*. He must, that is, investigate the origin of that project which, considered simply as a product, *is* "the meaning of his action." The search for the genuine because-motive occurs, therefore, when the Ego is engaged in a certain type of self-explication. For this type of self-explication it is essential that one start out with the in-order-to motive; in other words, from the project of the concrete action. This project is a constituted and complete meaning-context in relation to which all genuine because-motives are contemplated in the pluperfect tense. Therefore, the project is never related to the genuine because-motive as that which fulfills or fails to fulfill the latter: since the because-motives are pictured in the pluperfect tense, they are free from all protentions or anticipations; they are simply memories and have received their perspective-horizons, their highlights and shadows, from a Here and Now always later than the one in which the project was constituted.

We have already become acquainted with a typical case of the interpretation of such because-motives in our analysis of the process of choice preceding an action. We saw that it was by no means the case that two or more possibilities were presented to the actor within his stream of consciousness, possibilities between which he might make a selection. We saw further that what appear to be coexisting possibilities are really successive Acts of running through different projects. Once the die is cast, it does indeed seem that those possibilities between which the choice had stood detached had coexisted, as though a determining cause of the outcome had been present. We saw that this way of thinking led to a nest of pseudo-problems, but we did not pursue the matter any further. We are now in a position to explain this phenomenon also. All these possibilities between which a choice is made, and all those determining grounds which appear to have led to the selection of a certain project, disclose themselves to the backward-looking glance as genuine because-motives. They had no existence as discrete experiences as long as the Ego lived in them and therefore prephenomenally. They are only interpretations performed by the backward-looking glance when it is directed upon those conscious experiences which precede (in the pluperfect tense) the actual project. And since every interpretation in the pluperfect tense is determined by the Here and Now from which it is made, the choice of *which* past experiences are to be regarded as the genuine because-motive of the project depends on the cone of light which the Ego lets fall on its experiences preceding the project.

In a quite different area we come upon a similar problem, that is, when we study the question of the choice of problem and the constitution of the relevant interpretive schemes, which we explained in section 16. The correlation in question can be understood as a motivational context. If I ask what the intended meaning is of one of my lived experiences, my aim is to place the latter within the total context of my experience. Therefore I project the structure of an "in-order-to," and the choice of interpretive schemes is itself conditioned by the mode of the attention I give to my just completed lived experience and therewith, at the same time, to the total context of my experience. Once the choice of problem—which, as we saw, is a free Act of the Ego—has taken place, then, taking that as a vantage point, one can inquire into the "because" of the particular choice, picturing that ground in the pluperfect tense. Everything we have said, in fact, concerning the relation of the in-order-to motive to the genuine because-motive holds true on a higher level for the whole complex of topics involving the choice of problem and the choice of interpretive scheme. Whoever seeks to order a concrete lived experience within the total context of his experience orients his procedure according to an in-order-to motive of interpretation. He does this by choosing from all the interpretive schemes in the store of his past experience the one that is relevant for the solution of his problem. But the constitution of the in-order-to motive of self-interpretation, in other words, *the formulation of the problem itself*, takes place as the result of a genuine because-motive which one can picture only in the pluperfect tense. This complicated state of affairs is called "interest" in everyday life, and Weber adopts that loose word into his sociology. Of course, the term "interest" is ambiguous and covers in-order-to as well as genuine because-motives. Whoever asks what the intended meaning is of one of his lived experiences is "interested" in it first from the point of view of an already formulated problem. This is an "in-order-to" interest. But he is also interested in the problem itself, and this is a "because" interest. This however is a case of putting the conclusion before the premises, because the problem which is taken for granted, and the very selection of it as interesting or relevant, can only be the result of an ex post facto interpretation.

With this we bring to a close our study of the meaning-context of motive and the structure of the meaningful within the consciousness of the solitary Ego. We turn now to the sphere of social meaning and to the interpretation of the alter ego.

3 / Foundations of a Theory of Intersubjective Understanding

19. The General Thesis of the Alter Ego in Natural Perception

AS WE PROCEED TO OUR STUDY of the social world, we abandon the strictly phenomenological method.[1] We shall start out by simply accepting the existence of the social world as it is always accepted in the attitude of the natural standpoint, whether in everyday life or in sociological observation. In so doing, we shall avoid any attempt to deal with the problem from the point of view of transcendental phenomenology. We shall, therefore, be bypassing a whole nest of problems whose significance and difficulty were pointed out by Husserl in his *Formal and Transcendental Logic*, although he did not there deal with these problems specifically.[2] The question of the "meaning" of the "Thou" can only be answered by carrying out the analysis which he posited in that work. Even now, however, it can be stated with certainty that the concept of the world in general must be based on the concept of "everyone" and therefore also of "the other."[3] The same idea was expressed by Max Scheler in his "Erkenntnis und Arbeit":

> The reality of the world of contemporaries and community are taken for granted as *Thou-spheres* and *We-spheres*, first of all of the whole of nature both living and inorganic. . . . Furthermore, the reality of the "Thou" and of a community is taken for granted before the reality of the "I" in the sense of one's own Ego and its personal private experiences.[4]

1. See our APPENDED NOTE at the end of Chap. 1, p. 43, above.
2. In the *Cartesian Meditations*, especially in Meditation V, Husserl has given us a profound analysis of the general significance of these questions and has also given us the essential starting point from which they must be solved.
3. This follows from Husserl's method of dealing with the problem. Cf. *Logik*, p. 212.
4. *Die Wissensformen und die Gesellschaft* (Leipzig, 1926), II, pp. 475 f.

We must, then, leave unsolved the notoriously difficult problems which surround the constitution of the Thou within the subjectivity of private experience. We are not going to be asking, therefore, how the Thou is constituted in an Ego, whether the concept "human being" presupposes a transcendental ego in which the transcendental alter ego is already constituted, or how universally valid intersubjective knowledge is possible. As important as these questions may be for epistemology and, therefore, for the social sciences, we may safely leave them aside in the present work.[5]

The object we shall be studying, therefore, is the human being who is looking at the world from within the natural attitude. Born into a social world, he comes upon his fellow men and takes their existence for granted without question, just as he takes for granted the existence of the natural objects he encounters. The essence of his assumption about his fellow men may be put in this short formula: The Thou (or other person) is conscious, and his stream of consciousness is temporal in character, exhibiting the same basic form as mine. But of course this has implications. It means that the Thou knows its experiences only through reflective Acts of attention. And it means that the Acts of attention themselves will vary in character from one moment to the next and will undergo change as time goes on. In short, it means that the other person also experiences his own aging.

So, then, all that we said in Chapter 2 about the consciousness of the solitary Ego will apply quite as much to the Thou. Since the Thou also performs intentional Acts, it also bestows meaning. It also selects certain items from its stream of consciousness and interprets these items by placing them within one or another context of meaning. It also pictures as whole units intentional Acts that took place step by step. It also lays down meaning-contexts in layers, building up its own world of experience, which, like my own, always bears upon it the mark of the particular moment from which it is viewed. Finally, since the Thou interprets its lived experiences, it gives meaning to them, and this meaning is intended meaning.

In Chapter 1 we already saw the difficulties standing in the way of comprehending the intended meaning of the other self.[6] We found, in fact, that such comprehension could never be achieved and that the concept of the other person's intended meaning remains at best a limiting concept. Our temporal analysis has for the first time made clear the real reason why the postulate of comprehending the other person's intended meaning could never be carried out. For the postu-

---

5. [This paragraph is an adaptation.]
6. See pp. 38 f. and the APPENDED NOTE, pp. 43 f.

late *means that I am to explicate the other person's lived experiences
in the same way that he does.* Now we have seen that self-explication
is carried out in a series of highly complex Acts of consciousness.
These intentional Acts are structured in layers and are in turn the
objects of additional Acts of attention on the part of the Ego. Naturally, the latter are dependent upon the particular Here and Now
within which they occur. The postulate, therefore, that I can observe
the subjective experience of another person precisely as he does is
absurd. For it presupposes that I myself have lived through all the
conscious states and intentional Acts wherein this experience has been
constituted. But this could only happen within my own experience and
in my own Acts of attention to my experience. And this experience of
mine would then have to duplicate his experience down to the smallest
details, including impressions, their surrounding areas of protention
and retention, reflective Acts, phantasies, etc. But there is more to
come: I should have to be able to remember all his experiences and
therefore should have had to live through these experiences in the
same order that he did; and finally I should have had to give them
exactly the same degree of attention that he did. In short, my stream
of consciousness would have to coincide with the other person's, which
is the same as saying that I should have to *be* the other person. This
point was made by Bergson in his *Time and Free Will.*[7] "Intended
meaning" is therefore essentially subjective and is in principle confined to the self-interpretation of the person who lives through the
experience to be interpreted. Constituted as it is within the unique
stream of consciousness of each individual, *it is essentially inaccessible to every other individual.*

It might seem that these conclusions would lead to the denial of
the possibility of an interpretive sociology and even more to the denial
that one can ever understand another person's experience. But this is
by no means the case. We are asserting neither that your lived experiences remain in principle inaccessible to me nor that they are meaningless to me. Rather, the point is that the meaning I give to your
experiences cannot be precisely the same as the meaning you give to
them when you proceed to interpret them.

To clarify the distinction between the two types of meaning in-

7. Cf. also Husserl's *Ideen*, p. 167 [E.T., p. 241]: "Closer inspection would
further show that two *streams of experience* (spheres of consciousness for two
pure Egos) *cannot be conceived as having an essential content that is identically
the same*; moreover. . . . no *fully-determinate experience* of the one could ever
belong to the other; only experiences of identically the same specification can
be common to them both (although not common in the sense of being individually
identical), but never two experiences which in addition have absolutely the same
'setting.' "

volved, that is, between self-explication and interpretation of another person's experience, let us call in the aid of a well-known distinction of Husserl's:

> Under *acts immanently directed,* or, to put it more generally, under *intentional experiences immanently related,* we include those acts which are *essentially* so constituted *that their intentional objects, when these exist at all, belong to the same stream of* experiences as themselves. . . . Intentional experiences for which this does not hold good are *transcendently directed,* as, for instance, all acts directed . . . towards the intentional experiences of other Egos with other experience-streams.[8]

It goes without saying that, not only are intentional Acts directed upon another person's stream of consciousness transcendent, but my experiences of another person's body, or of my own body, or of myself as a psychophysical unity fall into the same class. So we are immediately faced with the question of the specific characteristics of that subclass of transcendent Acts which are directed toward the lived experiences of another person. We could say that we "perceive" the other's experiences if we did not imply that we directly intuited them in the strict sense but meant rather that we grasped them with that same perceptual intention (*anschauliches Vermeinen*) with which we grasp a thing or event as present to us. It is in this sense that Husserl uses the word "perception" to mean "taking notice of": "The listener notices that the speaker is expressing certain subjective experiences of his and in that sense may be said to notice *them;* but he himself does not live through these experiences—his perception is 'external' rather than 'internal.' "[9] This kind of perception which is signitive[10] in character should not be confused with that in which an object directly appears to us. I apprehend the lived experiences of another only through signitive-symbolic representation, regarding either his body or some cultural artifact he has produced as a "field of expression"[11] for those experiences.

Let us explain further this concept of signitive apprehension of another's subjective knowledge. The whole stock of my experience (*Erfahrungsvorrat*) of another from within the natural attitude consists of my own lived experiences (*Erlebnisse*) of his body, of his behavior, of the course of his actions, and of the artifacts he has produced. For the time being let us speak simply of the interpretation

8. *Ideen,* p. 68 [E.T., p. 124].

9. *Logische Untersuchungen,* II., i, 34.

10. ["The term 'signification' is the same as 'meaning' for Husserl. Similarly, he often speaks of *significative* or *signitive acts* instead of acts of meaning-intention, of meaning, and the like. Signitive is also good as expressing opposition to intuitive. A synonym for *signitive* is *symbolic*" (Farber, *Foundation of Phenomenology,* p. 402, n.).]

11. [Cf. above, sec. 3.]

of the other person's *course of action* without further clarification. My lived experiences of another's acts consist in my perceptions of his body in motion. However, as I am always interpreting these perceptions as "body of another," I am always interpreting them as something having an implicit reference to "consciousness of another." Thus the bodily movements are perceived not only as physical events but also as a sign that the other person is having certain lived experiences which he is expressing through those movements. My intentional gaze is directed right through my perceptions of his bodily movements to his lived experiences lying behind them and signified by them. The signitive relation is essential to this mode of apprehending another's lived experiences. Of course he himself may be aware of these experiences, single them out, and give them his own intended meaning. His observed bodily movements become then for me not only a sign of his lived experiences as such, but of those to which he attaches an intended meaning. How interpretation of this kind is carried out is something which we shall study in detail later on. It is enough to say at this point that the signitive experience (*Erfahrung*) of the world, like all other experience in the Here and Now, is coherently organized and is thus "ready at hand." [12]

Here it could be objected that the concept of lived experience excludes by definition everything but my own experience, since the very term "lived experience" is equivalent to "object of immanent awareness." A transcendent apprehension of someone else's lived experience would therefore be ruled out as absurd. For, the argument runs, it is only the indications of someone else's lived experience that I apprehend transcendently; having apprehended such indications, I infer from them the existence and character of the experiences of which they *are* indications. Against this point of view we should maintain emphatically that signitive apprehension of the other's body as an expressive field does not involve inference or judgment in the usual sense. Rather what is involved is a certain intentional Act which utilizes an already established code of interpretation directing us through the bodily movement to the underlying lived experience. [13]

12. Cf. sec. 15.

13. Cf. Husserl's *Méditations cartésiennes*, p. 97: "The organism of another person keeps demonstrating that it *is* a living organism solely by its changing but always consistent behavior. And it does that in the following way: the physical side of the behavior is the index of the psychic side. It is upon this 'behavior' appearing in our experience and verifying and confirming itself in the ordered succession of its phases . . . it is in this indirect but genuine accessibility of that which is not in itself directly accessible that the existence of the other is, for us, founded." [The English rendering here is our own. Cf. Cairns' translation (from the German), *Cartesian Meditations*, p. 114.]

In the everyday world in which both the I and the Thou turn up, not as transcendental but as psychophysical subjects, there corresponds to each stream of lived experience of the I a stream of subjective experience of the Thou. This, to be sure, refers back to my own stream of lived experience, just as does the body of the other person to my body. During this process, the peculiar reference of my own ego to the other's ego holds, in the sense that my stream of lived experience is for you that of another person, just as my body is another's body for you.[14]

20. The Other's Stream of Consciousness as Simultaneous with My Own

IF I WISH TO OBSERVE one of my own lived experiences, I must perform a reflective Act of attention. But in this case, what I will behold is a past experience, not one presently occurring. Since this holds true for all my Acts of attention to my own experiences, I know it holds true for the other person as well. You are in the same position as I am: you can observe only your past, already-lived-through experiences. Now, whenever I have an experience of you, this is still my own experience.[15] However, this experience, while uniquely my own, still has, as its signitively grasped intentional object, a lived experience of yours which you are having at this very moment. In order to observe a lived experience of my own, I must attend to it reflectively. By no means, however, need I attend reflectively to *my* lived experience *of you* in order to observe *your* lived experience. On the contrary, by merely "looking" I can grasp even those of your lived experiences which you have not yet noticed and which are for you still prephenomenal and undifferentiated. This means that, whereas I can observe my own lived experiences only after they are over and done with, I can observe yours as they actually take place. This in turn implies that you and I are in a specific sense "simultaneous," that we "coexist," that our respective streams of consciousness intersect. To be sure, these are merely images and are inadequate since they are spatial. However, recourse to spatial imagery at this point is deeply rooted. We are concerned with the synchronism of two streams of consciousness here, my own and yours. In trying to understand this synchronism we can

14. Cf. also, Husserl, *Logik*, p. 210.
15. [Or, literally, "all my experiences of the other self's experiences are still my own experiences" ("nun sind auch meine Erlebnisse von Fremden Erlebnissen noch immer je-meinige Erlebnisse.")]

hardly ignore the fact that when you and I are in the natural attitude we perceive ourselves and each other as psychophysical unities.

This synchronism or "simultaneity" is understood here in Bergson's sense:

> I call simultaneous two streams which from the standpoint of my consciousness are indifferently *one* or *two*. My consciousness perceives these streams as a single one whenever it pleases to give them an undivided act of attention; on the other hand it distinguishes them whenever it chooses to divide its attention between them. Again, it can make them both one and yet distinct from one another, if it decides to divide its attention while still not splitting them into two separate entities.[16]

I see, then, my own stream of consciousness and yours in a single intentional Act which embraces them both. The simultaneity involved here is not that of physical time, which is quantifiable, divisible, and spatial. For us the term "simultaneity" is rather an expression for the basic and necessary assumption which I make that your stream of consciousness has a structure analogous to mine. It endures in a sense that a physical thing does not: it subjectively experiences its own aging, and this experience is determinative of all its other experiences. While the duration of physical objects is no *durée* at all, but its exact opposite, persisting over a period of objective time,[17] you and I, on the other hand, have a genuine *durée* which experiences itself, which is continuous, which is manifold, and which is irreversible. Not only does each of us subjectively experience his own *durée* as an absolute reality in the Bergsonian sense, but the *durée* of each of us is given to the other as absolute reality. What we mean, then, by the simultaneity of two durations or streams of consciousness is simply this: the phenomenon of *growing older together*. Any other criterion of simultaneity presupposes the transformation of both durations into a spatio-temporal complex and the transformation of the real *durée* into a merely *constructed time*. This is what Bergson means by the time which is not experienced by you, nor by me, nor by anyone at all.[18] But in reality you and I can each subjectively experience and live through

16. *Durée et simultanéité: A propos de la théorie d'Einstein*, 2d ed. (Paris, 1923) p. 66.
17. [". . . ein Beharren im Ablauf der objektiven Zeit." The words here are reminiscent of Kant. Cf. the *Critique of Pure Reason* B 183: "The schema of substance is the permanence of the real in time" ("die Beharrlichkeit des Realen in der Zeit").]
18. Bergson, *op. cit.*, p. 88 and *passim*.

his own respective duration, each other's duration, and everyone's duration.[19]

I can therefore say without hesitation that the Thou is that consciousness whose intentional Acts I can see occurring as other than, yet simultaneous with, my own. Also I can say that I may become aware of experiences of the Thou which the latter never gets to notice: its prephenomenal subjective experiences. If, for instance, someone is talking to me, I am aware not only of his words but his voice. To be sure, I interpret these in the same way that I always interpret my own lived experiences. But my gaze goes right through these outward symptoms to the inner man of the person who is speaking to me. Whatever context of meaning I light upon when I am experiencing these outward indications draws its validity from a corresponding context of meaning in the mind of the other person. The latter context must be the very one within which his own present lived experience is being constructed step by step.[20]

What we have just described is the comprehension, at the very moment they occur, of the other person's intentional Acts, Acts which take place step by step and which result in syntheses of a higher order. Now, this is precisely what Weber means by observational as opposed to motivational understanding. But the essential thing about the simultaneity involved here is not bodily coexistence. It is not as if I could observationally understand only those whom I directly experience. Not at all. I can imaginatively place the minds of people of past ages in a quasisimultaneity with my own, observationally understanding them through their writings, their music, their art. We have yet to deal with the different forms taken on by this understanding in the different spheres of the social world.

The simultaneity of our two streams of consciousness, however,

19. Cf. Husserl, *Méditations cartésiennes*, p. 97: "From the phenomenological point of view, the other person is a modification of 'my' self."

20. Husserl comes to the same conclusion from an entirely different starting point: "It (the experience of the other person) establishes a connection between, on the one hand, the uninterrupted, unimpeded living experience which the concrete *ego* has of itself, *in other words, the ego's primordial sphere, and on the other hand* the alien sphere which appears within the latter by appresentation. It establishes this connection by means of a synthesis which identifies the primordially given animate body of the other person with his body as appresented under another mode of appearance. From there it reaches out to a synthesis of the same Nature, given and verified at once primordially (with pure sensuous originality) and in the mode of appresentation. Thus is definitely instituted for the first time *the coexistence of my 'I'* (as well as my concrete *ego* in general) and the 'I' *of the other person,* the coexistence of my intentional life and his, of my 'realities' and his; in short what we have here is the creation of a *common time-form* (*Méditations cartésiennes*, § 55, p. 108. [See also E.T., Cairns, p. 128. Cf. the next footnote for an explanation of what Husserl means by "a synthesis of the same Nature."]

does not mean that the same experiences are given to each of us. My lived experience of you, as well as the environment I ascribe to you, bears the mark of my own subjective Here and Now and not the mark of yours. Also, I ascribe to you an environment which has already been interpreted from my subjective standpoint. I thus presuppose that at any given time we are both referring to the same objects, which transcend the subjective experience of either of us.[21] This is so at least in the world of the natural attitude, the world of everyday life in which one has direct experience of one's fellow men, the world in which I assume that you are seeing the same table I am seeing. We shall also see, at a later point, the modifications this assumption undergoes in the different regions of the social world, namely, the world of contemporaries, the world of predecessors, and the world of successors.[22]

In what follows we shall be seeking confirmation for this general thesis of the other self in the concrete problems of understanding other people. However, even at this early point we can draw a few fundamental conclusions.

The self-explication of my own lived experiences takes place within the total pattern of my experience. This total pattern is made up of meaning-contexts developed out of my previous lived experiences. In these meaning-contexts all my past lived experiences are at least potentially present to me. They stand to a certain extent at my disposal, whether I see them once again in recognition or reproduction or whether, from the point of view of the already constituted meaning-context, I *can* potentially observe the lived experiences which they have built up. Furthermore, I can repeat my lived experiences in free reproduction (at least insofar as they have originated in spontaneous activities).[23] We say "in free reproduction" because I can leave unnoticed any phases whatsoever and turn my attention to any other

21. Husserl arrives at similar conclusions. He formulates the concept of the "intersubjective Nature" corresponding to the ordinary concept of environment, and he draws the profound distinction between apperception in the mode of the *"hic"* and of the *"illic."* "It (the other's body as it appears to me) appresents, first of all, the activity of the other person as controlling his body (*illic*) as the latter appears to me. But also, and as a result of this, it appresents his action through that body on the *Nature* which he perceives. This Nature is the *same* Nature to which that body (*illic*) belongs, *my own* primordial Nature. It is the same Nature but it is given to me in the mode of 'If I were over there looking out through his eyes.' . . . Furthermore, *my whole* Nature is the same as his. It is constituted in my primordial sphere as an identical unity of my multiple modes of givenness, identical in all its changing orientations from the point of view of my body, which is the zero point, the absolute *here* (hic)" (*Méditations cartésiennes*, p. 104). [Cf. also E.T., Cairns, p. 123.]

22. See Chap. 4, secs. 33–41.

23. For the sake of simplicity we are here leaving essentially actual lived experiences out of account.

phases previously unnoticed. In principle, however, the continuum which is my total stream of lived experience remains open in its abundance at all times to my self-explication.

Still, *your* whole stream of lived experience is *not* open to me. To be sure, your stream of lived experience is also a continuum, but I can catch sight of only disconnected segments of it. We have already made this point. If I could be aware of your whole experience, you and I would be the same person. But we must go beyond this. You and I differ from each other not merely with respect to how much of each other's lived experiences we can observe. We also differ in this: When I become aware of a segment of your lived experience, I arrange what I see within my own meaning-context. But meanwhile you have arranged it in yours. Thus I am always interpreting your lived experiences from my own standpoint. Even if I had ideal knowledge of all your meaning-contexts at a given moment and so were able to arrange your whole supply of experience, I should still not be able to determine whether the particular meaning-contexts of yours in which I arranged your lived experiences were the same as those which *you* were using. This is because your manner of attending to your experiences would be different from my manner of attending to them. However, if I look at my whole stock of knowledge of your lived experiences and ask about the structure of this knowledge, one thing becomes clear: *This is that everything I know about your conscious life is really based on my knowledge of my own lived experiences.* My lived experiences of you are constituted in simultaneity or quasisimultaneity with *your* lived experiences, to which they are intentionally related. It is only because of this that, when I look backward, I am able to synchronize *my* past experiences of you with *your* past experiences.

It might be objected that another person's stream of consciousness could still be constructed, without contradictions, as so synchronized with my own that they corresponded moment for moment. Furthermore, an ideal model might be constructed in which, at every moment, the Ego has lived experiences *of* the other self and is thereby simultaneously encountering the *other's* lived experiences. In other words, I might be able to keep track of your lived experiences *in their continuity* all through your lifetime. Yes, but only in their continuity, not in their completeness. For what I call the series of your lived experiences is merely one possible meaning-context which I have constructed out of a few of your lived experiences. I always fall far short of grasping the totality of your lived experience, which at this very moment is being transformed into a unique present moment for you. And, of course, what holds true of the series holds true of the single moment: comprehension falls short of fullness, even in simultaneity. In sum-

get the other in "segments"

mary it can be said that my own stream of consciousness is given to me continuously and in all its fullness but that yours is given to me in discontinuous segments, never in its fullness, and only in "interpretive perspectives."

But this also means that our knowledge of the consciousness of other people is always in principle open to doubt, whereas our knowledge of our own consciousness, based as it is on immanent Acts, is always in principle indubitable.[24]

The above considerations will prove to be of great importance for the theory of the other self's action, which will be a predominant concern of ours in the pages to follow. It is in principle doubtful whether your experiences, as I comprehend them, are seized upon by your reflective glance at all, whether they spring from your spontaneous Acts and are therefore really "behavior" in the sense we have defined, and consequently whether they are really action, since the latter is behavior oriented to a goal. And so, in the concept of the other self's action, we come up against a profound theoretical problem. The very postulate of the comprehension of the intended meaning of the other person's lived experiences becomes unfulfillable. Not only this, but it becomes in principle doubtful whether the other person attends to and confers meaning upon those of his lived experiences which I comprehend.

21. The Ambiguities in the Ordinary Notion of Understanding the Other Person

BEFORE WE PROCEED FURTHER, it would be well to note that there are ambiguities in the ordinary notion of understanding another person. Sometimes what is meant is intentional Acts directed toward the other self; in other words, my lived experiences of you. At other times what is in question is *your* subjective experiences. Then, the arrangements of all such experiences into meaning-contexts (Weber's comprehension of intended meaning) is sometimes called "understanding of the other self," as is the classification of others' behavior into motivation contexts. The number of ambiguities associated with the notion of "understanding another person" becomes even greater when we bring in the question of understanding the signs he is *Signs* using. On the one hand, what is understood is the sign itself, then again *what* the other person means by using this sign, and finally the significance of the fact *that* he is using the sign, here, now, and in this particular context.

24. Husserl, *Ideen*, p. 85 [E.T., p. 143].

In order to sort out these different levels in the meaning of the term, let us first give it a generic definition. Let us say that understanding (*Verstehen*) as such is correlative to meaning, for all understanding is directed toward that which has meaning (*auf ein Sinnhaftes*) and only something understood is meaningful (*sinnvoll*). In Chapter 2 we saw the implications for the sphere of the solitary Ego of this concept of that which has meaning (*des Sinnhaften*). In this sense, all intentional Acts which are interpretations of one's own subjective experiences would be called Acts of understanding (*verstehende Akte*). We should also designate as "understanding" all the lower strata of meaning-comprehension on which such self-explication is based.

The man in the natural attitude, then, understands the world by interpreting his own lived experiences of it, whether these experiences be of inanimate things, of animals, or of his fellow human beings. And so our initial concept of the understanding of the other self is simply the concept "our explication of our lived experiences *of* our fellow human beings as such." The fact that the Thou who confronts me is a fellow man and not a shadow on a movie screen—in other words, that he has duration and consciousness—is something I discover by explicating my own lived experiences of him.

Furthermore, the man in the natural attitude perceives changes in that external object which is known to him as the other's body. He interprets these changes just as he interprets changes in inanimate objects, namely, by interpretation of his own lived experiences of the events and processes in question. Even this second phase does not go beyond the bestowing of meaning within the sphere of the solitary consciousness.

The transcending of this sphere becomes possible only when the perceived processes come to be regarded as lived experiences belonging to another consciousness, which, in accordance with the general thesis of the other self, exhibits the same structure as my own. The perceived bodily movements of the other will then be grasped not merely as *my* lived experience of these movements within *my* stream of consciousness. Rather it will be understood that, simultaneous with *my* lived experience of you, there is *your* lived experience which belongs to you and is part of your stream of consciousness. Meanwhile, the specific nature of your experience is quite unknown to me, that is, I do not know the meaning-contexts you are using to classify those lived experiences of yours, provided, indeed, you are even aware of the movements of your body.

However, I can know the meaning-context into which I classify my own lived experiences of you. We have already seen that this is not your intended meaning in the true sense of the term. What can be comprehended is always only an "approximate value" of the limiting concept "the other's intended meaning."

However, talk about the meaning-context into which the Thou orders its lived experience is again very vague. The very question of whether a bodily movement is purposive or merely reactive is a question which can only be answered in terms of the other person's own context of meaning. And then if one considers the further questions that can be asked about the other person's schemes of experience, for instance about his motivational contexts, one can get a good idea of how complex is the theory of understanding the other self. It is of great importance to penetrate into the structure of this understanding far enough to show that we can only interpret lived experiences belonging to other people in terms of our own lived experiences of them.

In the above discussion we have limited our analysis exclusively to cases where other people are present bodily to us in the domain of directly experienced social reality. In so doing, we have proceeded as if the understanding of the other self were based on the interpretation of the movements of his body. A little reflection shows, however, that this kind of interpretation is good for only one of the many regions of the social world; for even in the natural standpoint, a man experiences his neighbors even when the latter are not at all present in the bodily sense. He has knowledge not only of his directly experienced consociates [25] but also about his more distant contemporaries. He has, in addition, empirical information about his historical predecessors. He finds himself surrounded by objects which tell him plainly that they were produced by other people; these are not only material objects but all kinds of linguistic and other sign systems, in short, artifacts in the broadest sense. He interprets these first of all by arranging them within his own contexts of experience. However, he can at any time ask further questions about the lived experiences and meaning-contexts of their creators, that is, about why they were made.

We must now carefully analyze all these complex processes. We shall do so, however, only to the extent required by our theme, namely, "the understanding of the other person within the social world." For this purpose we must begin with the lowest level and clarify those Acts of self-explication which are present and available for use in interpreting the behavior of other people. For the sake of simplicity, let us

25. [Schutz used the English term "consociates" (among others) to mean those whom we directly experience. We shall be using it in this technical sense to translate references to people in our *Umwelt* (domain of directly experienced social reality).]

assume that the other person is present bodily. We shall select our examples from various regions of human behavior by analyzing first an action without any communicative intent and then one whose meaning is declared through signs.

As an example of the "understanding of a human act" without any communicative intent, let us look at the activity of a woodcutter.

Understanding that wood is being cut can mean:

1. That we are noticing only the "external event," the ax slicing the tree and the wood splitting into bits, which ensues. If this is all we see, we are hardly dealing with what is going on in another person's mind. Indeed, we need hardly bring in the other person at all, for woodcutting is woodcutting, whether done by man, by machine, or even by some natural force. Of course, meaning *is* bestowed on the observed event by the observer, in the sense that he understands it as "woodcutting." In other words, he inserts it into his own context of experience. However, this "understanding" is merely the explication of his own lived experiences, which we discussed in Chapter 2. The observer perceives the event and orders his perceptions into polythetic syntheses, upon which he then looks back with a monothetic glance, and arranges these syntheses into the total context of his experience, giving them at the same time a name. However, the observer in our case does not as yet perceive the *woodcutter* but only *that the wood is being cut,* and he "understands" the perceived sequence of events as "woodcutting." It is essential to note that even this interpretation of the event is determined by the total context of knowledge available to the observer at the moment of observation. Whoever does not know how paper is manufactured will not be in a position to classify the component processes because he lacks the requisite interpretive scheme. Nor will he be in a position to formulate the judgment "This is a place where paper is manufactured." And this holds true, as we have established, for all arrangements of lived experiences into the context of knowledge.

But understanding that wood is being cut can also mean:

2. That changes in another person's body are perceived, which changes are interpreted as indications that he is alive and conscious. Meanwhile, no further assumption is made that an action is involved. But this, too, is merely an explication of the observer's own perceptual experiences. All he is doing is identifying the body as that of a living human being and then noting the fact and manner of its changes.

Understanding that someone is cutting wood can, however, mean:

3. That the center of attention is the woodcutter's own lived experiences as actor. The question is not one about external events but one about lived experiences: "Is this man acting spontaneously accord-

ing to a project he had previously formulated? If so, what is this project? What is his in-order-to motive? In what meaning-context does this action stand for *him*?" And so forth. These questions are concerned with neither the facticity of the situation as such nor the bodily movements as such. Rather, the outward facts and bodily movements are understood as indications (*Anzeichen*) of the lived experiences of the person being observed. The attention of the observer is focused not on the indications but on what lies behind them. This is *genuine understanding of the other person.*

Now, let us turn our attention to a case where signs are being used and select as our example the case of a person talking German. The observer can direct his attention:

1. Upon the bodily movements of the speaker. In this case he interprets his own lived experience on the basis of the context of experience of the present moment. First the observer makes sure he is seeing a real person and not an image, as in a motion-picture film. He then determines whether the person's movements are actions. All this is, of course, self-interpretation.

2. Upon the perception of the sound alone. The observer may go on to discover whether he is hearing a real person or a tape recorder. This, too, is only an interpretation of his own experiences.

3. Upon the specific pattern of the sounds being produced. That is, he identifies the sounds first as words, not shrieks, and then as German words. They are thus ordered within a certain scheme, in which they are signs with definite meanings. This ordering within the scheme of a particular language can even take place without knowledge of the meanings of the words, provided the listener has some definite criterion in mind. If I am traveling in a foreign country, I know when two people are talking to each other, and I also know that they are talking the language of the country in question without having the slightest idea as to the subject of their conversation.

In making any of these inferences, I am merely interpreting my own experiences, and nothing is implied as to a single lived experience of any of the people being observed.

The observer "understands," in addition:

4. The word as the sign of its own word meaning. Even then he merely interprets his own experiences by coordinating the sign to a previously experienced sign system or interpretive scheme, say the German language. As the result of his knowledge of the German language, the observer connects with the word *Tisch* the idea of a definite piece of furniture, which he can picture with approximate accuracy. It matters not at all whether the word has been uttered by another person, a phonograph, or even a parrot. Nor does it matter

whether the word is spoken or written, or, if the latter, whether it is traced out in letters of wood or iron.[26] It does not matter when or where it is uttered or in what context. As long, therefore, as the observer leaves out of account all questions as to why and how the word is being used on the occasion of observation, his interpretation remains self-interpretation. He is concerned with the *meaning of the word*, not the *meaning of the user of the word*. When we identify these interpretations as self-interpretations, we should not overlook the fact that all previous knowledge of the other person belongs to the interpreter's total configuration of experience, which is the context from whose point of view the interpretation is being made.

The observer can, however, proceed to the genuine understanding of the other person if he:

5. Regards the meaning of the word as an indication (*Anzeichen*) of the speaker's subjective experiences—regards the meaning, in short, as *what the speaker meant*. For instance, he can try to discover what the speaker intended to say and what he meant by saying it on this occasion. These questions are obviously aimed at conscious experiences. The first question tries to establish the context of meaning within which the speaker understands the words he is uttering, while the second seeks to establish the motive for the utterance. It is obvious that the genuine understanding of the other person involved in answering such questions can only be attained if the objective meaning of the words is first established by the observer's explication of his own experiences.

All these, of course, are only examples. Later we shall have repeated opportunity to refer to the essential point which they illustrate. Let us now state in summary which of our interpretive acts referring to another self are interpretations of our own experience. There is first the interpretation that the observed person is really a human being and not an image of some kind. The observer establishes this solely by interpretation of his own perceptions of the other's body. Second, there is the interpretation of all the external phases of action, that is, of all bodily movements and their effects. Here, as well, the observer is engaging in interpretation of his own perceptions, just as when he is watching the flight of a bird or the stirring of a branch in the wind. In order to understand what is occurring, he is appealing solely to his own past experience, not to what is going on in the mind of the observed person.[27] Finally, the same thing may be said of the percep-

26. Cf. Husserl, *Logische Untersuchungen* (3d ed.), II, ii, 89.

27. Of course, all such interpretations presume acceptance of the General Thesis of the Alter Ego, according to which the external object is understood to be animated, that is, to be the body of another self.

tion of all the other person's expressive movements and all the signs which he uses, provided that one is here referring to the general and objective meaning of such manifestations and not their occasional and subjective meaning.

But, of course, by "understanding the other person" much more is meant, as a rule. This additional something, which is really the only strict meaning of the term, involves grasping what is really going on in the other person's mind, grasping those things of which the external manifestations are mere indications. To be sure, interpretation of such external indications and signs in terms of interpretation of one's own experiences must come first. But the interpreter will not be satisfied with this. He knows perfectly well from the total context of his own experience that, corresponding to the outer objective and public mean- *inner subjective meaning* ing which he has just deciphered, there is this other, inner, subjective meaning. He asks, then, "What is that woodcutter really thinking about? What is he up to? What does all this chopping mean to him?" Or, in another case, "What does this person mean by speaking to me in this manner, at this particular moment? For the sake of what does he do this (what is his in-order-to motive)? What circumstance does he give as the reason for it (that is, what is his genuine because-motive)? What does the choice of these words indicate?" Questions like these point to the other person's *own* meaning-contexts, to the complex ways in which his own lived experiences have been constituted polythetically and also to the monothetic glance with which he attends to them.

22. The Nature of Genuine Intersubjective Understanding *have to start with you*

HAVING ESTABLISHED THAT all genuine understanding of the other person must start out from Acts of explication performed by the observer on his own lived experience, we must now proceed to a precise analysis of this genuine understanding itself. From the examples we have already given, it is clear that our inquiry must take two different directions. First we must study the genuine understanding of actions which are performed *without any communicative intent*. The action of the woodcutter would be a good example. Second we would examine cases where such communicative intent was present. The latter type of action involves a whole new dimension, the using [28] and interpreting of signs.

Let us first take actions performed without any communicative intent. We are watching a man in the act of cutting wood and wonder-

28. [*Setzung;* literally, "positing" or "establishing."]

ing what is going on in his mind. Questioning him is ruled out, because that would require entering into a social relationship [29] with him, which in turn would involve the use of signs.

Let us further suppose that we know nothing about our woodcutter except what we see before our eyes. By subjecting our own perceptions to interpretation, we know that we are in the presence of a fellow human being and that his bodily movements indicate he is engaged in an action which we recognize as that of cutting wood.

Now how do we know what is going on in the woodcutter's mind? Taking this interpretation of our own perceptual data as a starting point, we can plot out in our mind's eye exactly how *we* would carry out the action in question. Then we can actually imagine ourselves doing so. In cases like this, then, we project the other person's goal as if it were our own and fancy ourselves carrying it out. Observe also that we here project the action in the future perfect tense as completed and that our imagined execution of the action is accompanied by the usual retentions and reproductions of the project, although, of course, only in fancy. Further, let us note that the imagined execution may fulfill or fail to fulfill the imagined project.

Or, instead of imagining for ourselves an action wherein we carry out the other person's goal, we may recall in concrete detail how we once carried out a similar action ourselves. Such a procedure would be merely a variation on the same principle.

In both these cases, we put ourselves in the place of the actor and identify our lived experiences with his. It might seem that we are here repeating the error of the well-known "projective" theory of empathy. For here we are reading our own lived experiences into the other person's mind and are therefore only discovering our own experiences. But, if we look more closely, we will see that our theory has nothing in common with the empathy theory except for one point. This is the general thesis of the Thou as the "other I," the one whose experiences are constituted in the same fashion as mine. But even this similarity is only apparent, for we start out from the general thesis of the other person's flow of duration, while the projective theory of empathy jumps from the mere fact of empathy to the belief in other minds by an act of blind faith. Our theory only brings out the implications of what is already present in the self-explicative judgment "I am experiencing a fellow human being." We know with certainty that the other person's subjective experience of his own action is in principle different from our own imagined picture of what we would do in the same

project
others
goal as if
own

29. The term "social relationship" is here being used in Weber's vague colloquial sense. Later, in sec. 31, we expect to subject it to detailed analysis.

situation. The reason, as we have already pointed out, is that the intended meaning of an action is always in principle subjective and accessible only to the actor. The error in the empathy theory is two-fold. First, it naïvely tries to trace back the constitution of the other self within the ego's consciousness to empathy, so that the latter becomes the direct source of knowledge of the other.[30] Actually, such a task of discovering the constitution of the other self can only be carried out in a transcendentally phenomenological manner. Second, it pretends to a knowledge of the other person's mind that goes far beyond the establishment of a structural parallelism between that mind and my own. In fact, however, when we are dealing with actions having no communicative intent, all that we can assert about their meaning is already contained in the general thesis of the alter ego.

It is clear, then, that we imaginatively project the in-order-to motive of the other person as if it were our own and then use the fancied carrying-out of such an action as a scheme in which to interpret his lived experiences. However, to prevent misunderstanding, it should be added that what is involved here is only a reflective analysis of another person's completed act. It is an interpretation carried out after the fact. When an observer is directly watching someone else to whom he is attuned in simultaneity, the situation is different. Then the observer's living intentionality carries him along without having to make constant playbacks of his own past or imaginary experiences. The other person's action unfolds step by step before his eyes. In such a situation, the identification of the observer with the observed person is not carried out by starting with the goal of the act as already given and then proceeding to reconstruct the lived experiences which must have accompanied it. Instead, the observer keeps pace, as it were, with each step of the observed person's action, identifying himself with the latter's experiences within a common "we-relationship." We shall have much more to say about this later.[31]

So far we have assumed the other person's bodily movement as the only datum given to the observer. It must be emphasized that, if the bodily movement is taken by itself in this way, it is necessarily isolated from its place within the stream of the observed person's living experience. And this context is important not only to the observed person but to the observer as well. He can, of course, if he lacks other data, take a mental snapshot of the observed bodily movement and then try to fit it into a phantasied filmstrip in accordance with the way he thinks he would act and feel in a similar situation. However, the observer can

30. For a critique of the empathy theory see Scheler, *Wesen und Formen der Sympathie*, pp. 277 ff. [E.T., Heath, p. 241].
31. See below, Chap. 4, sec. 33.

draw much more reliable conclusions about his subject if he knows something about his past and something about the over-all plan into which this action fits. To come back to Max Weber's example, it would be important for the observer to know whether the woodcutter was at his regular job or just chopping wood for physical exercise. An adequate model of the observed person's subjective experiences calls for just this wider context. We have already seen, indeed, that the unity of the action is a function of the project's span. From the observed bodily movement, all the observer can infer is the single course of action which has directly led to it. If, however, I as the observer wish to avoid an inadequate interpretation of what I see another person doing, I must "make my own" all those meaning-contexts which make sense of this action on the basis of my past knowledge of this particular person. We shall come back later on to this concept of "inadequacy" and show its significance for the theory of the understanding of the other person.

23. Expressive Movement and Expressive Act

So FAR WE HAVE STUDIED only cases where the actor seeks merely to bring about changes in the external world. He does not seek to "express" his subjective experiences. By an "expressive" action we mean one in which the actor seeks to project outward (*nach aussen zu projizieren*) [32] the contents of his consciousness, whether to retain the latter for his own use later on (as in the case of an entry in a diary) or to communicate them to others. In each of these two examples we have a genuinely planned or projected action (*Handeln nach Entwurf*) whose in-order-to motive is that someone take cognizance of something. In the first case this someone is the other person in the social world. In the second it is oneself in the world of the solitary Ego. Both of these are expressive acts. We must clearly distinguish the "expressive act" (*Ausdruckshandlung*) from what psychologists call the "expressive movement" (*Ausdrucksbewegung*). The latter does not aim at any communication or at the expression of any thoughts for one's own use or that of others.[33] Here there is no genuine action in our sense, but only behavior: there is neither project nor in-order-to motive. Examples of such expressive movements are the gestures and facial expressions which, without any explicit intention, enter into every conversation.[34]

32. [It is perhaps needless to caution the reader against any confusion of this concept with Schutz's "to project" (*entwerfen*), which means "to plan" or "design" an act.]

33. Husserl, *Logische Untersuchungen*, II, 31.

34. *Ibid.*

From my point of view as observer, your body is presented to me as a field of expression on which I can "watch" the flow of your lived experiences. I do this "watching" simply by treating *both* your expressive movements and your expressive acts as indications of your lived experiences.[35] But we must look at this point in greater detail.

If I understand, as Weber says, certain facial expressions, verbal interjections, and irrational movements as an outbreak of anger, this understanding itself can be interpreted in several different ways. It can mean, for instance, nothing more than self-elucidation, namely my arrangement and classification of my own experiences of your body. It is only when I perform a further Act of attention involving myself intimately with *you*, regarding *your* subjective experiences as flowing simultaneously with *my* subjective experiences *of* you, that I really grasp or "get with" *your* anger. This turning to the genuine understanding of the other person is possible for me only because I have previously had experiences similar to yours even if only in phantasy, or if I have encountered it before in external manifestations.[36] The expressive movement does, then, enter into a meaning-context, but only for the *observer*, for whom it is an indication of the lived experiences of the person he is observing. The latter is barred from giving meaning to his own expressive movements as they occur, due to the fact that they are inaccessible to his attention, or prephenomenal.

Expressive movements, then, have meaning only for the observer, not for the person observed. It is precisely this that distinguishes them from expressive acts. The latter always have meaning for the actor. Expressive acts are always genuine communicative acts (*Kundgabehandlungen*) which have as a goal their own interpretation.

The mere occurrence of a piece of external behavior, therefore, gives the interpreter no basis for knowing whether he is dealing with an expressive movement or an expressive act. He will be able to determine this only by appealing to a different context of experience. For instance, the play of a man's features and gestures in everyday life may be no different from those of an actor on the stage. Now we look upon the facial expressions and gestures of the latter as set signs that the stage actor is utilizing to express certain subjective experiences. In everyday life, on the other hand, we never quite know whether another person is "acting" in this sense or not unless we pay attention to factors other than his immediate movements. For instance, he may be imitating someone else for our benefit, or he may be playing a

---

35. Cf. sec. 3, above.
36. For an adequate discussion of this point, we must await our analysis of the "world of contemporaries" in sec. 37.

joke on us, or he may be hypocritically feigning certain feelings in order to take advantage of us.

It is quite immaterial to the understanding of expressive acts whether they consist of gestures, words, or artifacts. Every such act involves the use of signs. We must, then, turn next to the problem of the nature of signs.

24. Sign and Sign System

WE MUST FIRST DISTINGUISH the concept of "sign" or "symbol" from the general concept of "indication" or "symptom." In so doing we will be following Husserl's First *Logical Investigation*.[37] By an "indication" Husserl means an object or state of affairs whose existence indicates the existence of a certain other object or state of affairs, in the sense that belief in the existence of the former is a nonrational (or "opaque") motive for belief in the existence of the latter. For our purposes the important thing here is that the relation between the two exists solely in the mind of the interpreter.

Now, it is obvious that Husserl's "motive of belief" has nothing to do with our "motive of action." Husserl's so-called "motive" is, like ours, *a complex of meaning* or meaning-context. But it is a complex consisting of at least two interpretive schemes. However, when we interpret an indication, we do not attend to this causal relation, hence the motive is not "rational." The connection between the indication and what it indicates is therefore a purely formal and general one; there is nothing logical about it. There is no doubt that Husserl would agree with this point. Both animate and inanimate objects can serve as indications. For the geologist, a certain formation in the earth's surface is an indication of the presence of certain minerals. For the mathematician, the fact that an algebraic equation is of an odd degree is an indication that at least it has a real root. All these are relations—or correlations—within the mind of the interpreter and as such may be called contexts of meaning for him. In this sense, the perceived movements of the other person's body are indications for the observer of what is going on in the mind of the person he is observing.

"Signifying signs," "expressions," or "symbols" are to be contrasted with "indications."

First of all, let us see how a sign gets constituted in the mind of the interpreter. We say that there exists between the sign and that which it signifies the relation of representation.[38] When we look at a symbol,

37. *Logische Untersuchungen*, II, i, 25–31.
38. Cf. Husserl's Sixth *Logical Investigation*.

which is always in a broad sense an external object, we do not look upon it *as object* but *as representative* of something else. When we "understand" a sign, our attention is focused not on the sign itself but upon that for which it stands. Husserl repeatedly points out that it belongs to the essence of the signitive relation that "the sign and what it stands for have nothing to do with each other." [39] The signitive relation is, therefore, obviously a particular relation between the interpretive schemes which are applied to those external objects here called "signs." When we understand a sign, we do not interpret the latter through the scheme adequate to it as an external object but through the schemes adequate to whatever it signifies. We are saying that an interpretive scheme is *adequate* to an experienced object if the scheme has been constituted out of polythetically lived-through experiences of this same object as a self-existent thing. For example, the following three black lines, **A**, can be interpreted (1) *adequately*, as the diagram of a certain black and white visual Gestalt, or (2) *nonadequately*, as a sign for the corresponding vocal sound. The adequate interpretive scheme for the vocal sound is, of course, constituted not out of visual but out of auditory experiences.

However, confusion is likely to arise out of the fact that the interpretation of signs in terms of what they signify is based on previous experience and is therefore itself the function of a scheme.[40]

What we have said holds true of all interpretation of signs, whether the individual is interpreting his own signs or those of others. There is, however, an ambiguity in the common saying "a sign is always a sign for something." The sign is indeed the "sign for" what it means or signifies, the so-called "sign meaning" or "sign function." But the sign is also the "sign for" what it expresses, namely, the subjective experiences of the person using the sign. In the world of nature there are no signs (*Zeichen*) but only indications (*Anzeichen*). A sign is by its very nature something used by a person to express a subjective experience. Since, therefore, the sign always refers back to an act of choice on the part of a rational being—a choice of this particular sign—the sign is also an indication of an event in the mind of the sign-user. Let us call this the "expressive function" of the sign.[41]

A sign is, therefore, always either an artifact or a constituted

39. *Ibid.*, II, ii, 55 [or II, 527 in the 1901 edition].
40. In effect, what we have here is a kind of metascheme connecting two others. This corresponds to Felix Kaufmann's so-called "coordinating scheme" (*Das Unendliche in der Mathematik und seine Ausschaltung* [Leipzig and Vienna, 1930], p. 42).
41. Our usage here diverges from the terminology of Husserl's *Logical Investigations*, I and VI.

act-object.[42] The boundary between the two is absolutely fluid. Every act-object which functions as a sign-object (for instance, my finger pointing in a certain direction) is the end result of an action. But I might just as well have constructed a signpost, which would, of course, be classified as an artifact. In principle it makes no difference whether the action culminates in an act-object or in an artifact.[43]

It should be noted that in interpreting a sign it is not necessary to refer to the fact that someone made the sign or that someone used it. The interpreter need only "know the meaning" of the sign. In other words, it is necessary only that a connection be established in his mind between the interpretive scheme proper to the object which is the sign and the interpretive scheme proper to the object which it signifies. Thus when he sees a road sign, he will say to himself, "Intersection to the left!" and not "Look at the wooden sign!" or "Who put that sign there?"

We can, therefore, define signs as follows: Signs are artifacts or act-objects which are interpreted not according to those interpretive schemes which are adequate to them as objects of the external world but according to schemes not adequate to them and belonging rather to other objects. Furthermore, it should be said that the connection between the sign and its corresponding non-adequate scheme depends on the past experience of the interpreter. As we have already said, the applicability of the scheme of that which is signified to the sign is itself an interpretive scheme based on experience. Let us call this last-named scheme the "sign system." A sign system is a meaning-context which is a configuration formed by interpretive schemes; the sign-user or the sign-interpreter places the sign within this context of meaning.

Now there is something ambiguous in this idea of a sign context. Surely no one will maintain that the connection in question exists independently of the actual establishment, use, or interpretation of the signs. For the connection is itself an example of meaning and therefore a matter of either prescription or interpretation. In a strict sense, therefore, meaning-connections hold, not between signs as such, but between their meanings, which is just another way of saying between the experiences of the knowing self establishing, using, or interpreting

---

42. [The words here translated "act-object" and "sign-object" are, respectively, *Handlungsgegenständlichkeit* and *Zeichengegenständlichkeit*. They refer to the act and sign considered as repeatable objects rather than as unique events.]

43. I cannot, therefore, admit as fundamental Hans Freyer's distinction between the physiognomic side of an action and its objectification in the material world. (See his *Theorie des objectiven Geistes* [Leipzig, 1923], pp. 29 ff.)

the signs. However, since these "meanings" are understood only in and through the signs, there holds between the latter the connection we call the "sign system."

The sign system is present to him who understands it as a meaning-context of a higher order between previously experienced signs. To him the German language is the meaning-context of each of its component words; the sign system of a map is the meaning-context of every symbol on that map; the system of musical notation is the meaning-context of every written note; and so forth.

Knowing that a sign belongs to a certain sign system is not the same thing as knowing *what* that sign means and for what subjective experience of its user it is the expressive vehicle. Even though I do not know shorthand, still I know shorthand when I see it. Even though I may not know how to play a card game, still I can recognize the cards as *playing* cards, etc. The placing of a sign within its sign system is something I do by placing it within the total context of my experience. In doing this, all that is necessary is that I find within the store of my experience such a sign system together with the rules on the basis of which it is constituted. I do not have to understand the meaning of the individual signs or be fully conversant with the sign system. For instance, I can see that certain characters are Chinese without understanding their meaning.

As an *established* sign every sign is meaningful and therefore in principle intelligible. In general it is absurd to speak of a meaningless sign. A sign can properly be called meaningless only with respect to one or more established sign systems. However, to say that a sign is alien to one such system only means that it belongs to another. For instance, the meaninglessness per se of a definite auditory-visual symbol can never be determined but only its meaninglessness within a definite "language," in the broadest sense of that term. A letter combination which is quite unpronounceable can have a code meaning. It can be put together by one person according to the rules of the code and can then be interpreted by another person who knows those same rules. More than that, however, the audio-visual symbol "Bamalip" seems at first quite meaningless so far as the European languages are concerned. But the person who knows that "Bamalip" is the scholastic term for an entity of formal logic, namely, the first mood of the fourth figure of the syllogism, will be able to place it quite precisely within the structure of his own native language.

From this it follows that the sign meaning within a certain sign system must have been experienced previously. It is a question just what this phrase, "have been experienced," means. If we ask ourselves in what circumstances we have experienced the connection between the term "Bamalip" and the first mood of the fourth figure, we will find that we have learned it from a teacher or from a book. To have experienced the connection, however, means that we must on that occasion have established in our minds the term "Bamalip" as the sign of the first mood of the fourth figure. Therefore, the understanding of a sign (to be more precise, the possibility of its interpretation within a given system) points back to a previous decision on our part to accept and use this sign as an expression for a certain content of our consciousness.

Every sign system is therefore a scheme of our experience. This is true in two different senses. First, it is an *expressive scheme;* in other words, I have at least once used the sign for that which it designates, used it either in spontaneous activity or in imagination. Second, it is an *interpretive scheme;* in other words, I have already in the past interpreted the sign as the sign of that which it designates. This distinction is important, since, as already shown, I can recognize the sign system as an interpretive scheme, but only know that others do so. In the world of the solitary Ego the expressive scheme of a sign and its corresponding interpretive scheme necessarily coincide. If, for instance, I invent a private script, the characters of that code are established by me while I am inventing the script or using it to make notes. It is for me at such moments an expressive scheme. But the same scheme functions as an interpretive one for me when I later read what I have written or use it to make further notes.

To master fully a sign system such as a language, it is necessary to have a clear knowledge of the meaning of the individual signs within the system. This is possible only if the sign system and its component individual signs are known both as expressive schemes and as interpretive schemes for previous experiences of the knower. In both functions, as interpretive scheme and as expressive scheme, every sign points back to the experiences which preceded its constituting. As expressive scheme and as interpretive scheme a sign is only intelligible in terms of those lived experiences constituting it which it designates. Its meaning consists in its translatibility, that is, its ability to lead us back to something known in a different way. This may be either that scheme of experience in which the thing designated is understood, or another sign system. The philologist Meillet explains this point clearly as far as languages are concerned:

> We cannot apprehend the sense of an unknown language intuitively. If we are to succeed in understanding the text of a language whose tradition has been lost, we must either have a faithful translation into a known language, that is, we must be closely related to one or more

languages with which we are familiar. In other words, *we must already know it.*[44]

This property of "being already known" amounts to this: the meaning of the sign must be discoverable somewhere in the past experience of the person making use of the sign. To be fully conversant with a language, or in fact with any sign system, involves familiarity with given interpretive schemes on the basis of one's preceding experiences—even though this familiarity may be somewhat confused as to the implications of the schemes. It also involves the ability to transform these constituted objects into active experience of one's own,[45] that is, in the ability to use expressively a sign system that one knows how to interpret.

We are now getting close to an answer to the question of what is meant by "connecting a meaning with a sign." Surely this involves something more than connecting words with behavior, which, as we pointed out in our Introduction,[46] is a mere figure of speech. A meaning is connected with a sign, insofar as the latter's significance within a given sign system is understood both for the person using the sign and for the person interpreting it. Now we must be quite clear as to what we mean by speaking of the established membership of a sign in a given sign system. A sign has an "objective meaning" within its sign system when it can be intelligibly coordinated to what it designates within that system independently of whoever is using the sign or interpreting it. This is merely to say that he who "masters" the sign system will interpret the sign in its meaning-function to refer to that which it designates, regardless of who is using it or in what connection. The indispensable reference of the sign to previous experience makes it possible for the interpreter to repeat the syntheses that have constituted this interpretive or expressive scheme. Within the sign system, therefore, the sign has the ideality of the "I can do it again." [47]

However, this is not to say that the signs within the previously known sign system cannot be understood without an Act of attention to those lived experiences out of which the knowledge of the sign was constituted. On the contrary: as a genuine interpretive scheme for previous lived experiences, it is invariant with respect to the lived experiences of the I in which it was constituted.

44. Quoted in Vossler, *Geist und Kultur in der Sprache* (Heidelberg, 1925), p. 115. [E.T., Oscar Oeser, *The Spirit of Language in Civilization* (London, 1932), p. 104. The reference is to A. Meillet, *Aperçu d'une histoire de la langue grecque* (Paris, 1913), p. 48.]
45. See above, sec. 14.
46. See above. sec. 6.
47. Cf. Husserl, *Logik*, p. 167; see also above, sec. 14.

What we have been considering is the objective meaning of the sign. The objective meaning is grasped by the sign-interpreter as a part of his interpretation of his own experience to himself. With this objective meaning of the sign we must contrast the sign's expressive function. The latter is its function as an indication of what actually went on in the mind of the communicator, the person who used the sign; in other words, of what was the communicator's own meaning-context.

If I want to understand the meaning of a word in a foreign language, I make use of a dictionary, which is simply an index in which I can see the signs arranged according to their objective meaning in two different sign systems or languages. However, the total of all the words in the dictionary is hardly the language. The dictionary is concerned only with the objective meanings of the words, that is, the meanings which do not depend on the users of the words or the circumstances in which they use them. In referring to subjective meanings, we do not here have in mind Husserl's "essentially subjective and occasional expressions," which we mentioned earlier.[48] Such essentially subjective expressions as "left," "right," "here," "there," "this," and "I" can, of course, be found in the dictionary and are in principle translatable; however, they also havè an objective meaning insofar as they designate a certain relation to the person who uses them. Once I have spatially located this person, then I can say that these subjective occasional expressions have objective meaning. However, *all* expressions, whether essentially subjective in Husserl's sense or not, have for both user and interpreter, over and above their objective meaning, a meaning which is both subjective and occasional. Let us first consider the *subjective* component. Everyone using or interpreting a sign associates with the sign a certain meaning having its origin in the unique quality of the experiences in which he once learned to use the sign. This added meaning is a kind of aura surrounding the nucleus of the objective meaning.[49] Exactly what Goethe means by "demonic"[50] can only be deduced from a study of his works as a whole. Only a careful study of the history of French culture aided by linguistic tools can permit us to understand the subjective meaning

48. Sec. 5, p. 33.

49. In fact, we can even say that the understanding of the objective meaning is an unrealizable ideal, which means merely that the subjective and occasional component in the sign's meaning should be explained with the utmost clarity by means of rational concepts. That language is "precise" in which all occasional subjective meanings are adequately explained according to their circumstances.

50. It was Jaspers who first called attention to the central importance of this concept in Goethe's image of the world. See his *Psychologie der Weltanschauung*, 3d ed. (Berlin, 1925).

of the word "civilization" in the mouth of a Frenchman.[51] Vossler applies this thesis to the whole history of language in the following way: "We study the development of a word; and we find that the mental life of all who have used it has been precipitated and crystallized in it." [52] However, in order to be able to "study" the word, we must be able to bring to bear from our previous experience a knowledge of the mental structure of all those who have used it. The particular quality of the experiences of the user of the sign at the time he connected the sign and the *signatum* is something which the interpreter must take into account, over and above the objective meaning, if he wishes to achieve true understanding.

We have said that the added meaning is not only subjective but *occasional*. In other words, the added meaning always has in it something of the context in which it is used. In understanding someone who is speaking, I interpret not only his individual words but his total articulated sequence of syntactically connected words—in short, "what he is saying." In this sequence every word retains its own individual meaning in the midst of the surrounding words and throughout the total context of what is being said. Still, I cannot really say that I understand the word until I have grasped the meaning of the whole statement. In short, what I need at the moment of interpretation is the total context of my experience. As the statement proceeds, a snythesis is built up step by step, from the point of view of which one can see the individual acts of meaning-interpretation and meaning-establishment. Discourse is, therefore, itself a kind of meaning-context. For both the speaker and the interpreter, the structure of the discourse emerges gradually. The German language expresses the point we are making precisely in its distinction between *Wörter* ("unconnected words") and *Worte* ("discourse"). We can, in fact, say that when unconnected words receive occasional meaning, they constitute a meaningful whole and become discourse.

But what is that synthesis, what is that superimposed meaning-context which serves as an interpretive scheme for the understanding of a sign's occasional meaning? The answer is this: discourse is a sign-using act. The unity of a given speaker's discourse is, from his point of view, simply the unity that belongs essentially to every act. We have already seen in what this unity consists.[53] It arises from the sign-user's own project or plan of action. It follows that the interpreter cannot grasp that unity until the act itself is completed. All he can do is arrive at an approximation based on his previous knowledge. This

51. Curtius, *Frankreich* (Stuttgart, 1930), I, 2 ff.
52. Vossler, *Geist und Kultur in der Sprache*, p. 117 [E.T., p. 106].
53. See sec. 9, p. 62.

limitation, in fact, applies to the interpretation of objective as well as occasional meaning. One always has to wait until the last word has been said if one expects to make an effective interpretation. And it always remains a question of fact *what the unit is* whose end has to be awaited: whether it is a sentence, a book, the complete works of an author, or a whole literary movement.

The problem of the subjective and occasional meaning of signs is only one aspect of the larger problem of the distinction between objective and subjective meaning. It is to this dichotomy that we must now turn our attention.

25. Meaning-Establishment and Meaning-Interpretation

WE HAVE NOW SEEN that the sign has two different functions. First it has a *significative function.* By this we mean that it can be ordered by an interpreter within a previously learned sign system of his own. What he is doing here is interpreting the sign as an item of his own experience. His act is just another example of what we call self-interpretation. But there is a second kind of interpretation in which he can engage. He can inquire into the subjective and occasional meaning of the sign, in short, the *expressive* function which it acquires within the context of discourse. This subjective meaning can be his own, in which case he must go back in memory to the experiences he had at the moment of using the sign and establishing its meaning. Or it can be someone else's, in which case he must try to find out about the other person's subjective experiences when *he* used the sign. But in any case, when interpreting signs used by others, we will find two components involved, the objective and the subjective. Objective meaning is the meaning of the sign as such, the kernel, so to speak; whereas subjective meaning is the fringe or aura emanating from the subjective context in the mind of the sign-user.

Let us take a conversation between two people as an example. As one person speaks, thoughts are building up in his mind, and his listener is following him every step of the way just as the thoughts occur. In other words, none of the thoughts come out as prefabricated unities. They are constructed gradually, and they are interpreted gradually. Both speaker and listener live through the conversation in such a manner that on each side Acts of meaning-establishment or meaning-interpretation are filled in and shaded with memories of what has been said and anticipations of what is yet to be said. Each of these Acts can in turn be focused upon introspectively and analyzed as a unit in itself. The meaning of the speaker's discourse consists for him *and* for his listener in his individual sentences and these, in turn, in their component words as they come, one after another. The sentences for both of them serve as the meaning-contexts of the words, and the whole discourse as the meaning-context of the separate sentences.

Understanding the conscious Acts of another person who is communicating by means of signs does not differ in principle from understanding his other Acts (sec. 22). Like the latter, it occurs in the mode of simultaneity or quasi-simultaneity. The interpreter puts himself in the place of the other person and imagines that he himself is selecting and using the signs. He interprets the other person's subjective meaning as if it were his own. In the process he draws upon his whole personal knowledge of the speaker, especially the latter's ways and habits of expressing himself. Such personal knowledge continues to build itself up in the course of a conversation.

The same process goes on in the mind of the speaker. His words will be selected with a view to being understood by his listener. And the meaning he seeks to get across will not only be objective meaning, for he will seek to communicate his personal attitude as well. He will sketch out his communicative aim in the future perfect tense, just as he does the project of any other act. His choice of words will depend on the habits he has built up in interpreting the words of others, but it will, of course, also be influenced by his knowledge of his listener.

However, if the speaker is focused on what is going on in the mind of his listener, his knowledge of the latter is still quite uncertain. He can only estimate how much he is actually getting across. Any such estimate is necessarily vague, especially considering the fact that the listener's interpretation is always subsequent to the choice of words and fulfills or fails to fulfill the speaker's project in making that choice.

The listener is in a different position. For him the actual establishment of the meaning of the words has already occurred. He can start out with the objective meaning of the words he has heard and from there try to discover the subjective meaning of the speaker. In order to arrive at that subjective meaning, he imagines the project which the speaker must have had in mind. However, this picturing of the project starts out from the speaker's already spoken words. Contrary to the case of the speaker who is picturing something future on the basis of something present, the listener is picturing something pluperfect on the basis of something past. Another difference is that he is starting from words which have either succeeded or failed in fulfilling the speaker's project, and he is trying to uncover that project. The speaker, on the other hand, starts out with his own project as datum and tries to estimate whether it is going to be fulfilled by the listener's future interpretation.

Now since the words chosen by the speaker may or may not express his meaning, the listener can always doubt whether he is understanding the speaker adequately. The project of the speaker is always a matter of imaginative reconstruction for his interpreter and so is attended by a certain vagueness and uncertainty.

To illustrate what we mean, consider the fact that, in a conversation, thoughts like the following may run through the heads of the participants. The person about to speak will say to himself, "Assuming that this fellow speaks my kind of language, I must use such and such words." A moment later his listener will be saying to himself, "If this other fellow is using words the way I understand them, then he must be telling me such and such." The first statement shows how the speaker always chooses his words with the listener's interpretation in mind. The second statement shows how the listener always interprets with the speaker's subjective meaning in mind. In either case an intentional reference to the other person's scheme is involved, regardless of whether the scheme is interpretive or expressive.

As the speaker chooses his words, he uses, of course, his own interpretive scheme. This depends partly upon the way he himself usually interprets words and partly upon his knowledge of his listener's interpretive habits. When I read over a letter I have written to someone, I tend to interpret it just as if I were the receiver and not the sender. Now, my purpose in writing the letter was not merely to communicate an objective meaning to the reader but my subjective meaning as well. To put it in another way, I want him to rethink my thoughts. It may very well be, therefore, that when I read over my letter I shall decide that it falls short of this purpose. Knowing the person to whom I am writing and knowing his customary reactions to certain words and phrases, I may decide that this or that expression is open to misinterpretation or that he will not really be in a position to understand this or that thought of mine. Or I may fear that he will, as he reads, miss the point I am trying to make due to some subjective bias or some failure of attention on his part.

On the other hand, the recipient of the letter can carry out the opposite process. He can take a sentence and imagine that he himself wrote it. He can try to reconstruct the intention of the writer by guessing at some possible intentions and then comparing them with the actual propositional content of the sentence. He may conclude, "I see what he was trying to say, but he really missed his mark and said something else. If I had been he, I should have put it in such and such a way." Or the reader may say to himself instead, "My friend always uses that term in an odd way, but I see what he means, since I know the way he thinks. It's lucky that I am the one reading the letter. A third party would have been thrown off the track entirely at this point." In the last case, the reader really carries out a threefold interpretation. First, he interprets the sentence objectively on the basis of his ordinary habits of interpretation. Second, from his knowledge of the writer, he reconstructs what must be the latter's real meaning. Third, he imagines how the ordinary reader would understand the sentence in question.

These considerations hold true quite generally for all cases in which signs are either used or interpreted. This being the case, it ought to be clear that in interpreting the subjective meaning of the signs used by someone else, or in anticipating someone else's interpretation of the subjective meaning of our own signs, we must be guided by our knowledge of that person. Naturally, therefore, the degree of intimacy or anonymity in which the person stands to us will have a great deal to do with the matter. The examples we have just used were all cases where knowledge of the other person was derived from direct contact; they belong to what we call the domain of directly experienced social reality. However, the use and interpretation of signs are to be found in the other areas of social life as well, such as the worlds of contemporaries and of predecessors, where direct knowledge of the people with whom we are dealing is minimal or even absent. Our theory of the establishment and interpretation of the meaning of signs will naturally undergo various modifications as it is applied to these areas. We shall see what these modifications are when we come to Chapter 4. Even in the direct social relations we have used as examples, it was obviously impossible for the participants to "carry out the postulate of grasping each other's intended meaning," a point that we discussed in section 19. The subjective meaning that the interpreter *does* grasp is at best an approximation to the sign-user's intended meaning, but never that meaning itself, for one's knowledge of another person's perspective is always necessarily limited. For exactly the same reason, the person who expresses himself in signs is never quite sure of how he is being understood.

What we have been discussing is the content of communication. But we must remember that the actual *communicating* is itself a meaningful act and that we must interpret that act and the way it is done as things in their own right.

26. The Meaning-Context of Communication. Recapitulation

ONCE THE INTERPRETER has determined both the objective and subjective meanings of the content of any communication, he may proceed to ask why the communication was made in the first place. He is then seeking the in-order-to motive of the person communicating. For it is essential to every act of communication that it have an extrinsic goal. When I say something to you, I do so for a reason, whether to evoke a particular attitude on your part or simply to explain something to you. Every act of communication has, therefore, as its in-order-to motive the aim that the person being addressed take cognizance of it in one way or another.

The person who is the object or recipient of the communication is frequently the one who makes this kind of interpretation. Having settled what are the objective and subjective meanings of the content of the communication by finding the corresponding interpretive or expressive schemes, he proceeds to inquire into the reason why the other person said this in the first place. In short, he seeks the "plan" behind the communication.

However, the seeker of the in-order-to motive need not be the person addressed at all. A nonparticipant observer may proceed to the same kind of interpretation. I can, indeed I must, seek the in-order-to motive of the communication if I am ever to know the goal toward which the communication is leading. Furthermore, it is self-evident that one can seek the in-order-to motives even of those acts of other people which have no communicative intent. We have already seen this in section 22. What an actor's subjective experience actually is we can only grasp if we find his in-order-to motive. We must first light upon his project and then engage in a play-by-play phantasy of the action which would fulfill it. In the case of action without communicative intent, the completed act itself is properly interpreted as the fulfillment of the in-order-to motive. However, if I happen to know that the completed act is only a link in a chain of means leading to a further end, then what I must do is interpret the subjective experiences the other person has of that further goal itself.

Now, we have already seen that we can go beyond the in-order-to motive and seek out the because-motive. Of course, knowledge of the latter presupposes in every case knowledge of the former. The subjective meaning-context which is the in-order-to motive must first be seen and taken for granted as an already constituted object in itself before any venture into deeper levels is undertaken. To speak of such deeper levels *as existing* by no means implies that the actor actually experiences them subjectively as meaning-contexts of his action. Nor does it mean that he can become aware even retrospectively of those polythetic Acts which, according to my interpretation, have constituted the in-order-to motive. On the contrary, there is no evidence to support the view that the actor ever has any awareness of the because-motive of his action. This applies to one who is establishing a meaning as well as to any other actor. To be sure, he lives through the subjective experiences and intentional Acts which I have interpreted as his because-motive. However, he is not as a rule aware of them, and, when he is, it is no longer as actor. Such awareness, when it occurs, is a separate intentional Act independent of and detached from the action it is interpreting. It is then that a man can be said to understand himself. Such self-understanding is essentially the same as understanding others, with this difference—that usually, but not always, we have at our disposal a much richer array of information about ourselves and our past than others do.

Later on we shall describe the relation of the in-order-to motive to the because-motives in the various regions of the social world. At this point we shall merely try to recapitulate the complex structures involved in understanding another person insofar as these bear on communication and the use of signs. For to say, as we do, that for the user of the sign the sign stands in a meaning-context involves a number of separate facts which must be disentangled.

First of all, whenever I make use of a sign, those lived experiences signified by that sign stand for me in a meaning-context. For they have already been constituted into a synthesis, and I look upon them as a unit.

In the second place, for me the sign must already be part of a sign system. Otherwise I would not be able to use it. A sign must already have been interpreted before it can be used. But the understanding of a sign is a complicated synthesis of lived experiences resulting in a special kind of meaning-context. This meaning-context is a configuration involving two elements: the sign as object in itself and the *signatum,* each of which, of course, involves separate meaning-contexts in its own right. The total new meaning-context embracing them both we have called the "coordinating scheme" [54] of the sign.

Third, the Act of selecting and using the sign is a special meaning-context for the sign-user to the extent that each use of a sign is an expressive action. Since every action comprises a meaning-context by virtue of the fact that the actor visualizes all the successive lived experiences of that action as one unified act, it follows that every expressive action is therefore a meaning-context. This does not mean that every case of sign-using is *ipso facto* a case of communication. A person may, talking to himself for instance, use a sign purely as an act of self-expression without any intention of communication.

Fourth, the meaning-context "sign-using as act" can serve as the

54. [Cf. p. 119.]

basis for a superimposed meaning-context "sign-using as communicative act" without in any way taking into account the particular person addressed.

Fifth, however, this superimposed meaning-context can enter into a still higher and wider meaning-context in which the addressee *is* taken into account. In this case the communicating act has as its goal not merely that someone take cognizance of it but that its message should motivate the person cognizing to a particular attitude or piece of behavior.

Sixth, the fact that this particular addressee is communicated with *here, now,* and *in this way* can be placed within a still broader context of meaning by finding the in-order-to motive of that communicative act.

All these meaning-contexts are in principle open to the interpreter and can be uncovered systematically by him. Just which ones he does seek to inquire into will depend upon the kind of interest he has in the sign.[55]

However, the statement that all these meaning-contexts in principle lie open to interpretation requires some modification. As we have said repeatedly, the structure of the social world is by no means homogeneous. Our fellow men and the signs they use can be given to us in different ways. There are different approaches to the sign and to the subjective experience it expresses. Indeed, we do not even need a sign in order to gain access to another person's mind; a mere indication can offer us the opening. This is what happens, for instance, when we draw inferences from artifacts concerning the experiences of people who lived in the past.

27. Subjective and Objective Meaning. Product and Evidence

WE HAVE NOW SEEN the different approaches to the genuine understanding of the other self. The interpreter starts with his own experience of the animate body of the other person or of the artifacts which the latter has produced. In either case he is interpreting Objectivations in which the other's subjective experiences manifest themselves. If it is the body of the other that is in question, he concerns himself with act-objectifications, i.e., movements, gestures, or the results of action. If it is artifacts that are in question, these may be either signs in the narrower sense or manufactured external objects

55. We have previously noted how, in such cases, the selection of questions to be answered actually occurs. See above, sec. 16, p. 85, and sec. 18, p. 95.

such as tools, monuments, etc. All that these Objectivations have in common is that they exist only as the result of the action of rational beings. Because they are products of action, they are *ipso facto* evidence of what went on in the minds of the actors who made them. It should be noted that *not all evidences are signs, but all signs are evidences.* For an evidence to be a sign, it must be capable of becoming an element in a sign system with the status of coordinating scheme. This qualification is lacking in some evidence. A tool, for instance, although it is an evidence of what went on in the mind of its maker, is surely no sign. However, under "evidences" we mean to include not only equipment [56] that has been produced by a manufacturing process, but judgment that has been produced by thought, or the message content which has been produced by an act of communication.

The problematic of subjective and objective meaning includes evidences of all sorts. That is to say, anyone who encounters a given product can proceed to interpret it in two different ways. First, he can focus his attention on its status as an object, either real or ideal, but at any rate independent of its maker. Second, he can look upon it as evidence for what went on in the mind of its makers at the moment it was being made. In the former case the interpreter is subsuming his own experiences (*erfahrende Akte*) of the object under the interpretive schemes which he has at hand. In the latter case, however, his attention directs itself to the constituting Acts of consciousness of the producer (these might be his own as well as those of another person).

This relation between objective and subjective meaning will be examined in a more detailed way at a later point. *We speak, then, of the subjective meaning of the product if we have in view the meaning-context within which the product stands or stood in the mind of the producer. To know the subjective meaning of the product means that we are able to run over in our own minds in simultaneity or quasi-simultaneity the polythetic Acts which constituted the experience of the producer.*

We keep in view, then, the other person's lived experiences as they are occurring; we observe them being constituted step by step. For us, the other person's products are indications of those lived experiences. The lived experiences stand for him, in turn, within a meaning context. We know this by means of a particular evidence, and we can in an act of genuine understanding be aware of the constituting process in his mind.

Objective meaning, on the contrary, we can predicate only of the

56. *Zeug.* This is the term used by Heidegger for those objects of the external world which are "ready to hand." Cf. *Sein und Zeit,* p. 102 [E.T., *Being and Time,* Macquarrie and Robinson, p. 135].

product as such, that is, of the already constituted meaning-context of the thing produced, whose actual production we meanwhile disregard. The product is, then, in the fullest sense the end result of the process of production, something that is finished and complete. It is no longer part of the process but merely points back to it as an event in the past. The product itself is, however, not an event but an entity (*ein Seiendes*) which is the sediment of past events within the mind of the producer. To be sure, even the interpretation of the objective meaning of the product occurs in step-by-step polythetic Acts. Nevertheless, it is exhausted in the ordering of the interpreter's experiences of the product within the total meaning-context of the interpretive act. And, as we have said, the interpreter leaves the original step-by-step creation of the product quite out of account. It is not that he is unaware that it has occurred; it is just that he pays no attention to it. Objective meaning therefore consists only in a meaning-context within the mind of the interpreter, whereas subjective meaning refers beyond it to a meaning-context in the mind of the producer.

A subjective meaning-context, then, is present if what is given in an objective meaning-context was created as a meaning-context by a Thou on its own part. Nothing, however, is thereby implied either about the particular kind of meaning-context into which the Thou orders its lived experiences or about the quality of those experiences themselves.

We have already noted that the interpreter grasps the other person's conscious experiences in the mode of simultaneity or quasi-simultaneity. Genuine simultaneity is the more frequent, even though it is a special case of the process. It is tied to the world of directly experienced social reality and presupposes that the interpreter witnesses the actual bringing-forth of the product. An example would be a conversation, where the listener is actually present as the speaker performs Acts that bring forth meaningful discourse and where the listener performs these Acts with and after the speaker. A case of quasi-simultaneous interpretation would be the reading of a book. Here the reader relives the author's choice of words as if the choice were made before his very eyes. The same would hold for a person inspecting some artifacts, such as tools, and imagining to himself how they were made. However, in saying that we can observe such subjective experiences on the part of the producer, we only meant that we can grasp the fact *that* they occur. We have said nothing about how we understand *what* experiences occur, nor how we understand *the way in which* they are formed. We shall deal with these problems when we analyze the world of contemporaries, the world of direct social experience, and the world of the genuine We-relationship. Still, it can be said even at this point that what is essential to this further knowledge is a knowledge of the <u>person being interpreted</u>. When we ask what the subjective meaning of a product is, and therefore what conscious experiences another person has, we are asking what particular poly-thetically constructed lived experiences are occurring or have occurred in a particular other person. This other person, this Thou, has his own unique experiences and meaning-contexts. No other person, not even he himself at another moment, can stand in his shoes at this moment.

The objective meaning of a product that we have before us is, on the other hand, by no means interpreted as evidence for the particular lived experience of a particular Thou. Rather, it is interpreted as already constituted and established, abstracted from every subjective flow of experience and every subjective meaning-context that could exist in such a flow. It is grasped as an objectification endowed with "universal meaning." Even though we implicitly refer to its author when we call it a "product," still we leave this author and everything personal about him out of account when we are interpreting objective meaning. He is hidden behind the impersonal "one" (someone, some-one or other). This anonymous "one" is merely the linguistic term for the fact that a Thou exists, or has once existed, of whose particularity we take no account. I myself or you or some ideal type or Everyman could step into its shoes without in any way altering the subjective meaning of the product. We can say nothing about the subjective processes of this anonymous "one," for the <u>latter has no duration</u>, and the temporal dimension we ascribe to it, being a logical fiction, is in principle incapable of being experienced. But precisely for this reason the objective meaning remains, from the point of view of the inter-preter, invariant for all possible creators of the meaningful object. Insofar as that object contains within its very meaning the ideality of the "and so forth" and of the "I can do it again," to that extent is that meaning independent of its maker and the circumstances of its origi-nation. The product is abstracted from every individual consciousness and indeed from every consciousness as such. Objective meaning is merely the interpreter's ordering of his experiences of a product into the total context of his experience.

It follows from all we have said that every interpretation of subjec-tive meaning involves a reference to a particular person. Furthermore, it must be a person of whom the interpreter has some kind of experi-ence (*Erfahrung*) and whose subjective states he can run through in simultaneity or quasi-simultaneity, whereas objective meaning is ab-stracted from and independent of particular persons. Later we shall study this antithesis in greater detail, treating it as a case of polar opposition. Between the understanding of subjective meaning and the understanding of pure objective meaning there is a whole series of intermediate steps based on the fact that the social world has its own unique structure derived, as it is, from the worlds of direct social experience, of contemporaries, of predecessors, and of successors. We shall devote Chapter 4 to the study of these different worlds, meanwhile paying special attention to the process of anonymization in each. We shall explain the polar opposition between subjective and objective meaning as an ideal-typical formulation of heuristic principles of meaning-interpretation.

28. Excursus: A Few Applications of the Theory of Objective and Subjective Meaning in the Field of the Cultural Sciences

THE THEORY OF THE two different types of meaning-interpretation of products which we have just developed is of great significance for the cultural sciences (*Geisteswissenschaften*) and not for these only. First of all, let us consider what are called "cultural objects," in other words, such ideal objectivities as "state," "art," "language," and so forth. These are all products according to our theory, for they bear upon them the mark of their production by our fellow men and are evidences of what went on in the minds of our fellow men. All cultural Objectivations can, therefore, be interpreted in a twofold manner. One interpretation treats them as completely constituted objectifications as they exist for us the interpreters, either now, as contemporaries in the present, or as coming later in history. These objectifications can be described quite simply or can be subjected to theoretical elaboration as objects of essential knowledge; that is, one can study the state as such, art as such, language as such.

All these products can, however, be treated as evidences for what went on in the minds of those who created them. Here highly complex cultural objects lend themselves to the most detailed investigation. The state can be interpreted as the totality of the acts of those who are oriented to the political order, that is, of its citizens; or it can be interpreted as the end result of certain historical acts and therefore itself as a historical object; or it can be treated as the concretization of a certain public-mindedness on the part of its rulers, and so forth. The art of a particular era can be interpreted as the expression of a particular artistic tendency of the time or as the expression of a particular interpretation of the world preceding and determining all artistic expression, in other words, as an expression of a particular way of "seeing." However, it can further be interpreted as a historical development which comes about in the form of a variation on the known style of an earlier epoch, whether due to the succession of schools or simply of generations. These are mere samples of the numerous possibilities of interpretation, and to each of them corresponds a special interpretive scheme and way of giving meaning to the object of interpretation.

We have already noted that the meaning-content of a product is more or less independent of what went on in the mind of the person creating it, according to whether the latter is understood by his interpreter in greater or lesser anonymity. In order to grasp a certain objectification in the ideality of the "I can do it again," one must conceive the author of that objectification simply as "one." Let us see how this works out in the field of economic theory. The so-called "principles of catallactics" [57] certainly have as their subject matter human acts considered as finished products, not actions in progress. The meaning-content of these principles is exhausted in the subsumption of such acts under the interpretive schemes of economic theory. To be sure, no economic act is conceivable without some reference to an economic actor, but the latter is absolutely anonymous; it is not you, nor I, nor an entrepreneur, nor even an "economic man" as such, but a pure universal "one." [58] This is the reason why the propositions of theoretical economics have just that "universal validity" which gives them the ideality of the "and so forth" and the "I can do it again." However, one can study the economic actor as such and try to find out what is going on in his mind; of course, one is not then engaged in theoretical economics but in economic history or economic sociology, of which Weber has furnished us an unparalleled example in the first book of his *Wirtschaft und Gesellschaft*. However, the statements of these sciences can claim no universal validity, for they deal either with the economic sentiments of particular historical individuals or with types of economic activity for which the economic acts in question are evidence.

To give examples from other fields of the significance of this question, we need only point out the importance of drawing a sharp

57. [The theory of exchange. This term, originated by Whately, plays a major part in the economic thought of Ludwig von Mises, to which Schutz often refers. See Mises' *Human Action* (New Haven, 1966), esp. Part IV. Catallactics for Mises is part of a pure a priori theory of action considered as abstracted from its psychological and historical circumstances; Mises' concept is therefore especially useful as an example at this point. For a very recent major economic treatise based on the same concept see Murray N. Rothbard, *Man, Economy and the State* (Princeton, 1962).]

58. See the discussion of the anonymity of the world of contemporaries, sec. 39, below, for a further analysis of this concept of "one."

distinction between subjective and objective meaning in those sciences which are interpretive in the narrow sense, namely, philology and jurisprudence. In philology it is always a basic question whether what is being studied is the objective meaning of a word at a definite time within a definite language area or, second, the subjective meaning which the word takes on in the usage of a particular author or of a particular circle of speakers or, third, the occasional meaning which it takes on in the context of discourse. Again, every student of law is familiar with the distinction between considering a point of law as a proposition within the legal system in accordance with philological and juridical canons of interpretation, on the one hand, and asking, on the other hand, what "the intention of the legislator" was. All these differences come down to the distinction between the objective and subjective meaning of the product, with which we have just been dealing.

One more point before we conclude this chapter. The tendency to look for a subjective meaning for everything in existence is so deeply rooted in the human mind, the search for the meaning of every object is so tied up with the idea that that object was once given meaning by some mind, that everything in the world can be interpreted as a product and therefore as evidence for what went on in the mind of God. Indeed, the whole universe can be regarded as the product of God, to whose creative act it bears witness. This is only to make a passing reference, of course, to a whole area of problems that lie outside the strict sciences. In any case, the problem of subjective and objective meaning is the open door to every theology and metaphysics.

4 / The Structure of the Social World: The Realm of Directly Experienced Social Reality, the Realm of Contemporaries, and the Realm of Predecessors

[A] INTRODUCTION

29. Preliminary Survey of the Problem

IN CHAPTER 3 we outlined the main features of a theory of our knowledge of other selves. We considered the general understanding we have of the other person's subjective experiences, and we found that this understanding is based on our own subjective experiences of him. Once the existence of the Thou is assumed, we have already entered the realm of intersubjectivity. The world is now experienced by the individual as shared by his fellow creatures, in short, as a *social* world. And, as we have already said repeatedly, this social world is by no means homogeneous but exhibits a multiform structure. Each of its spheres or regions is both a way of perceiving and a way of understanding the subjective experiences of others.

The present chapter will be devoted to a study of this multiform structure. We shall try to answer these questions: first, how such an inner differentiation is possible; second, what grounds we have for supposing that the social world has both unity and inner differentiation; and third, which of these differentiations may usefully serve as a basis for our analysis of understanding the other self. Only after we have answered these questions shall we be able to describe the different ways of understanding the other self peculiar to the different regions.

Even after having satisfied ourselves on these points, however, we should still be far from our main goal. As we have already seen, the question of the proper scientific approach to understanding others—a problem that is crucial for each of the social sciences—depends on a previous question. This is the question of the nature of intended meaning. For there is a difference in kind between the type of naïve understanding of other people we exercise in everyday life and the type of understanding we use in the social sciences. It is our task to find what distinguishes two sets of categories from each other: (1) those categories in terms of which the man in the natural standpoint understands the social world and which, in fact, are given to the social sciences as material with which to begin, and (2) those categories which the social sciences themselves use to classify this already preformed material.

However, the two spheres overlap. For in a certain sense I am a social scientist in everyday life whenever I reflect upon my fellow men and their behavior instead of merely experiencing them. I live with them as a man among men, I encounter them continually in direct experience. My awareness of their presence and of their personal characteristics [1] is immediate. It is no less immediate, and indeed no less integral to my consciousness, than is my awareness of the physical world surrounding me, to the extent that this world is spatial; it includes both my own body and those of others, together with their movements. Your body, for instance, is spatial, not merely in the sense of being a physical object or even a physiological one, but in the sense of being a psychophysical object, that is, a field for the expression of your subjective experiences. And, in accordance with the general thesis of the other self, I not only consciously experience you, but I live with you and grow old with you. I can attend to your stream of consciousness, just as I can attend to my own, and I can, therefore, become aware of what is going on in your mind. In the living intentionality of this experience, I "understand" you without necessarily paying any attention to the acts of understanding themselves. This is because, since I live in the same world as you, I live *in* the acts of understanding you. You and your subjective experiences are not only "accessible" to me, that is, open to my interpretation, but are taken for granted by me together with your existence and personal characteristics. And this in the strict sense of our definition: while I am directly experiencing you and talking with you, the whole complicated substructure of my own interpretation of you escapes my attention. I am not interested in such matters; my living intentionality, my *attention à la vie*, has other goals at the moment. However, I can at any given time change all this and bring these acts within the focus of my gaze. For instance, I may ask, "Have I understood you correctly?" "Don't you mean something else?" "What do you mean by such and such action?" These are typical of the questions that I am forced to ask every day in

1. ["Meine Erlebnisse von ihrem Dasein und Sosein. . . ."]

my relations with other people. The moment I raise such questions, I have abandoned my simple and direct awareness of the other person, my immediate grasp of him in all his subjective particularity. I have abandoned the living intentionality of our confrontation. The light in which I am looking at him is now a different one: my attention has shifted to those deeper layers that up to now had been unobserved and taken for granted. I no longer experience my fellow man in the sense of sharing his life with him; instead I "think about him." But now I am acting like a social scientist. For the latter (when he is acting *as a social scientist* and not just as an ordinary human being) gains access to the subjective experiences of others by treating them as objects of thought rather than by immediately grasping them as they occur. We see, then, that the whole problem of the social sciences and their categories has already been posed in the prescientific sphere, i.e., in the midst of life in the social world. To be sure, it is posed here in a very primitive form. The social scientist, as we shall see, utilizes methods and concepts which are quite different from the ordinary person who is simply observing another.

Abstracting, however, from the refinements which occur once the scientific stage is reached, it is quite clear that the *starting point* of social science is to be found in ordinary social life. Our fellow men are not only objects of experience in everyday life but are also objects of thought. Now, this kind of everyday thinking about our fellow men can be an end in itself, or it can serve as a means to further ends, thereby entering into a broader meaning-context. For instance, we may want to adjust our own behavior to that of others, or we may want to influence their thoughts or their behavior. In such cases, we formulate our project in the future perfect tense, using our knowledge of what is in other people's minds as a means to our end.

However, this is not to say that all action oriented toward others or even all action designed to change their behavior necessarily (or even usually) presupposes a previous direction of the attention toward the lower levels of their consciousness. On the contrary: even though I am acting upon my fellow men and trying to influence their behavior, still, to the extent that I am living with them and directly grasping their subjective experiences, I can hardly be paying attention to the lower levels of their consciousness at the same time.

Since our aim is to illuminate just these constitutive processes of understanding others, our task will be in each case the description and clarification of these lower layers. We shall, to begin with, put aside any effort to describe those acts (*Handlungen*) of the ego in whose project the subjective experiences of the Thou are included. We shall, above all, come to terms with Max Weber's concept of *social action* and then proceed to analyze critically his concept of *social relation-ship*. At this point we shall be able to make a close study of the peculiar backward reference which the subjective experiences of the other person included in the project of my action have to my own subjective experiences. All of these analyses, will, however, be merely preparatory to a further study of the general problem of life in the social world. To begin with, let us consider the fact that I face my fellow men in quite different and finely differentiated ways. For instance, I understand them in different conceptual perspectives. Again, I live through their subjective experiences in various degrees of intimacy. These are not merely differences in the way in which I grasp intentionally the other person's subjective experiences. They extend even to the very content of my act of grasping—to the intentional object itself. And, of course, others as well as myself experience these differences. For we have in common the same world of directly experienced social reality: the world surrounding me in my Here and Now corresponds to the one surrounding you in your Here and Now. My Here and Now includes you, together with your awareness of my world, just as I and my conscious content belong to your world in your Here and Now. However, this *domain (or realm) of directly experienced social reality* (as we intend to call it) is only one among many social realms. Just as the world of my actual perception is only a fragment of the whole world of my experience, and this in turn is but a fragment of the world of my possible experience, so likewise the social world (itself a portion of this "whole world") is only directly experienced by me in fragments as I live from moment to moment. This directly experienced social world is again, on its side, segmented according to conceptual perspectives. Beyond this domain of directly experienced social reality to which I am anchored by spatiotemporal community, there are still other social realms. Some of these I have once directly experienced and *can* in principle repeatedly re-experience in the same direct fashion. Others I can experience directly if I choose, but have not yet done so. These realms we will consider as one and call the *social world of contemporaries (soziale Mitwelt)*. The social world of contemporaries coexists with me and is simultaneous with my duration. However, even though living *with* it, I do not live *through* it as a matter of direct experience. Let us call the other selves of the world of directly experienced social reality my "fellow men" (*Mitmenschen*) and the other selves of the world of contemporaries my "contemporaries" (*Nebenmenschen*). We can then say that, living with my fellow men, I directly experience them and their subjective experiences. But of my contemporaries we will say that, while living among them, I do not directly and immediately grasp their subjective experiences but instead infer, on the basis of indirect evidence, the typical subjective experiences they must be having. Inferences of this kind, of course, can be well founded. Now, we have already seen that in the domain of directly experienced social reality I can be both observer and actor. This is also true of the world of contemporaries. Here, too, I can not only observe, but also act, making the behavior and subjective experience of my contemporaries the in-order-to motives of my action.

But in addition to these two worlds, I can also be cognizant of a social world that existed before I myself did and which at no point overlaps with any part of my own life. With respect to this realm, *the social world of predecessors (Vorwelt)*, or *history*, I can only be an observer and not an actor. Finally, I know that there is yet another world, one also inhabited by others, that will exist when I am no more, *a social world of successors (Folgewelt)*,[2] men of whom I know nothing as individuals and with whose subjective experiences I can have no personal acquaintance. As a matter of fact, I only know their typical experiences by supposing that the latter will be the same as those of my contemporaries and my predecessors. This is a world which I can only vaguely grasp but never directly experience.

In using the term "world" for these domains or realms, we mean only that different people are consociates, contemporaries, predecessors, or successors to one another and that they accordingly experience one another and act upon one another in the different ways in question.

All these considerations merely serve to outline the vast theoretical field of the social world, the methodical exploration of which is the task of the social sciences. Throughout this book we shall be limiting ourselves to the theory of the understanding of other people in the broadest sense of such understanding, a theory which also embraces the use and interpretation of signs as well as the creation of other products and their interpretation. Our path is clearly set before us. We shall have to ascertain how our knowledge of each of these regions draws its original claim from the general thesis of the other self, in other words, from the simultaneity or quasi-simultaneity of the other self's consciousness with my own. We shall also have to discover the proper approach to the subjective meaning of the products of each of these worlds. We shall have to find how the phenomena of meaning-determination and meaning-interpretation are carried out in the spheres in question. We shall have to discover the principles of conti-

2. The striking expression *Folgewelt*, which is greatly preferable to *Nachwelt* (world to come), is taken from Schiller's inaugural lecture, *Was heisst und zu welchem Ende studiert man Universalgeschichte?* [Schiller's *Werke*, ed. Ludwig Bellermann and Benno von Wiese (Leipzig, 1936–37), Vol. IX.]

nuity between the spheres. We shall have to determine which spheres are alone accessible to the methods of the social sciences. Finally, we shall have to get clear as to what methods the social sciences should employ in order to carry out research adequate to their objects.

[B] SOCIAL BEHAVIOR, SOCIAL ACTION, SOCIAL RELATIONSHIP

30. Max Weber's Concept of "Social Action." Other-Orientation and Affecting-the-Other

WE HAVE ALREADY CONSIDERED, in our preliminary study in Chapter 1, Weber's definition of social action: [3] "Action is social insofar as, by virtue of the subjective meaning attached to it by the acting individual (or individuals), it takes account of the behavior of others, and is thereby oriented in its course." We must bear in mind that Weber, when he speaks about social action, does not mean that action which we have distinguished (in Chapter 2) from "behavior in the broadest sense." Instead, for him, action of any sort means inner or outer "behavior" in a still unclear sense, provided that "meaning" can be attributed to the person behaving. Accordingly, there fall under this concept not only all intentional Acts deriving from spontaneous activity, whether or not they be projected beforehand and thus qualify as action, but also all passively emerging subjective experiences which are only in a general sense intentionally related to another person.

Following the logic of our own terminology, we prefer to take as our starting point, not social action or social behavior, but *intentional conscious experiences directed toward the other self.* However, we include here only those intentional experiences which are related to the other *as other,* that is, as a conscious living being. We are leaving out of account intentional Acts directed only to the other person's body as a physical object rather than as a field of expression for his subjective experiences. Conscious experiences intentionally related to another self which emerge in the form of spontaneous activity we shall speak of as *social behavior.* If such experiences have the character of being previously projected, we shall speak of them as *social action.* Social behavior so defined will embrace all specific Ego-Acts (*Ich-Akte*) which are intentionally directed upon a Thou as upon another self having consciousness and duration. Here we include experiences such as feelings of sympathy and antipathy, erotic attitudes, and feeling-activities of all kinds. All these subjective experiences of con-

---

3. See sec. 2, p. 15.

sciousness would no doubt be called social action by Weber, if we are to judge by the examples he adduces. On the other hand, this would be limited to *previously* projected behavior by his definition of it as action oriented to the behavior of the other person. For only a previously projected piece of behavior can be oriented, since orientation necessarily presupposes a project. However, even then, not every such previously projected action "toward another" would be social action. Suppose, for instance, that I act toward the other person as if he were merely a physical thing, paying no attention to his subjective experiences as another self. My own conscious experiences accompanying my action are here not, following the above definition, intentionally directed toward the other self. My action, therefore, is in this case no social action. Weber would apparently agree with this point. Remember that he said the collision of two bicycles does not have the status of social action but that the conversation that follows is indeed social action. The doctor who performs an operation on an anaesthetized patient truly acts "upon the body" of that patient, but this is not social action in Weber's sense. The soldier keeping in step with the man in front of him is not engaging in social action either, for, as a rule, he is orienting his behavior not to the other man's consciousness but to his body, and then only to his bodily movements as such, and not as clues to his conscious experiences.

However, our interpretation of the experiences of consciousness related intentionally to the other self does not completely fulfill the requirements of Weber's definition. For, according to this definition, social action must be related to the other's *behavior* and not merely to his being there or having the characteristics he has. And here we encounter further difficulties. One difficulty lies in the fact that Weber's concept of behavior is itself totally unclear. In fact, according to him, behavior need not even be meaningful. Now, indeed, it is possible to interpret him in such a way that his "orientation to the other's behavior" is equivalent to our "general thesis of the other self." In other words, it would be orientation to the fact that *the Thou has duration*, that it has certain subjective experiences and is conscious of them. If we accepted this interpretation, we could go on to say that social behavior must be oriented to the behavior of the other person in the sense that it is oriented to his consciousness and the subjective experiences being constituted therein. It would now become quite immaterial whether the Thou was actually "behaving" in our sense, that is, producing conscious experiences out of spontaneous activity.

Fritz Sander [4] has submitted Max Weber's concept of social behav-

4. Sander, "Der Gegenstand der reinen Gesellschaftslehre," *Archiv für Sozialwissenschaften*, LIV (1925), 329 ff., esp. 335.

ior to a critique that is ingenious and in many ways decisive. He points out that, according to Weber's definition, every perception of another's body is already social action and that this concept is therefore too broad and imprecise to determine the object of social science.[5] Sander's example is very instructive. No doubt even the interpretive perception of the other person's conscious experiences is a meaningful action related and therefore oriented to the other's behavior. It is, therefore, by Weber's definition a social action. Then too, according to our terminology, it is a conscious experience intentionally related to another self, provided always that it is a question of genuine interpretation of the other. (Acts of interpretation of one's own experiences of the other self would as such not qualify as Acts intentionally related to the other self.) Any conscious experiences arising from spontaneous activity and directed toward another self are, by our definition, social behavior. If this social behavior is antecedently projected, it is social action. An example of the latter would be my turning my attention to another's consciousness *in order to* note what occurred therein. Here the goal of the act (*Handlungsziel*) is merely to understand the other person's subjective experiences, and the in-order-to motive (with its corresponding attentional modifications) is entirely exhausted in that goal. I do not go beyond that goal and seek to modify the other person's subjective experiences.

We have engaged in this analysis of the perception of another self in order to clarify the basic nature of all experiences intentionally directed toward the other self, whether these experiences are behavior or not. They are all distinguished by a certain attitude of the ego toward the other person's duration. This attitude is founded on the general thesis of the other self as a being itself both conscious and experiencing. We shall call this attitude "Other-orientation." Other-orientation can come into existence in the social sphere only if it is founded not merely on the positing of the transcendental alter ego but on that of the mundane alter ego. It is based, however, on the positing of the latter's existence (*Daseinssetzung*), not on the positing of its particular characteristics (*Soseinssetzung*). It postulates that a Thou lives, endures, and has consciously lived experiences; just which experiences these are and what implications they have remains undetermined. Furthermore, Other-orientation *can* in principle be one-sided: while it pertains to its essence to be related to an Other, it can both exist and continue without any reciprocation on the part of the Other.

5. Lack of space unfortunately rules out a detailed account of Sander's argument, with which I by no means agree on all points. The specialist will easily spot the points of deviation.

Therefore, Other-orientation does not have an external effect in the usual sense of the word. It may exist without any communicative act and without any expressive action. No use may be made of signs, nor any interpretation of them. Other-orientation in principle includes no more and no less than all the attitudinal acts of the Ego related to a Thou and therefore also all feeling-activities, such as love and hate. One may question, of course, whether it is really appropriate to call all acts of Other-orientation "social acts."

However, when Weber speaks of the meaningful relationship of social action to the behavior of others, he is hardly thinking of Other-orientation in the broad sense defined above. Nevertheless, there does seem to be hovering before his mind a specific type of connection between the social action and a piece of behavior on the part of the other person. Social action no doubt exists for him only in two types of situation: either (a) where the social actor intends by means of his action to induce the other person to behave in a particular way—if, that is, the goal of his action is to produce a certain effect on the other person's consciousness; or (b) if this same social action was induced by the other person's behavior—if, in other words, the perception and interpretation of the already enacted behavior of the other person is the genuine because-motive of the social actor. Weber's concept of social action covers both of these cases. Social action can, as he puts it, "be oriented to the past, present, or expected future behavior of others." [6] Once again we see coming to the fore that conceptual ambiguity which we noted several times before: Weber fails to distinguish between orientation to the past action and orientation to the future action of the other person; he fails to distinguish between genuine because-motives and in-order-to motives and, as a result, includes situations quite unlike one another under the same basic concept. But let us return to the main course of our analysis.

The intentional Acts (*Akte*) directed to an Other, insofar as they are projected acts (*Handlungen*), that is, spontaneous behavior according to an antecedent project, can have as their in-order-to motive the bringing-about of a certain conscious experience in the other person. We shall call a social action of this kind "affecting-the-Other" (*Fremdwirken*). Every such action is performed within an Other-orientation and in fact is a social action, but not every Other-orientation or even every social action involves affecting-the-Other. It is easy to see that affecting-the-Other is confined to antecedently projected social Acts (*Akte*) arising from spontaneous activity, in other words,

---

6. *Wirtschaft und Gesellschaft,* p. 11 [E.T., p. 112].

genuine social action (*Handeln*) in the sense of our own definition, given above. In order to act socially upon an Other's consciousness, I must pay attention to the flow of his consciousness as it occurs. Further, I must have anticipated in phantasy in the project of my act (in the future perfect tense) the conscious experiences to be brought about in the Other either as my final goal or as one of my intermediate goals. If my in-order-to motive is merely to get the other person to understand me, then, of course, what I manage to bring about in his consciousness is my final goal. But what I can get him to think or feel is only a means if what I am really interested in is influencing his behavior. A piece of social *behavior* in the significant sense lacks the character of having been projected and is for that very reason not a case of affecting-the-Other. Goethe's famous line, "And if I love you, what business is it of yours?" is a good example of feeling that is Other-oriented yet not at all seeking to affect the other person.

Obviously, it is the affecting of the other person, or, as we shall call it from now on, "social affecting" (*soziales Wirken*), which has served as the model for Weber's concept of social action. Once we realize this, we can without difficulty translate his definition into our terminology. The fact that social action is meaningfully related to the behavior of others implies that the actor (since he is Other-oriented in his action) turns his attention to the subjective experiences of the Other in their constitutive structure. The fact that the social actor meaningfully orients his action to the other's behavior as it occurs implies that the attention so given takes place within a special motivational context. Within this motivational context the other person's subjective experiences are anticipated in the future perfect tense as part of the actor's project.

However, we are speaking here only of the expectation of another's *future* subjective experiences, through which expectation one's own action is given an in-order-to motive. Now, Weber insists emphatically that social action can also be oriented to the past behavior of others. If he were right, we should have a case of social action if one's attention to another person's subjective experiences functioned as the genuine because-motive of one's own action.[7] However, our study of the genuine because-motive has shown that the meaning-context of the latter can only be constituted out of the *already motivated* subjective experience *in the past*. In this connection, it is always possible that the coordination of an action to a genuine because-motive is itself on hand in the form of a "maxim" in experience. This is true universally and in no

7. Cf. Sander's distinction between Acts directed to the future behavior of others and Acts directed to the past behavior of others, *op. cit.* p. 361.

way depends on whether the motivating experience is related to an Other or not. In every case one can ask meaningfully what the genuine because-motive was only after the action has occurred, or at least after the project has been formed. Suppose, to use an example of Weber's, that I wish to avenge myself for a past attack. In such a case, my purpose is projected before one can meaningfully say that it was motivated by the attack, i.e., before one can say that it was revenge for the attack. I could, as a matter of fact, hesitate between retaliating and overlooking the attack. In fact I could even submit to the attack without contemplating revenge at all. Now, surely what makes my action social is not that its *activating stimulus* was someone else's behavior as opposed to a natural event. What makes my behavior social is the fact that its intentional object is the expected behavior of another person.

We should not, therefore, place actions which affect others on an equal plane with actions which are affected by others. This term "action affected by another" (*fremdbewirktes Handeln*) is the term we shall apply to an action motivated in a genuine "because-fashion" by the actor's attention to another's already past subjective experiences. This does not mean that such an action can occur without Other-orientation. Rather, while attending to the other person's subjective experiences at the time of the production of the synthetic because-context, I am, of course, performing intentional Acts directed toward another person. Also, the because-context itself depends on the attentional modifications of my experiences of the Other, which I now look upon in the pluperfect tense. However, if I look for the because-motive, then my action was already projected before I performed an Act (*Akt*) of orientation toward another person. But this action is for just that reason not an Other-oriented Act (*Akt*) and is therefore not social behavior. The projected action is one thing; quite another thing is that specific attention to the constituted project or the finished act (*Handlung*) in which the meaning-context of the true because-motivation is constituted. In the case of an action affected by another person, it is not the action itself but the meaning-context of its because-motivation that takes place within Other-orientation. We shall go more deeply into this when we deal with social relationship.

It is clear that we could set up a continuous series beginning with conscious experiences intentionally related to another person, going on through social behavior and social action, and ending finally with social affecting. It is not without reason that we have drawn a contrast between the latter and all the other members of the series, namely, those covered by the term Other-orientation. Let us try to make this distinction a little clearer by taking another glance at meaning-establishment and meaning-interpretation.

In the final paragraph of Chapter 3 we spoke of the subjective meaning which I attribute to each product I take as evidence of what goes on in another's mind. We now see that my attention to someone else's subjective meaning always takes place in, and draws its validity from, an Act of Other-orientation. Every product and therefore every sign that I see has, apart from any Other-orientation, an objective meaning for me; but by interpreting it as a sign of another's conscious experiences, I can bring it within an Other-orientation. Notice that we say "within an Act of Other-orientation," not "within an Act of affecting-the-Other." For when I read a book, rehearse another's train of thought, or seek to discover the origin of a tool, I am merely oriented to others; I am not in any way affecting them.

But if I originate a sign for someone else to interpret, it is different. Now I am Other-oriented, to be sure, but it is a specific kind of Other-orientation. I am now affecting another. Had I merely originated the sign for my own use, i.e., without any Other-orientation, I should not have been involved in affecting another. But the origination of a sign within an attitude of Other-orientation is an *act of communication*. The in-order-to motive of this act is the bringing-about of certain conscious experiences in the mind of the person to whom it is addressed. We can therefore say that *all communication is social affecting* and that *all heeding of communication presupposes Other-orientation*. The same holds true for all other products. If I make a tool for others to use, then I "see to it," in the future perfect tense, that they know what the tool is for.

Our next step will be to show that, within each of the social spheres, Other-orientation and affecting-the-Other occur in correspondingly different forms. The most striking difference lies in the degree of anonymity of the object. Our views here stand in contrast to those of Max Weber, for whom it is a matter of indifference whether the "others" which are the object of social action are "individual persons and . . . known to the actor as such . . . or constitute an indefinite plurality and [are] entirely unknown as individuals." [8] Nor does Weber tell us how, if at all, the quality of my acquaintance with the other person modifies my "orientation" (*Orientierung*) toward him. We, on the other hand, will seek to work out in detail the different forms of Other-orientation and affecting-the-Other to be found in the world of directly experienced social reality and the world of mere contemporaries.

8. *Wirtschaft und Gesellschaft*, p. 11 [E.T., p. 112].

31. Weber's Concept of Social Relationship. Orientation Relationship and Social Interaction

THERE WERE TWO NOTABLE omissions in the preceding section. Nothing was said about the other person's conscious experiences while I am oriented toward him. And nothing was said about the experiences which I seek to bring about in him when I affect him. For what is essential to Other-orientation is that the other person *exist*, not that he have characteristics of one kind or another. As a matter of fact, both Other-orientation and affecting-the-Other can, in principle, be one-sided. In neither the concept of affecting-the-Other nor in that of Other-orientation is it implied that the partner must respond by an Other-orientation of his own. This is also true of Weber's concept of social action. But of course such a response *can* always occur: this indeed follows from the general thesis of the alter ego and from the fact that the two partners are contemporaries. As a matter of fact, whenever we engage in social behavior, we take into account the possibility of such response.

When two people do become reciprocally oriented toward each other, we have what Weber calls a "social relationship." By this he means "the behavior of a plurality of actors in so far as, in its meaningful content, the action of each *takes account of* that of the others, and is oriented in these terms." He continues,

> The social relationship thus consists entirely and exclusively in the existence of a probability [*in der Chance*] that there will be, in some meaningfully understandable sense, a course of social action. For purposes of definition there is no attempt to specify the basis of this probability.[9]

Weber's view that a social relationship exists only where there is social action in a meaningful sense itself contains an ambiguity, as we have shown in Chapter 1. The ambiguity spreads from this point to almost all the basic concepts of his sociology. It is based on his failure to make a clear distinction between the subjective comprehension of other people that takes place in everyday life and the objective interpretation of them and their experiences that takes place in the social sciences. Let us look again at his statement that a "social relationship consists entirely and exclusively in the existence of a probability that there will be . . . social action." *For whom does this*

9. *Ibid.*, p. 13, sec. 3 [E.T., p. 118].

probability exist—the actor, or the social scientist who observes him?
In attempting to answer this, Weber advances two contradictory views
on the same page. First he says that the two parties are socially related
to each other "insofar as even though, partly or wholly erroneously,
one party *presumes* a particular attitude toward him on the part of the
other and orients his action to this expectation. This can and usually
will have consequences for the course of action and the form of the
relationship." [10] What Weber is referring to here is what is sometimes
called "subjective probability," namely, the subjective expectation on
the part of the one party that the other will manifest a reciprocal
orientation. But in the very next paragraph he proceeds to say,

> It is *only* the existence of the *probability* that a certain type of action
> will take place which constitutes the "existence" of the social relation-
> ship. Thus that a "friendship" or a "state" exists or has existed means
> only this: that *we the observers* judge that there is or has been a
> *probability* that on the basis of certain kinds of known subjective attitude
> of certain individuals there will result *in the average sense* a certain
> specific type of action.

This second kind of probability naturally has nothing to do with the
first, which consists in a context of meaning in the minds of one or
both of the parties to the social relationship. It is rather part of the
context of what is judged by an external observer, that is, a social
scientist. In other words, what we have in this second case is objective
probability. Now, what all this amounts to is that Weber's very concept
of social relationship itself becomes ambiguous. He is really dealing
with two different kinds of situation and calling them both "social
relationship." In the first case, the actor's subjective expectation establishes the probability of a reciprocal orientation, which by definition means that a social relationship exists. In the second case, it is
the outside observer's "objective" judgment which establishes this
probability and *eo ipso* the relationship.

These two situations are by no means identical. For it can hardly
be said that, just because an observer can see a social relationship
existing, therefore the participant in the same relationship will also be
aware of it. Nor is the opposite the case: what the participant sees, or
thinks he sees, may be quite hidden from the observer. We must,
therefore, seek the criterion on the basis of which the participant, on
the one hand, or the observer, on the other, may conclude that such a
relationship exists.

Let us begin with the situation confronting the external observer,

10. *Ibid.*, p. 14, point 3 [E.T., p. 119].

the situation which we, following Weber, have called the *objective probability* of the existence of a social relationship. The observer sees various indications of the existence of such and such subjective experiences of the observed person. The latter's body is, from the point of view of the observer, the field of expression of these subjective experiences. His bodily movements are indications of those subjective experiences arising from spontaneous activity. The cultural products he brings forth are signs of the constitutive processes going on in his mind. Now, what is meant by the statement that the *conscious experiences* of two or more persons under observation are *mutually related?* Apparently nothing more than that *for the observer* the outward indications he sees before him stand in a relation of correspondence to certain conscious processes. Perhaps the observer notices that the two people he is watching are united in a common task or are exerting a common influence on the external world. Or perhaps he sees that when *A* acts in a certain way, *B* follows in a certain other way. However, these series of acts are mere indications for the observer of what is going on in the minds of the actors. He is interpreting his own experiences of them, and doing so in such a way as to establish the meaning-contexts in which these conscious experiences must exist in the minds of the observed persons. He seeks to interpret the in-order-to and because-motives of their actions and to establish which goals are primary and which are intermediate, etc. In doing so, he imaginatively re-establishes the constitutive structure of these meaning-contexts, arriving at interpretations which are consistent, first, with his total experience of the social world and, second, with his knowledge of the character of the observed person. All this will hold true quite generally, whether it is a question of observing the individual conscious processes of one or more other people or of observing average or typical conscious processes. It will hold true regardless of whether the observed persons belong to the observer's world of directly experienced social reality, his world of mere contemporaries, or his world of predecessors. In every case the observer assumes an Other-orientation with respect to the observed, and it is this Other-orientation, of course, which alone makes possible the comprehension of subjective meaning.

The observer, therefore, seeks also to discover the conscious experiences for which the indications stand, and, from the correspondence he finds, he draws his conclusions concerning the social relationship. But the correspondence is then for him no longer an *objective probability* that the conscious processes of the people observed are really related to one another. For it is a part of the very concept of the *correspondence* of the *indications* that the latter can be established only between events already lying in the past. It is only by taking the reaction as already given that the observer can establish that it corresponds to the Action (*Aktion*) preceding it. The statement asserting the existence of the correspondence is, therefore, in principle a statement in the pluperfect tense about events in the past. Of course, this does not prevent the establishment of a correspondence in simultaneity between the events in question. For the existence of such a correspondence can, as a repeatable maxim of experience, as an already constituted interpretive scheme in the consciousness of the observer, be part of his stock of knowledge, "ready to hand" [11] for him.

However, there are different degrees of certainty with which an observer can conclude that a social relationship exists. This is based on the fact that the sureness with which the outward indications can be connected with inward subjective states itself depends on how well the observer knows the person he is observing. And, of course, the correspondence relation itself depends on this sureness. And so we have, in fact, *degrees of interpretability*. When I am observing my fellow men as they go about their ordinary activities, it is no great problem for me to decide whether they are or are not engaged in social relationships. I see these relationships in the sequence of their actions and reactions, in the coordination of the because-motive of the one to the in-order-to motive of the other. The same is true if I observe communicative acts such as the use of signs, even if I am not the person addressed. Granted that I know the interpretive schemes of the signs, I can treat the communicative acts in question as indications of the existence of a correspondence relation. More generally we can say that any social relationship within which a case of affecting-the-Other occurs can be identified as such with greater confidence than a social relationship in which no more takes place than intentional Acts of Other-orientation. The first type of social relationship we shall from now on call "social interaction" (*Wirkensbeziehung*),[12] and the second, "orientation-

11. Cf. sec. 27, p. 133.
12. [Literally, "relationship of affecting." It is our view, in agreement with Luckmann (cf. Schutz, *Collected Papers*, II, 23), that the term "social interaction" as used later by Schutz is an acceptable approximate rendering of *Wirkensbeziehung*. Cf. Schutz's essay "Making Music Together," *ibid.*, p. 160: "When sociologists speak of social interaction, they usually have in mind a set of interdependent actions of several human beings, mutually related by the meaning which the actor bestows upon his action and which he supposes to be understood by his partner," as in the case of two chess players. However, even though the extension of *Wirkensbeziehung* usually coincides with that of "social interaction," Schutz seems to have in mind a more generic concept for which there is no term in English. He explains this below on page 158, where he says that every *Wirkensbeziehung* is an act of affecting another with the *aim* of leading the other to have conscious experiences of a desired sort. It is not necessary that the other act at all, far less *react upon* the actor in the dictionary sense of "interaction." In other words, Schutz's concept of *Wirkensbeziehung* here seems to be broader than his

relationship" (*Einstellungsbeziehung*). It is easier to observe the effect that the action of one person has on that of another than it is to observe the attitudes they may have toward each other, e.g., sympathy or antipathy. In other words, it is easier for me to state with objective probability that two people are socially interacting than it is for me to say that they are merely oriented toward each other in a certain way. Any such conclusion must depend for its reliability upon how well the observed is known by the observer. Between them there are countless degrees of interpretability. Suppose, for instance, that a social relationship is based not on Acts of reciprocal affecting (*Akte wechselseitigen Fremdwirkens*) but on the fact that the partners merely carry out the same kind of action. By "the same kind of action" we mean actions oriented to a common interpretive scheme (such as a language, a legal system, a common conception of art, a shared fashion, common habits of life). In a case like this, if the observer is to estimate the objective probability of the existence of the social relationship, then his argument must take more factors into account. It must, of course, proceed according to the method of the "correspondence of indications" discussed above. But it will also be based on the observer's previous knowledge of the common interpretive scheme in question. Also it must include the interpretive scheme in the project of the actors who are being observed.

Now, how is that presumption—for that is what objective probability amounts to—of the existence of a social relationship transformed into certainty? Let us suppose that both action and reaction have occurred as expected; for example, A has asked B a question, and B has replied. At this point, what had previously been a matter of conjecture has become probable. But notice that it is still less than certain. Whether A and B really understand each other is something only they can say. What is needed is a statement from A saying that when he spoke he was really asking a question of B, and then a statement from B saying that when *he* spoke he was answering A. Both would, in short, have to testify that their actions were Other-oriented. Therefore, it is only by questioning the observed persons that the observer can be certain of the existence of a social relationship between them. However, no sooner does he start questioning them than he himself enters into a social relationship with one or both of them. More than this, whatever judgment the observer may make concerning the probability, possibility, or conceivability of the exist-

---

later "social interaction" and far broader than any "reciprocal affecting" (*Wechselwirkung*). Yet Schutz sometimes seems to imply that reciprocal acts of affecting-the-Other (*Akte wechselseitigen Fremdwirkens*) were involved in *Wirkensbeziehung*. See a few lines below this point.]

ence of any social relationship derives whatever validity it has from the possibility of thus questioning the person or persons who may be involved in that relationship. This very "possibility of being questioned" (*Befragbarkeit*) is a specific characteristic of the object of direct social observation.

Having settled the question of what the observer's criterion is for the existence of a social relationship, we must now try to determine the participant's criterion.

We have already seen that a social relationship exists for me if I, while maintaining an Other-orientation toward my partner, ascertain that he is, on his part, experiencing an Other-orientation toward me. I can ascertain that my partner is oriented toward me, therefore, only if I first orient myself toward him.

My partner's Other-orientation toward me is something I can come to know in several different ways. For instance, he may affect me, and I may then become aware of that fact. Or I may turn my attention to him and find that his attention is already on me. In both these cases, the social relationship is constituted through my own Act of attention. On the other hand, I can intend to affect my partner in such a way that his own attention to me is required if the project or purpose behind the act of affecting is to be carried out. But all this is not so much a description of how a person knows he is in a social relationship as it is a description of how such a relationship is generated. To use a good expression of Wiese, it is a description of the *action of contact* and of the *contact situation* (*des Kontakthandelns und der Kontaktsituation*).

There are two ways in which a person living in the social world can become aware that his intentional Acts of consciousness directed upon another person are reciprocated. He can either *live in* these mutually related conscious experiences or, stepping out, so to speak, of the social relationship, he can *contemplate* them as objects of observation. An example of the first case would be the following. I take up an Other-orientation toward my partner, who is in turn oriented toward me. Immediately, and at the same time, I grasp the fact that he, on his part, is aware of my attention to him. In such cases I, you, *we*, live in the social relationship itself, and that is true in virtue of the intentionality of the living Acts directed toward the partner. I, you, we, are by this means carried from one moment to the next in a particular attentional modification of the state of being mutually oriented to each other. The social relationship in which we live is constituted, therefore, by means of the attentional modification undergone by my Other-orientation, as I immediately and directly grasp within the latter the very living reality of the partner as one who is in turn oriented toward me. We will call such a social relationship a "living social relationship."

The living social relationship can occur in several different forms. In its purity and fullness, as we shall show later in detail, it is tied to the bodily givenness of the Thou in the face-to-face situation. As such, it is a living face-to-face relationship or a pure We-relationship. From it derive their validity all intentional Acts of Other-orientation not belonging to the domain of directly experienced social reality, all ways of interpreting subjective meaning, and all possibilities of attending to the worlds of mere contemporaries and of predecessors. One of our primary tasks in this chapter will be to clarify the social relationships we have to the worlds of mere contemporaries and of predecessors on the basis of the pure We-relationship and to demonstrate how the former is deduced from the latter.

But I, who have been living within the social world, can also turn my attention to it by stepping outside it and transforming it into an object of observation or thought. What happens then is that I attend in the pluperfect tense to the intentional Acts I have already performed while Other-oriented and to what I have grasped in those Acts, namely, the Other's orientation toward me. I can, on the basis of this attention, then proceed to judge the objective probability of a mutual orientation. When I do this, I am, in a sense, engaging in self-observation. If, for instance, I try to affect another, it is only after my action is over and done with—and therefore already a success or failure—that I can know whether that person has oriented himself toward me. Of course, the project of my social affecting was accompanied by protentions anticipating such reciprocation. However, only if these protentions have been fulfilled can I, as an observer, make a "rational surmise" that a social relationship really exists here. My attitude is the same in this case as that of an outside observer. Also, from my point of view as observer, the presence at hand of an Other-orientation on the part of my partner—in short, of a social relationship—is a purely objective probability. The relationship, therefore, appears to me in different degrees of evidence and interpretability. Of course, there is a very significant difference between self-observation in such a situation and observation by a third party external to the relationship. For, as I look back on my project, I know with certainty the in-order-to motive of my action. I can, therefore, clarify for myself, in a kind of imaginative re-enactment, the meaning-context of the motivation, even if I have only a vague and confused awareness of it. I can, by observing the course of the action, ascertain whether my project has been fulfilled. Furthermore, I can call to mind the broader goal with respect to which my action on the other person was only an intermediate goal. Finally, I can recall the attentional modifications undergone during the action by my intentional Acts as they were directed toward the other person. In the case of these complex processes of self-observation, the same interpretive principles apply as in the case of observation by a third party. The constitution of a social interaction is incomparably easier to discern than that of a simple orientation relationship. And there are many different stages in between these, it should be noted.

In the preceding paragraphs we have been seeking the criterion by which a person living in the social world knows that he is in a social relationship. We have still to deal with the second state of affairs which Weber includes in his concept of social relationship, the case, namely, where the actor orients his action to the subjective probability of the existence of a social relationship. Now it is by no means true that all behavior within a social relationship is oriented to the existence of that relationship. For this reason we must distinguish between (1) those Acts (*Akte*) which have been intentionally directed toward the partner and which have as their essential presupposition an Other-orientation on his part and (2) all other Acts (*Akte*) performed in Other-orientation within a social relationship. Only by doing this will we be able to ascertain in what sense it can be said that an actor assumes that his partner is oriented toward him and orients his own behavior to that assumption.

With respect to this point, our previous distinction between orientation relationship and interaction is of great importance. Let us take as an example of the first a love of whose reciprocation the lover is uncertain. In order for me to have a loving orientation toward my partner, it is by no means necessary that I know whether and how she is oriented toward me. My knowledge of my partner's attitude is purely secondary. No doubt I do, in certain circumstances, desire the other person to pay attention to me, to know of my love and to return it; but there may be other circumstances in which I desire no such thing. As the example shows, it is not essential to the Acts (*Akte*) of the orientation relationship that they be based on the knowledge of the existence or nonexistence of a reciprocal attitude. To be sure, my aim may be to bring about precisely this reciprocal attitude in the other person, and I may be concerned with the success or failure of this undertaking. In such a case, the pure orientation relationship is transformed into an interaction, which gives us quite a different situation. An interaction, then, exists if one person acts upon another with the expectation that the latter will respond, or at least notice. It is not necessary that the partner reciprocally affect the actor or even act himself. All that is required is that the partner be aware of the actor and interpret what he does or says as evidence for what is going on in his mind. All the partner's subjective experiences will, naturally, be modified by his attention to the actor.

Every interaction is, therefore, based on an action of affecting another within a social situation. The *object* of the action is to lead the partner to have conscious experiences of a desired sort. The *necessary condition* of the action is that the partner be paying attention to the actor. But not every act of affecting-the-Other is carried out within a relationship of interaction, or indeed within any social relationship whatever; not every act of affecting-the-Other presupposes that the Other is oriented toward me. On the contrary, there are cases where affecting another presupposes precisely the latter's lack of awareness of me, presupposes that I remain unnoticed and anonymous, behind the scenes, so to speak. But cases like this are a derivative form of the pure situation of affecting-the-Other. In this derivative form I seek only to perform an act which induces certain conscious experiences in my partner, an act, however, which could just as well be performed by someone else and in different circumstances.

But whenever in affecting another I intend him to know that I am affecting him,[13] then we have the relationship of interaction. His attentional attitude toward me has now entered into the very project of my act. It has become my in-order-to motive. It has become the "for-the-sake-of-which" of my affecting him, in the sense that it is either my final goal or my intermediate goal. Every time I establish a meaning, therefore, I will be looking forward to its interpretation by my partner. This expectation of mine will enter into the broader goal-context within which the meaning-establishment takes place. *Social interaction is, accordingly, a motivational context and, in fact, an intersubjective motivational context.* It is essential to the constitution of interaction that each act of affecting the partner be undertaken in order to bring about a certain reciprocal Other-orientation on his part. Let us now examine the unique structure of this motivational context.

32. The Motivational Context of Social Interaction

I MAY SO PROJECT my action that I picture you as being moved to a certain kind of behavior as soon as you have grasped what I am doing. I am then picturing your interpretation of my action as the because-motive of your behavior. Suppose, for instance, that I ask you

---

13. Whether in such a situation I am experienced by my partner as physically present or merely as an ideal type depends upon whether the interaction is one of direct or indirect social experience ["ob es sich um eine umweltliche oder mitweltliche Wirkensbeziehung handelt"].

a question. My in-order-to motive is not merely that you understand the question but that I get an answer from you. Your answer is the reason why (the "for-the-sake-of-which") of my question. Already in my project I had pictured the question as having been asked and you as having understood it and persuaded by that understanding to reply. What is pictured beforehand is *that* you will answer. Of course *what* you will answer remains undetermined within this particular context of meaning (putting a question and waiting for the answer). No doubt every such phantasying and every such expectation is accompanied by a wish, a feeling-tendency striving toward the consummation of the already sketched-out project. But it is quite certain that I perform a judgment in phantasy to the effect that my questioning will evoke a definite reaction from you. This judgment is detachable from the wish which is based on it, and can be studied separately. Let us therefore ignore the feeling-activity and ask what is meant by saying that an action I perform within a social relationship (which is, therefore, interactional) will induce the person to whom the action is addressed to behave in a certain way.

Let us keep to the example of question and answer. The questioner phantasies in the future perfect tense that the person questioned will have answered him. He phantasies, therefore, that his questioning will become a genuine because-motive for the other person's replying, and he keeps that in mind as he formulates the question. Now, this seems to contradict our earlier statement [14] that a because-motive can only be grasped in the pluperfect tense and within an Act of attention that takes as given a motivated act already performed. One could reply that the person who is phantasying pictures within his project in the future perfect tense that an (unspecified) answer has already been given. The act of answering thus appears as past to the questioner, and the answerer's motive appears in the pluperfect. However, this does not satisfy the demands of exact analysis. For how does the questioner know that his own question is the answerer's genuine because-motive? This is a presupposition of his, and indeed it seems to be presupposed in every question. The judgment that the question will probably motivate the answer is, in fact, the in-order-to motive of the questioner. The questioner "knows" that this is probably the case, just as he knows anything else from experience. He knows that, whenever in the past he himself replied to a question, the question was the genuine because-motive of his answer. He answered *because* he was asked. And he knows that the same is true of his friends and acquaintances. From

14. Cf. sec. 18, p. 95.

the whole context of his past experience, then, he derives the general maxim that the question is a genuine because-motive of the answer.

Of course the questioner does not really know that his question will actually enter the other person's consciousness when and if he does answer. Nor is he even sure that it has, once the answer has been given. To be sure, the answer fulfills the questioner's project together with the latter's empty protentions and anticipations. But it is still uncertain whether the person questioned has looked upon the question as the genuine because-motive of his answer. It remains uncertain whether the utterance which the questioner interprets as an answer is "based" on the question or occurs "independently" of it, that is, without any meaning connected with it. In other words, it is not known whether it was really meant as an answer. There is still more: when the person questioned replies, he does so in accordance with his interpretation of the question and with the aim of communicating something to the questioner. This project of answering takes place in free spontaneity in a pure in-order-to context. But he who answers must first understand the question and must, therefore, be oriented to his questioner. And his answer must be such that the questioner will accept it as a real reply to his question. The orientation of the answerer, therefore, reflects that of the questioner. But the answerer is enabled to see that the question was his genuine because-motive only if he gives special attention to his project of replying, which is already past, and to his interpretation of the question, which preceded that. This attention he can give, if at all, not as actor, but as a person reviewing his own behavior and freshly interpreting it. This becomes quite clear if we complete the picture by bringing in the elements of feeling which we previously left out of account. We then note that the questioner *wishes* an answer and that the person questioned *is disposed* to reply. But the latter is not aware of his disposition; he merely carries it out by answering. Only later does he realize that his own readiness to answer served as the because-motive of the actual reply. He can see this only by looking at the project of the reply or at the reply itself. Only then can he detect the wish of his questioner as the genuine because-motive behind the triggering of his own disposition to answer.

However, great caution is to be observed here. The very concept of an answer presupposes that a question has been asked. And it presupposes also that the questioner will interpret his partner's behavior subsequent to the question as the answer to that question. The completed situation in which we find question and answer confronting each other is, therefore, merely an abbreviation of a highly complex state of affairs, within which involved processes of meaning-establishment and meaning-interpretation are elaborately interwoven with one another. We have already analyzed simpler examples of such processes. Nevertheless, we can be quite clear about the sense in which the question is the because-motive of the answer and the answer is the in-order-to motive of the question. What is essential is that the person who is interacting with another should anticipate the in-order-to motives of his own action as the genuine because-motives of the expected behavior of his partner and, conversely, that he should be prepared to regard the in-order-to motives of his partner as the genuine because-motives of his own behavior. This insight is of great importance, for it indicates the methods which are used in both everyday life and interpretive sociology to disclose the motives of the other person. Any affecting of the partner within a social relationship, therefore, presupposes that the partner is oriented to the actor in a special way. This orientation is such that the actor's in-order-to motives become the because-motives of the partner. Now, the actor need not be aware of this situation. All that is necessary is that at any moment he can bring it into focus by attending to it. But an Act of attention of this nature requires the actor to step outside the social relationship and interpret his own action within that relationship. In all such cases he can discover within his past experience the context of motivation constituting the partner's reaction. This may be specific experience of this particular partner, or it may be knowledge of the typical reactions one can expect when one affects another person in a typical way. We always carry about with us the knowledge of rules of this kind. We simply take them for granted, and, since we have no reason to question them, we never even bother to ask where we learned them. The amount of experience one has had of another person depends, of course, upon the social realm to which he belongs in relation to us: whether he is a fellow man in direct experience, a mere contemporary of ours, one of our predecessors, or one of our successors. The degree of accuracy with which we can estimate his reaction will depend upon which of these realms he inhabits. The motivational context of the interaction itself derives its validity from the direct social relationship, of which all other interactions are mere modifications. In the living intentionality of the direct social relationship, the two partners are face to face, their streams of consciousness are synchronized and geared into each other, each immediately affects the other, and the in-order-to motive of the one becomes the because-motive of the other, the two motives complementing and validating each other as objects of reciprocal attention.

The path is now open to the understanding of the structure of the social world. We shall begin with the domain of directly experienced social reality and the pure We-relationship which constitutes it.

[C] THE WORLD OF DIRECTLY EXPERIENCED SOCIAL REALITY

33. The Face-to-Face Situation and the We-Relationship

I SPEAK OF ANOTHER PERSON as within reach of my direct experience when he shares with me a community of space and a community of time. He shares a community of space with me when he is present in person and I am aware of him as such, and, moreover, when I am aware of him as this person *himself,* this *particular* individual, and of his body as the field upon which play the symptoms of his inner consciousness. He shares a community of time [15] with me when his experience is flowing side by side with mine, when I can at any moment look over and grasp his thoughts as they come into being, in other words, when we are growing older together. Persons thus in reach of each other's direct experience I speak of as being in the "face-to-face" situation. The face-to-face situation presupposes, then, an actual simultaneity with each other of two separate streams of consciousness. We have already made this point clear in section 20 of Chapter 3, when we were dealing with the general thesis of the alter ego. We are now adding to it the corollary of the spatial immediacy of the Other, in virtue of which his body is present to me as a field of expression for his subjective experiences.

This spatial and temporal immediacy is essential to the face-to-face situation. All acts of Other-orientation and of affecting-the-other, and therefore all orientations and relationships within the face-to-face situation, derive their own specific flavor and style from this immediacy.

Let us first look at the way in which the face-to-face situation is constituted from the point of view of a participant in that situation. In order to become aware of such a situation, the participant must become intentionally conscious of the person confronting him. He must assume a face-to-face Other-orientation toward the partner. We shall term this attitude "Thou-orientation," and shall now proceed to describe its main features.

First of all, the Thou-orientation is the pure mode in which I am aware of another human being as a person.[16] I am already Thou-oriented from the moment that I recognize an entity which I directly

---

15. Cf. sec. 20, p. 102.
16. [Literally, "the pure form in which he appears to me" (*reine Erscheinungsform*).]

experience as a fellow man (as a Thou), attributing life and consciousness to him. However, we must be quite clear that we are *not* here dealing with a conscious *judgment*. This is a prepredicative experience in which I become aware of a fellow human being *as a person*. The Thou-orientation can thus be defined as the intentionality of those Acts whereby the Ego grasps the existence of the other person in the mode of the original self.[17] Every such external experience in the mode of the original self presupposes the actual presence of the other person and my perception of him as there.

Now, we wish to emphasize that it is precisely the being there (*Dasein*) of the Other toward which the Thou-orientation is directed, not necessarily the Other's specific characteristics. The concept of the Thou-orientation does not imply awareness of what is going on in the Other's mind. In its "pure" form the Thou-orientation consists merely of being intentionally directed toward the pure being-there of another alive and conscious human being. To be sure, the "pure" Thou-orientation is a formal concept, an intellectual construct, or, in Husserl's terminology, an "ideal limit." [18] In real life we never experience the "pure existence" of others; instead we meet real people with their own personal characteristics and traits. The Thou-orientation as it occurs in everyday life is therefore not the "pure" Thou-orientation but the latter *actualized* and *rendered determinate* to some degree or other.

Now the fact that I look upon you as a fellow man does not mean that I am also a fellow man for you, unless you are aware of me. And, of course, it is quite possible that you may not be paying any attention to me at all. The Thou-orientation can, therefore, be either one-sided or reciprocal. It is one-sided if only one of us notices the presence of the other. It is reciprocal if we are mutually aware of each other, that is, if each of us is Thou-oriented toward the other. In this way there is constituted out of the Thou-orientation the face-to-face relationship (or directly experienced social relationship). We have already, in section 31, formulated the criteria for calling a person a partner in such a relationship. The face-to-face relationship in which the partners are aware of each other and sympathetically participate in each other's lives for however short a time we shall call the "pure We-relationship." But the "pure We-relationship" is likewise only a limiting concept. The directly experienced social relationship of real life is the pure We-relationship concretized and actualized to a greater or lesser degree and filled with content.

17. This originality is, of course, not "primary," since the conscious life of the other person is in principle inaccessible to me in direct perception. It is in Husserl's terminology a "secondary" originality (Husserl, *Logik*, p. 206).

18. *Ideen*, p. 138 [E.T., p. 208].

Let us illustrate this with an example. Suppose that you and I are watching a bird in flight. The thought "bird-in-flight" is in each of our minds and is the means by which each of us interprets his own observations. Neither of us, however, could say whether our lived experiences on that occasion were identical. In fact, neither of us would even try to answer that question, since one's own subjective meaning can never be laid side by side with another's and compared.[19]

Nevertheless, during the flight of the bird you and I have "grown older together"; our experiences have been simultaneous. Perhaps while I was following the bird's flight I noticed out of the corner of my eye that your head was moving in the same direction as mine. I could then say that the two of us, that *we*, had watched the bird's flight. What I have done in this case is to coordinate temporally a series of my own experiences with a series of yours. But in so doing I do not go beyond the assertion of a mere *general* correspondence between my perceived "bird in flight" and your experiences. I make no pretense to any knowledge of the content of your subjective experiences or of the particular way in which they were structured. It is enough for me to know that you are a fellow human being who was watching the same thing that I was. And if you have in a similar way coordinated my experiences with yours, then we can both say that *we* have seen a bird in flight.

The basic We-relationship is already given to me by the mere fact that I am born into the world of directly experienced social reality. From this basic relationship is derived the original validity of all my direct experiences of particular fellow men and also my knowledge that there is a larger world of my contemporaries whom I am not now experiencing directly. In this sense Scheler is right when he says that the experience of the We (*die Erfahrung vom Wir*) in the world of immediate social reality is the basis of the Ego's experience (*die Erfahrung des Ich*) of the world in general.[20] Of course we do not have the space in the present study to deal with the difficult phenomenological questions of how this We is constituted from the transcendental Subject or how the psychophysical Thou refers back to the psychophysical Ego.[21] In fact, however, we can for our purposes leave these questions aside. We can begin with the assumption of the mundane existence of other people and then proceed to describe how our experiences of them are constituted from the pure We-relationship.

19. Cf. above, sec. 19, p. 99.
20. Scheler, "Erkenntnis und Arbeit," *Die Wissensform und die Gesellschaft* (Leipzig, 1926), II, 475 f.
21. For a treatment of these questions cf. Husserl's *Cartesian Meditations*, IV and V.

To explain how our experiences of the Thou are rooted in the We-relationship, let us take conversation as an example. Suppose you are speaking to me and I am understanding what you are saying. As we have already seen, there are two senses of this understanding. First of all I grasp the "objective meaning" of your words, the meaning which they would have had, had they been spoken by you or anyone else. But second, of course, there is the subjective meaning, namely, what is going on in your mind as you speak. In order to get to your subjective meaning, I must picture to myself your stream of consciousness as flowing side by side with my own. Within this picture I must interpret and construct your intentional Acts as you choose your words. To the extent that you and I can mutually experience this simultaneity, growing older together for a time, to the extent that we can live in it together, to *that* extent we can live in each other's subjective contexts of meaning. However, our ability to apprehend each other's subjective contexts of meaning should not be confused with the We-relationship itself. For I get to your subjective meaning in the first place only by starting out with your spoken words as given and then by asking how you came to use those words. But this question of mine would make no sense if I did not already assume an actual or at least potential We-relationship between us. For it is only within the We-relationship that I can concretely experience you at a particular moment of your life. To put the point in terms of a formula: I can live in your subjective meaning-contexts only to the extent that I directly experience you within an actualized content-filled We-relationship.[22]

This is true for all stages of understanding another person in which attention to his subjective meaning is involved. For all my lived experiences of the other person (above all the directly apprehended other person), whether they manifest agreement or discrepancy, have their origin in the sphere of the We-relationship. Attention to the We-relationship in turn broadens the objective knowledge of other people which I have gained from the interpretation of my own experiences of them. It likewise broadens my objective knowledge of the particular person involved with me in this particular We-relationship. Thus the contents of the one undivided stream of the We are always enlarging and contracting. In this sense the We resembles my stream of consciousness in the flow of its duration. But this similarity is balanced by a difference. The We-relationship is spatial as well as temporal. It embraces the body of the other person as well as his consciousness. And because I grasp what is going on in his mind only through the medium of his perceived bodily movements, this Act of

22. [This paragraph is a paraphrase of the original.]

grasping is for me a lived experience that transcends my own stream of consciousness. Nevertheless, it should be emphasized that, among all self-transcending experiences, the We-experience remains closest to the stream of consciousness itself.

Moreover, while I am living in the We-relationship, I am really living in *our* common stream of consciousness. And just as I must, in a sense, step outside my own stream of consciousness and "freeze" my subjective experiences if I am going to reflect on them, the same requirement holds for the We-relationship. When you and I are immediately involved with each other, every experience is colored by that involvement. To the extent that we are going to think about the experiences we have together, we must to that degree withdraw from each other. If we are to bring the We-relationship into the focus of our attention, we must stop focusing on each other. But that means stepping out of the face-to-face relationship, because only in the latter do we live *in* the We. And here we can apply at a higher level everything that we said about phenomenal time in our analysis of the solitary Ego. Attention to the lived experiences of the We-relationship likewise presupposes that these experiences are full blown and have already elapsed. And our retrospective grasp of the We-experiences can fall anywhere in the continuum from maximum clarity to complete confusion. And it can be characterized by all degrees of consciousness, just as self-awareness can. In particular, the greater my awareness of the We-relationship, the less is my involvement in it, and the less am I genuinely related to my partner. The more I reflect, the more my partner becomes transformed into a mere object of thought.

Having defined the concept of the We-relationship, let us now describe the specific characteristics that distinguish it from all other social relationships.

34. Analysis of the Face-to-Face Relationship

IN THE PRECEDING SECTION we described the special form taken on by Other-orientation and social relationship in the direct presence of the other person. This description in effect defined the new concepts of Thou-orientation and We-relationship, separating them out from the more general concepts of Other-orientation and social relationship as such. It is these concepts which give us the basis for our analysis of the directly experienced Other-orientation and the face-to-face situation.

If the *pure* We-relationship were merely a modification of social relationship in general, it could be identified equally with direct social orientation and with social interaction. But, strictly speaking, the pure We-relationship is given *prior* to either of these. The pure We-relationship is merely the reciprocal form of the pure Thou-orientation, that is, the pure awareness of the *presence* of another person. His presence, it should be emphasized, not his specific traits. The pure We-relationship involves our awareness of each other's presence and also the knowledge of each that the other is aware of him. But, if we are to have a social relationship, we must go beyond this. What is required is that the Other-orientation of each partner become colored by a specific knowledge of the specific manner in which he is being regarded by the other partner. This in turn is possible only within directly experienced social reality. Only here do our glances actually meet; only here can one actually note how the other is looking at him.

But one cannot become aware of this basic connection between the pure We-relationship and the face-to-face relationship while still a participant in the We-relationship. *One must step out of it and examine it.* The person who is still a participant in the We-relationship does not experience it in its pure form, namely, as an awareness *that* the other person is there. Instead, he simply lives within the We-relationship in the fullness of its concrete content. In other words, the pure We-relationship is a mere limiting concept which one uses in the attempt to get a theoretical grasp of the face-to-face situation. But there are no specific concrete experiences which correspond to it. For the concrete experiences which do occur within the We-relationship in real life grasp their object—the We—as something unique and unrepeatable. And they do this in *one* undivided intentional Act.

Concrete We-relationships exhibit many differences among themselves. The partner, for instance, may be experienced with different degrees of immediacy, different degrees of intensity, or different degrees of intimacy. Or he may be experienced from different points of view. He may appear within the center of attention or at its periphery.

These distinctions apply equally to orientation relationships and to social interactions, determining in each of them the directness with which the partners "know" each other. Compare, for instance, the knowledge two people have of each other in conversation with the knowledge they have of each other in sexual intercourse. What different degrees of intimacy occur here, what different levels of consciousness are involved! Not only do the partners experience the We more deeply in the one case than in the other, but each experiences himself more deeply and his partner more deeply. It is not only the *object*, therefore, that is experienced with greater or lesser directness; it is the *relationship* itself, the being turned toward the object, the relatedness.

These are only two *types* of relationship. But now consider the different ways in which they can actually take place! The conversation, for instance, can be animated or offhand, eager or casual, serious or light, superficial or quite personal.

The fact that we may experience others with such different degrees of directness is very important. It is, as a matter of fact, the key to understanding the transition from the direct experience of others to the indirect which is characteristic of the world of mere contemporaries. We shall be coming to this transition very shortly,[23] but meanwhile let us continue our examination of direct social experience by describing the nature of the face-to-face relationship.

First of all, let us remember that in the face-to-face situation I literally see my partner in front of me. As I watch his face and his gestures and listen to the tone of his voice, I become aware of much more than what he is deliberately trying to communicate to me. My observations keep pace with each moment of his stream of consciousness as it transpires. The result is that I am incomparably better attuned to him than I am to myself. I may indeed be more aware of my own past (to the extent that the latter can be captured in retrospect) than I am of my partner's. Yet I have never been face to face with myself as I am with him now; hence I have never caught myself in the act of actually living through an experience.

To this encounter with the other person I bring a whole stock of previously constituted knowledge. This includes both general knowledge of what another person is as such and any specific knowledge I may have of the person in question. It includes knowledge of other people's interpretive schemes, their habits, and their language. It includes knowledge of the taken-for-granted in-order-to and because-motives of others as such and of this person in particular. And when I am face to face with someone, my knowledge of him is increasing from moment to moment. My ideas of him undergo continuous revision as the concrete experience unfolds. For no direct social relationship is one isolated intentional Act. Rather it consists of a continuous series of such Acts. The orientation relationship, for instance, consists of a continuous series of intentional Acts of Other-orientation, while social interaction consists in a continuous series of Acts of meaning-establishment and meaning-interpretation. All these different encounters with my fellow man will be ordered in multiple meaning-contexts: they are encounters with a human being as such, with this particular human being, and with this particular human being at this particular moment of time. And these meaning-contexts of mine will be "subjec-

23. Cf. sec. 36, below, p. 177.

tive" to the extent that I am attending to your actual conscious experiences themselves and not merely to my own lived experiences of you. Furthermore, as I watch you, I shall see that you are oriented to me, that you are seeking the subjective meaning of my words, my actions, and what I have in mind insofar as you are concerned. And I will in turn take account of the fact that you are thus oriented to me, and this will influence both my intentions with respect to you and how I act toward you. This again you will see, I will see that you have seen it, and so on. This interlocking of glances, this thousand-faceted mirroring of each other, is one of the unique features of the face-to-face situation. We may say that it is a constitutive characteristic of this particular social relationship. However, we must remember that the pure We-relationship, which is the very form of every encounter with another person, is not itself grasped *reflectively* within the face-to-face situation. Instead of being observed, it is lived through. The many different mirror images of Self within Self are not therefore caught sight of one by one but are experienced as a continuum within a single experience. Within the unity of this experience I can be aware simultaneously of what is going on in my mind and in yours, *living through* the two series of experiences as one series—what we are experiencing together.

This fact is of special significance for the face-to-face situation. Within the face-to-face situation I can be a witness of your projects and also of their fulfillment or frustration as you proceed to action. Of course, once I know what you are planning to do, I may momentarily *suspend* the We-relationship in order to estimate *objectively* your chances of success. But it is only within the intimacy of the We-relationship itself that one can actually *live through* a course of action from its birth as a project to its ultimate outcome.

It is further essential to the face-to-face situation that you and I have the same environment.[24] First of all I ascribe to you an environment corresponding to my own.[25] Here, in the face-to-face situation, but only here, does this presupposition prove correct, to the extent that I can assume with more or less certainty within the directly experienced social realm that the table I see is identical (and identical in all its perspective variations [26]) with the table you see, to the extent that I can assume this even if you are only my contemporary or my predecessor. Therefore, when I am in a face-to-face situation with you, I can

24. By "environment" I mean that part of the external world which I can directly apprehend. This would include not only the physical but also the social environment with all of its cultural artifacts, languages, etc.

25. See sec. 20, above, pp. 104–5.

26. [Cf. Husserl, *Ideas*, § 41.]

point to something in our common environment, uttering the words "this table here" and, by means of the identification of lived experiences in the environmental object, I can assure the adequacy of my interpretive scheme to your expressive scheme. For practical social life it is of the greatest significance that I consider myself justified in equating my own interpretation of my lived experiences with your interpretation of yours on those occasions when we are experiencing one and the same object.

We have, then, the same undivided and common environment, which we may call "our environment." The world of the We is not private to either of us, but is our world, the one common intersubjective world which is right there in front of us. It is only from the face-to-face relationship, from the common lived experience of the world in the We, that the intersubjective world can be constituted. This alone is the point from which it can be deduced.[27]

I can constantly check my interpretations of what is going on in other people's minds, due to the fact that, in the We-relationship, I share a common environment with them. In principle, it is only in the face-to-face situation that I can address a question to you. But I can ask you not only about the interpretive schemes which you are applying to our common environment. I can also ask you how you are interpreting your lived experiences, and, in the process, I can correct, expand, and enrich my own understanding of you. This becoming-aware of the correctness or incorrectness of my understanding of you is a higher level of the We-experience. On this level I enrich not only my experience of you but of other people generally.

If I know that you and I are in a face-to-face relationship, I also know something about the manner in which each of us is attuned to his conscious experiences, in other words, the "attentional modifications" of each of us. This means that the way we attend to our conscious experiences is actually modified by our relationship to each other. This holds for both of us. For there is a true social relationship only if you reciprocate my awareness of you in some manner or other. As soon as this happens, as soon as we enter the face-to-face situation, each of us begins to attend to his own experiences in a new way. This particular attentional modification in which the two partners of a directly experienced social relationship are mutually aware of each other has special implications for the social interaction which occurs in that situation. *Whenever I am interacting with anyone, I take for granted as a constant in that person a set of genuine because- or in-order-to motives.* I do this on the ground of my own past experience

27. Cf. Husserl, *Cartesian Meditations,* § 55.

of that particular person as well as of people generally. My own behavior toward that person is based in the first instance upon this taken-for-granted constellation of motives, regardless of whether they are his real motives or not. And here emerges the peculiarity of face-to-face interaction. It consists not in a specific structure of the reciprocal motivation context itself but in a specific *disclosure* of the motives of the other person. Even in face-to-face interactions I only project in phantasy the behavior of the other person as I plan my own action. This phantasy is, of course, merely the other's *expected* behavior, without the details as yet filled in and without, as yet, any confirmation. I have yet to see what my partner will actually do. But because he and I continually undergo modifications of attention with respect to each other in the We-relationship, I can actually live through and participate in the constitution of his motivational context. I interpret the present lived experiences which I impute to you as the in-order-to motives of the behavior I expect from you or as the consequences of your past experiences, which I then regard as their because-motives. I "orient" my action to these motivational contexts of yours, as you "orient" yours to mine. However, this "orienting oneself" takes place within the directly experienced social realm in the particular mode of "witnessing." When interacting with you within this realm, I *witness* how you react to my behavior, how you interpret my meaning, how my in-order-to motives trigger corresponding because-motives of your behavior. In between my expectation of your reaction and that reaction itself I have "grown older" and perhaps wiser, taking into account the realities of the situation, as well as my own hopes of what you would do. But in the face-to-face situation you and I grow older together, and I can add to my expectation of what you are going to do the actual sight of you making up your mind, and then of your action itself in all its constituent phases. During all this time we are aware of each other's stream of consciousness as contemporaneous with our own; we share a rich, concrete We-relationship without any need to reflect on it. In a flash I see your whole plan and its execution in action. This episode of my biography is full of continuous lived experiences of you grasped within the We-relationship; meanwhile, you are experiencing me in the same way, and I am aware of the fact.

35. Direct Social Observation

So FAR WE HAVE BEEN studying the directly experienced social relationship in order to bring out the peculiar characteristics of the face-to-face situation in its purest form. Our analysis would, however, be incomplete unless we dealt with the case where I am aware of someone else while knowing that he is *unaware* of me. Especially important under this heading is the observation of another's behavior. The analysis of such observation is, as a matter of fact, the key to the understanding of the manner in which the data of the social sciences are established. We have already, in Chapter 3, explained how the interpretation of the Other's behavior is actually carried out. At this point our task will be to throw light upon the special kind of Thou-orientation which the observer takes up toward the person he is directly observing. We shall be paying special attention to the ways in which his interpretive schemes differ from those used in the face-to-face relationship.

In the face-to-face relationship the Thou-orientation is *reciprocal* between the two partners. In direct social observation, however, it is *one-sided*. Let us imagine that we have a case of the latter. Say that I am observing someone else's behavior and that he either does not know that he is being observed or is paying no attention to it. Now the problem is, How do I know what is going on in his mind? Well, even if I am merely observing him, his body is still a field of expression for his inner life. I may, as I watch him, take my own perceptions of his body as signs of his conscious experiences. In so doing, I will take his movements, words, and so forth, into account as evidence. I will direct my attention to the subjective rather than to the objective meaning-contexts of the indications I perceive. As a direct observer I can thus in one glance take in both the outward manifestations—or "products"—and the processes in which are constituted the conscious experiences lying behind them. This is possible because the lived experiences of the Other are occurring simultaneously with my own objective interpretations of his words and gestures.

The other person is quite as much present in a bodily sense to the observer as he is to someone who is participating in a social relationship with him. His words can be heard and his gestures seen: there is as great a wealth of indications of his inner life as in the case of a direct relationship. Every additional experience the observer has of the other person increases his knowledge of the latter. Their two environments are congruent, and therefore their conscious experiences probably correspond. But this probability cannot in principle be raised to certainty. Here the situation differs from what obtains in a face-to-face relationship. In the latter I can, at will, verify my assumption that my experiences correspond to those of the other person. I can do this by direct appeal to an object of the external world which is common to both of us. But in any direct social observation carried on outside a social relationship, my interpretation of another's behavior cannot be

checked against his own self-interpretation, unless of course I exchange my role as an observer for that of a participant. *When I start
asking questions of the person observed, I am no longer a mere
observer.*[28] Still the point must be stressed that direct social observation can be converted at will into a face-to-face relationship, thereby
making such interrogation possible, whereas that cannot be said of
observation of one's mere contemporaries or predecessors.

Since the observer's Thou-orientation to his subject is one-sided,
the subjective meaning-context in which he interprets the lived experiences of the other person has no opposite number. Absent, therefore, is
the many-faceted mutual mirroring characteristic of the face-to-face
relationship, in which the conscious content of the two partners is
mutually identified. The behavior of the observed person, instead of
being oriented to the observer's behavior, is completely independent of
the latter. The participant in the face-to-face relationship knows with
probability or certainty that his partner's behavior is oriented to his
own, and he is even aware of the modifications of attention underlying
his partner's conscious experiences. He can compare these modifications of attention with his own toward the partner. The observer lacks
this access to the other person's attentional modifications; he can at
least acquire no information about these modifications from looking
into his own consciousness. Nor is he in a position to influence the
behavior of the observed nor to be influenced by him. He cannot
project his own in-order-to motive in such a way as to have it become
the because-motive of the observed. The observer cannot judge from
the mere behavior of the Other whether the latter is succeeding in
carrying out his plans or not. In extreme cases, as when seeing an
expressive movement, he can even be in doubt whether he is observing
an action at all. Perhaps it is pure purposeless behavior that he is
watching.

The observer who seeks to interpret his subject's motives will have
to be satisfied with three indirect approaches:

1. He can search his memory for similar actions of his own and,
finding such, can draw from them a general principle concerning the
relation of their in-order-to and because-motives. He can then assume
that this principle holds true for the other person's actions as well as
for his own and can proceed to interpret the other person's actions by
"putting himself in his place." This reading of one's own hypothetical
motives into another's behavior can take place either at once, on the

---

28. ["Das Du ist für den Beobachter als Beobachter wesensmässig unbefrag-
bar."]

spot, or through a later consideration of what could have made the person act as he did.[29]

2. Lacking such a guideline, he can resort to his own knowledge of the customary behavior of the person observed and from this deduce the latter's in-order-to and because-motives. If a visitor from Mars were to enter a lecture hall, a courtroom, and a church, the three places would seem quite the same to him in outward appearance. From the internal arrangements of none of the three would he be able to comprehend what the presiding official was about. But let him be told that one is a professor, another a judge, and the third a priest, and he would then be able to interpret their actions and assign motives to them.

3. But it may be that the observer lacks significant information about the person he is observing. His last resort will then be to try to infer the in-order-to motive from the act by asking whether such and such a motive would be furthered by the act in question.[30] He must, while observing the ongoing action, interpret it in terms of the effect which it actually has and assume that the effect is what was intended.

It is obvious that these three types of motivational understanding are not equally reliable. The further away from the concrete We-relationship (and, therefore, the more abstract) the interpretation is, the less chance it has of hitting its mark. The second type of understanding would, for instance, come up against this kind of pitfall: the priest speaking from the pulpit might not be delivering a sermon at all. The third type must face the hazard of the leap from the completed act to its in-order-to motive, a hazard still greater, since the act may not have turned out as the actor intended.

In the case of trying to discover the genuine because-motives of another, the contrast between participation and mere observation is considerably lessened. Here the observer is not much worse off than the participant in the face-to-face relationship. Even the latter is forced to reconstruct the motives of his partner ex post facto. The only advantage the direct participant has is that the data with which he starts are more vivid.

The direct observation of social relationships is, to be sure, more complicated than the observation of individual behavior. However, it

29. Weber would call the first "observational," the second "motivational," understanding. But from a structural point of view it makes no difference whether this attribution of one's own hypothetical motives to another takes place in a flash or through a chain of inferences. Here again we see the lack of depth in Weber's distinction between the two types of understanding.

30. This is the method in terms of which penology prefers to analyze an action. Cf. Felix Kaufmann, *Strafrechtsschuld*, p. 86.

does not differ in principle. Here, too, the observer must fall back upon his experience of social relationships in general, of this particular social relationship, and of the particular partners now involved. The observer's interpretive schemes cannot be identical with those of either of the partners in the relationship for the simple reason that his modifications of attention differ from theirs in a fundamental way. Moreover, he is aware of both of them, whereas they are aware only of each other. It can even happen that he knows one of the two people better than the latter is known by his partner and, therefore, is better acquainted with his interpretive schemes. Thus the nonparticipating listener can realize that two partners to a discussion are merely talking past one another, whereas they themselves may be totally unaware of this. On the other hand, the observer is at a disadvantage as compared to the participants: since he is not always sure of the in-order-to motives of one participant, he can hardly identify them with the because-motives of the other.

Of course, everything that we have been saying presupposes that the observer has some way of gaining access to the expressive schemes of the participants in the relationship. If this is not the case, he must resort to filling in the blank spaces out of his own past experiences in a way analogous to the procedure, previously described, of coming to know the motives of another person.

[D] THE WORLD OF CONTEMPORARIES AS A STRUCTURE OF IDEAL TYPES

36. The Transition from Direct to Indirect Social Experience. Continuous Social Relationships

WE HAVE ALREADY NOTED that the We-relationship can occur with varying degrees of concreteness. We have seen that in the relationship we may experience our fellow men with greater or lesser directness, intimacy, or intensity. However, in the face-to-face situation, directness of experience is essential, regardless of whether our apprehension of the Other is central or peripheral and regardless of how adequate our grasp of him is. I am still "Thou-oriented" even to the man standing next to me in the subway. When we speak of "pure" Thou-orientation or "pure" We-relationship, we are ordinarily using these as limiting concepts referring to the simple givenness of the Other in abstraction from any specification of the degree of concreteness involved. But we can also use these terms for the lower limits of experience obtainable in the face-to-face relationship, in other words, for the most peripheral and fleeting kind of awareness of the other person.

We make the transition from direct to indirect social experience simply by following this spectrum of decreasing vividness. The first steps beyond the realm of immediacy are marked by a decrease in the number of perceptions I have of the other person and a narrowing of the perspectives within which I view him. At one moment I am exchanging smiles with my friend, shaking hands with him, and bidding him farewell. At the next moment he is walking away. Then from the far distance I hear a faint good-by, a moment later I see a vanishing figure give a last wave, and then he is gone. It is quite impossible to fix the exact instant at which my friend left the world of my direct experience and entered the shadowy realm of those who are merely my contemporaries. As another example, imagine a face-to-face conversation, followed by a telephone call, followed by an exchange of letters, and finally messages exchanged through a third party. Here too we have a gradual progression from the world of immediately experienced social reality to the world of contemporaries. In both examples the total number of the other person's reactions open to my observation is progressively diminished until it reaches a minimum point. It is clear, then, that the world of contemporaries is itself a variant function of the face-to-face situation. They may even be spoken of as two poles between which stretches a continuous series of experiences.

It would be the task of a detailed survey of the social world to study these transformations of direct social experience in terms of their specific meaning-content. The studies of "contact situations," especially those lying in the intermediate zone between direct and indirect social experience, and the studies of men's behavior toward and with respect to one another—in short, Wiese's whole "theory of relationships"—are now shown to be well founded and justified. They belong to the special theory of the social world. It was the great merit of Wiese, and recently also of Sander,[31] to have seen these problems and to have made valuable contributions toward their solution.

Our purpose in this work, however, is not to set forth such a special theory of the social world. Nor is it our purpose even to formulate the basic principles of such a theory. But it is quite clear that before we describe the situation of being a contemporary, we must first discover how this is constituted out of the face-to-face situation.

In everyday life there seems to be no practical problem of where the one situation breaks off and the other begins. This is because we

---

31. In his still too little appreciated *Allgemeine Gesellschaftslehre* (Jena, 1930).

interpret both our own behavior and that of others within contexts of meaning that far transcend the immediate here and now. For this reason, the question whether a social relationship we participate in or observe is direct or indirect seems to be an academic one. But there is a yet deeper reason for our customary indifference to this question. Even after the face-to-face situation has receded into the past and is present only in memory, it still retains its essential characteristics, modified only by an aura of pastness. Normally we do not notice that our just-departed friend, with whom we have a moment ago been interacting, perhaps affectionately or perhaps in an annoyed way, now appears to us in a quite different perspective. Far from seeming obvious, it actually seems absurd that someone we are close to has somehow become "different" now that he is out of sight, except in the trite sense that our experiences of him bear the mark of pastness. However, we must still sharply distinguish between such memories of face-to-face situations, on the one hand, and an intentional Act directed toward a mere contemporary, on the other. The recollections we have of another bear all the marks of direct experience. When I have a recollection of you, for instance, I remember you as you were in the concrete We-relationship with me. I remember you as a unique person in a concrete situation, as one who interacted with me in the mode of "mutual mirroring" described above. I remember you as a person vividly present to me with a maximum of symptoms of inner life, as one whose experiences I witnessed in the actual process of formation. I remember you as one whom I was for a time coming to know better and better. I remember you as one whose conscious life flowed in one stream with my own. I remember you as one whose consciousness was continuously changing in content. However, now that you are out of my direct experience, you are no more than my contemporary, someone who merely inhabits the same planet that I do. I am no longer in contact with the living you, but with the you of yesterday. You, indeed, have not ceased to be a living self, but you have a "new self" now; and, although I am contemporaneous with it, I am cut off from vital contact with it. Since the time we were last together, you have met with new experiences and have looked at them from new points of view. With each change of experience and outlook you have become a slightly different person. But somehow I fail to keep this in mind as I go about my daily round. I carry your image with me, and it remains the same. But then, perhaps, I hear that you have changed. I then begin to look upon you as a contemporary—not any contemporary, to be sure, but one whom I once knew intimately.

Examples of this situation are those social relationships within which, according to Weber, "there is a probability of the repeated occurrence of the behavior which corresponds to its subjective meaning, behavior which is an understandable consequence of the meaning and hence is expected." [32] We tend to picture marriage or friendship as primarily face-to-face relationships, especially intimate ones at that. We do this because of a tendency we have to conceive the actions of the partners as integrated into the larger unity of the relationship and goal-directed toward that unity.

In actual life, however, a marriage or a friendship is made up of many separate events occurring over a long period of time. Some of these events involve face-to-face situations, in others the partners simply exist side by side as contemporaries. To call such social relationships as these "continuous" is erroneous in the extreme,[33] since discontinuity and repeatability are included in their very definition. What, then, do friends mean when they speak of their "friendship"? We can distinguish three different meanings they may have in mind.

1. When *A* speaks of his friendship with *B*, he may be thinking of a series of past face-to-face relationships which he shared with *B*. We say "series," because *A* does remember that during the course of his friendship with *B* he did spend some time alone or with other people.

2. When *A* speaks of his friendship with *B*, he may mean that, over and above such face-to-face situations, his behavior is oriented to *B*'s expected behavior or to the fact that *B* exists—that he is the kind of man he is. In this case, *A* is oriented toward *B* as a contemporary, and their relationship is the kind that exists between contemporaries. This relationship can be either one of orientation or of social interaction.[34] For instance, *A* may perform a certain action because he thinks it will please *B* as soon as the latter finds out about it. Whereas in the face-to-face situation he would literally see *B*'s reaction, here he is confined to merely imagining it. Within the "friendship" such contemporary-oriented acts are inserted between consociate-oriented acts. Face-to-face interaction involves mutual engagement in which the partners can witness the literal coming-to-birth of each other's experiences. Interaction between contemporaries, however, merely involves the expectation on the part of each partner that the other will respond in a relevant way. But this expectation is always a shot in the dark

---

32. Weber; *Wirtschaft und Gesellschaft*, p. 14, point 4 [E.T., p. 119].

33. [There is an unfortunate linguistic ambiguity here. A friendship, it is true, is (happily) not a continu*ous* series of contacts in the Cantorian sense that between any two contacts there is another. It is a series of continu*al* or recurring contacts. But, although it is not a continu*ous series*, it can be spoken of as a continu*ous relationship* unless every *au revoir* is a temporary "breaking-off" of the friendship.]

34. The different forms of orientation relationships and social interaction in the world of contemporaries remain to be described exactly.

compared to the knowledge one has of one's consociate in the face-to-face situation. Actions between contemporaries are only mutually *related,* whereas actions between consociates are mutually *interlocked.*[35] The being related to each other of contemporaries occurs in imagination, whereas the interlocking mutual engagement of the We-relationship is a matter of immediate experience. Between these two situations we find many intermediate degrees. For instance, think of the gradually decreasing immediacy of the following: (a) carrying on an imagined conversation with a friend, (b) wondering what my friend would say if I were to do such and such, (c) doing something "for him."

3. When *A* speaks of his friendship with *B*, he may be referring to the fact that, external obstacles aside, they can always get together again and begin where they have left off. This is parallel to what happens in the sphere of judgment. We showed in our analysis of the concept "knowledge" that the latter refers to a sum of already constituted objectified judgments [or judgment-objectivities—*Urteilsgegenständlichkeiten*]. Knowledge, then, is a storehouse which can be drawn on at any time by the reactivation of the judgments in question. In the same way, when *A* speaks of his friendship with *B*, he is referring to a storehouse of past experiences of *B*. But he is assuming at the same time that these experiences can be reactivated in a revived We-relationship and that, on that basis, both parties can proceed as before. What is here revived, of course, is not so much the specific lived experiences that previously occurred within the We-relationship but the lived experience of the We-relationship itself.

In the last few pages we have been describing the intermediate zone between the face-to-face situation and the situation involving mere contemporaries. Let us continue our journey. As we approach the outlying world of contemporaries, our experience of others becomes more and more remote and anonymous. Entering the world of contemporaries itself, we pass through one region after another: (1) the region of those whom I once encountered face to face and could encounter again (for instance, my absent friend); then (2) comes the region of those once encountered by the person I am now talking to (for instance, your friend, whom you are promising to introduce to me); next (3) the region of those who are as yet *pure* contemporaries but whom I will soon meet (such as the colleague whose books I have read and whom I am now on my way to visit); then (4) those contemporaries of whose existence I know, not as concrete individuals, but as points in social space as defined by a certain function (for

35. ["Aufeinanderbezogen . . . aufeinander eingestellt."]

instance, the postal employee who will process my letter); then (5) those collective entities whose function and organization I know while not being able to name any of their members, such as the Canadian Parliament; then (6) collective entities which are by their very nature anonymous and of which I could never in principle have direct experience, such as "state" and "nation"; then (7) objective configurations of meaning which have been instituted in the world of my contemporaries and which live a kind of anonymous life of their own, such as the interstate commerce clause and the rules of French grammar; and finally (8) artifacts of any kind which bear witness to the subjective meaning-context of some unknown person. The farther out we get into the world of contemporaries, the more anonymous its inhabitants become, starting with the innermost region, where they can almost be seen, and ending with the region where they are by definition forever inaccessible to experience.

37. The Contemporary as an Ideal Type. The Nature of the They-Relationship

MY MERE CONTEMPORARY (or "contemporary"), then, is one whom I know coexists with me in time but whom I do not experience immediately. This kind of knowledge is, accordingly, always indirect and impersonal. I cannot call my contemporary "Thou" in the rich sense that this term has within the We-relationship. Of course, my contemporary may once have been my consociate or may yet become one, but this in no way alters his present status.

Let us now examine the ways in which the world of contemporaries is constituted and the modifications which the concepts "Other-orientation" and "social relationship" undergo in that world. These modifications are necessitated by the fact that the contemporary is only indirectly accessible and that his subjective experiences can only be known in the form of *general types* of subjective experience.

That this should be the case is easy to understand if we consider the difference between the two modes of social experience. When I encounter you face to face I know you as a person in one unique moment of experience. While this We-relationship remains unbroken, we are open and accessible to each other's intentional Acts. For a little while we grow older together, experiencing each other's flow of consciousness in a kind of intimate mutual possession.

It is quite otherwise when I experience you as my contemporary. Here you are not prepredicatively given to me at all. I do not even directly apprehend your existence (*Dasein*). My whole knowledge of you is mediate and descriptive. In this kind of knowledge your "characteristics" are established for me by inference. From such knowledge results the indirect We-relationship.

To become clear about this concept of "mediacy," let us examine two different ways in which I come to know a contemporary. The first way we have already mentioned: my knowledge is derived from a previous face-to-face encounter with the person in question. But this knowledge has since become mediate [36] or indirect because he has moved outside the range of my direct observation. For I make inferences as to what is going on in his mind under the assumption that he remains much the same [37] since I saw him last, although, in another sense, I know very well that he must have changed through absorbing new experiences or merely by virtue of having grown older. But, as to how he has changed, my knowledge is either indirect or nonexistent.

A second way in which I come to know a contemporary is to construct a picture of him from the past direct experience of someone with whom I am now speaking (for example, when my friend describes his brother, whom I do not know). This is a variant of the first case. Here too I apprehend the contemporary by means of a fixed concept, or type, derived ultimately from direct experience but now held invariant. But there are differences. First, I have no concrete vivid picture of my own with which to start: I must depend on what my friend tells me. Second, I have to depend on my friend's assumption, not my own, that the contemporary he is describing has not changed.

These are the modes of constitution of all the knowledge we have of our contemporaries derived from our own past experience, direct or indirect, and of all the knowledge we have acquired from others, whether through conversation or through reading. It is clear, then, that indirect social experiences derive their original validity from the direct mode of apprehension. But the instances cited above do not exhaust all the ways by which I can come to know my contemporaries. There is the whole world of cultural objects, for instance, including everything from artifacts to institutions and conventional ways of doing things. These, too, contain within themselves implicit references to my contemporaries. I can "read" in these cultural objects the subjective experiences of others whom I do not know. Even here, however, I am making inferences on the basis of my previous direct experience of others. Let us say that the object before me is a finished product. Once,

36. We are here using "immediacy" in such a way as to include what Husserl calls "experience in a secondary originality" (*Logik*, p. 206); cf. above, sec. 33, p. 164.

37. On this point, as well as on the problem of the anonymity of the ideal type, see the sketchy but important contribution of Felix Kaufmann, 'Soziale Kollektiva," *Zeitschrift für Nationalökonomie*, I, 294–308.

perhaps, I stood by the side of a man who was manufacturing something just like this. As I watched him work, I knew exactly what was going on in his mind. If it were not for this experience I would not know what to make of the finished product of the same kind that I now see. I might even fail to recognize it as an artifact at all and would treat it as just another natural object, like a stone or a tree. For what we have called the general thesis of the alter ego, namely, that the Thou coexists with me and grows older with me, can only be discovered in the We-relationship. Even in this instance, therefore, I have only an indirect experience of the other self, based on past direct experiences either of a Thou as such or of a particular Thou. My face-to-face encounters with others have given me a deep prepredicative knowledge of the Thou as a self. But the Thou who is *merely* my contemporary is never experienced personally as a self and never prepredicatively. On the contrary, all experience (*Erfahrung*) of contemporaries is predicative in nature. It is formed by means of interpretive judgments involving all my knowledge of the social world, although with varying degrees of explicitness.

Now this is real Other-orientation, however indirect it may be. And under this indirect Other-orientation we will find the usual forms of simple Other-orientation, social behavior and social interaction. Let us call all such intentional Acts directed toward contemporaries cases of "They-orientation," [38] in contrast to the "Thou-orientation" of the intentional Acts of direct social experience.

The term "They-orientation" serves to call attention to the peculiar way in which I apprehend the conscious experiences of my contemporaries. For I apprehend them as anonymous processes.[39] Consider the contrast to the Thou-orientation. When I am Thou-oriented, I apprehend the other person's experiences within their setting in his stream of consciousness. I apprehend them as existing within a subjective context of meaning, as being the unique experiences of a particular person. All this is absent in the indirect social experience of the They-orientation. Here I am not aware of the ongoing flow of the Other's consciousness. My orientation is not toward the existence (*Dasein*) of a concrete individual Thou. It is not toward any subjective experiences now being constituted in all their uniqueness in another's mind nor toward the subjective configuration of meaning in which they are taking place. Rather, the object of my They-orientation is my own experience (*Erfahrung*) of social reality in general, of human

38. [*Ihreinstellung* in the original. We are adopting Luckmann's rendering "They-orientation" as the best English expression of the "distancing" that Schutz wished to emphasize here.]

39. On this point see below, sec. 39, p. 194.

beings and their conscious processes as such, in abstraction from any individual setting in which they may occur. My knowledge of my contemporaries is, therefore, inferential and discursive. It stands, by its essential nature,[40] in an objective context of meaning and only in such. It has within it no intrinsic reference to persons nor to the subjective matrix within which the experiences in question were constituted. However, it is due to this very abstraction from subjective context of meaning that they exhibit the property which we have called their "again and again" character. They are treated as typical conscious experiences of "someone" and, as such, as basically homogeneous and repeatable. The unity of the contemporary is not constituted originally in his own stream of consciousness. (Indeed, whether the contemporary has any stream of consciousness at all is a difficult question and one which we shall deal with later.) Rather, the contemporary's unity is constituted in my own stream of consciousness, being built up out of a synthesis of my own interpretations of his experiences. This synthesis is a synthesis of recognition in which I monothetically bring within one view my own conscious experiences of someone else. Indeed, these experiences of mine may have been of more than one person. And they may have been of definite individuals or of anonymous "people." It is in this synthesis of recognition that the *personal ideal type* is constituted.

We must be quite clear as to what is happening here. The subjective meaning-context has been abandoned as a tool of interpretation. It has been replaced by a series of highly complex and systematically interrelated objective meaning-contexts. The result is that the contemporary is anonymized in direct proportion to the number and complexity of these meaning-contexts. Furthermore, the synthesis of recognition does not apprehend the unique person as he exists within his living present. Instead it pictures him as always the same and homogeneous, leaving out of account all the changes and rough edges that go along with individuality. Therefore, no matter how many people are subsumed under the ideal type, it corresponds to no one in particular. It is just this fact that justified Weber in calling it "ideal."

Let us give a few examples to clarify this point. When I mail a letter, I assume that certain contemporaries of mine, namely, postal employees, will read the address and speed the letter on its way.[41] I am not thinking of these postal employees as individuals. I do not know them personally and never expect to. Again, as Max Weber pointed

40. Nevertheless, I can simultaneously experience someone as a mere contemporary and endow him with an enduring self having his own subjective contexts of meaning which are open to my inspection. See below, p. 186.
41. The example is taken from Felix Kaufmann, "Soziale Kollektiva," p. 299.

out, whenever I accept money I do so without any doubt that others, who remain quite anonymous, will accept it in turn from me. To use yet another Weberian example,[42] if I behave in such a way as to avoid the sudden arrival of certain gentlemen with uniforms and badges, in other words, to the extent that I orient myself to the laws and to the apparatus which enforces them, here, too, I am relating myself socially to my contemporaries conceived under ideal types.

On occasions like these I am always expecting others to behave in a definite way, whether it be postal employees, someone I am paying, or the police. My social relationship to them consists in the fact that I interact with them, or perhaps merely that, in planning my actions, I keep them in mind. But they, on their part, never turn up as real people, merely as anonymous entities defined exhaustively by their functions. Only as bearers of these functions do they have any relevance for my social behavior. How they happen to feel as they cancel my letter, process my check, or examine my income-tax return—these are considerations that never even enter my mind. I just assume that there are "some people" who "do these things." Their behavior in the conduct of their duty is from my point of view defined purely through an objective context of meaning. In other words, when I am They-oriented, I have "types" for partners.

The use of ideal types is not limited to the world of contemporaries. It is to be found in our apprehension of the world of predecessors as well. Moreover, since ideal types are interpretive schemes for the social world in general, they become part of our stock of knowledge about that world. As a result, we are always drawing upon them in our face-to-face dealings with people. This means that ideal types serve as interpretive schemes even for the world of *direct* social experience. However, they are carried along with and modified by the We-relationship as it develops. In the process they cease to be mere types and "return to reality" again. Let us give an example.

Sometimes I am face to face with several people at once. Thus, in a sense, we have here a *direct* They-relationship. But this "They" can always be broken down into a Thou and Thou and Thou, with each of whom I can enter into a We-relationship. Suppose, for instance, that I am watching a group of men playing cards. I can pay special attention to any one of them. As I do so, I am aware of him as a Thou. No longer, now, am I seeing him as "man playing cards," which would merely be an interpretation of my own perceptions. Rather, I am now aware of the way he plays the game. I follow his every move with interest, guessing what is going on in his mind at each particular play.

42. Weber, "R. Stammlers Überwindung der materialistischen Geschichtsauffassung," *Gesammelte Aufsätze zur Wissenschaftslehre,* p. 325.

And, as I observe the other partners, I find that they too are playing the game out of their own unique contexts of meaning.

But suppose I suspend for a moment my participation in this vivid We-relationship. Suppose I shift my mode of observation, transporting the players into my world of contemporaries. I can then make a statement like "They are playing a game of poker." This statement will apply to each individual player only to the extent that the course-of-action type "poker game" corresponds to a series of conscious experiences in his mind and stands in a subjective meaning-context for him. In this way the action of each player will be "oriented" to the rules of poker.[43] But what we have here is really a postulate: "If A, B, and C are playing poker, then their behavior is oriented to a certain action-model M." This postulate of course does not apply merely to A, B, and C. Rather it defines the ideal type "poker player." And the postulate will apply to A, B, and C only insofar as they exemplify individually that ideal type. But insofar as I myself look upon the players as examples of an ideal type, to the same extent must I disregard their individuality. No concrete lived experience of A is ever either identical or commensurable with one of B. For these experiences, belonging as they do to different streams of consciousness, are unique, unrepeatable, and incapable of being juxtaposed. *The typical and only the typical is homogeneous*, and it is always so. In the typifying synthesis of recognition I perform an act of anonymization in which I abstract the lived experience from its setting within the stream of consciousness and thereby render it impersonal.

The opposite process is also possible. The objective meaning-context defining the subjective experiences of an ideal type can be translated back into a subjective meaning whenever I apply it to an individual in a concrete situation. Thus I may say, "Oh, he's one of those!" or "I've seen that type before!" This is the explanation for the fact that I experience my contemporary as an individual with an ongoing conscious life, yet one whose experiences I know by inference rather than by direct confrontation. Therefore, even though I think of him as an individual, still he is for me an individual exhaustively defined by his type, an "anonymous" individual.

38. The Constitution of the Ideal-Typical Interpretive Scheme

IN THE FOREGOING SECTION we have described how we understand the behavior of others in terms of ideal types. We saw that

43. Even the cheater is oriented to the rules; otherwise he could not really cheat.

the process consisted essentially of taking a cross-section of our experience of another person and, so to speak, "freezing it into a slide." We saw that this is done by means of a synthesis of recognition. However, there is something ambiguous about this concept of an ideal type of human behavior.[44] It denotes at one and the same time ideal types covering (1) pregiven objective meaning-contexts, (2) products, (3) courses of action, and (4) real and ideal objects, whenever any of the above are the result of human behavior. Included also would be interpretations of the products of ideal-typical behavior. The latter are the interpretations to which we resort when we know nothing of the individual experiences of those who created these products. Whenever we come upon any ordering of past experience under interpretive schemes, any act of abstraction, generalization, formalization, or idealization, whatever the object involved, there we shall find this process in which a moment of living experience is lifted out of its setting and then, through a synthesis of recognition, frozen into a hard and fast "ideal type." Insofar as the term "ideal type" can be applied to any interpretive scheme under which experience is subsumed—as in Max Weber's early writings—it raises no special problem for the social scientist. We could speak in exactly the same sense of ideal types of physical objects and processes, of meteorological patterns, of evolutionary series in biology, and so forth. How useful the concept of ideal types would be in these fields is not for us to say, since we are concerned here with a specific group of problems in the social sciences.

The concept "ideal type of human behavior" can be taken in two ways. It can mean first of all the ideal type of another person who is expressing himself or has expressed himself in a certain way. Or it may mean, second, the ideal type of the expressive process itself, or even of the outward results which we interpret as the signs of the expressive process. Let us call the first the "personal ideal type" and the second the "material" or "course-of-action *type*." [45] Certainly an inner relation exists between these two. I cannot, for instance, define the ideal type of a postal clerk without first having in mind a definition of his job. The latter is a course-of-action type, which is, of course, an objective context of meaning. Once I am clear as to the course-of-action type, I can construct the personal ideal type, that is "the person who performs this job." And, in doing so, I imagine the corresponding subjective meaning-contexts which would be in his mind, the subjective contexts that would have to be adequate to the objective

44. [*Idealtypus fremden menschlichen Verhaltens:* literally, "ideal type of the human behavior of another person."]
45. [Schutz also called this the "action-pattern type."]

contexts already defined. The personal ideal type is therefore *derivative,* and the course-of-action type can be considered quite independently as a purely objective context of meaning.

By looking at language we can see the personal ideal type in the very process of construction. I am referring to those nouns which are merely verbs erected into substantives. Thus every present participle is the personal typification of an act in progress, and every past participle is the ideal type of a completed act. Acting is that act maybe. Consequently, when I seek to understand another's behavior in ideal-typical fashion, a twofold method is available to me. I can begin with the finished act, then determine the type of action that produced it, and finally settle upon the type of person who must have acted in this way. Or I can reverse the process and, knowing the personal ideal type, deduce the corresponding act. We have, therefore, to deal with two different problems. One problem concerns which aspects of a finished act [46] are selected as typical and how we deduce the personal type from the course-of-action type. The other problem concerns how we deduce specific actions from a given personal ideal type. The first question is a general question about the genesis of the typical. It has to do with the constitution of ideal types—whether course-of-action types or personal types—from given concrete acts. The second question has to do with the deduction of an action from a personal ideal type, and we shall deal with it under the heading "the freedom of the personal ideal type."

Let us first clarify the point that the understanding of personal ideal types is based on the understanding of course-of-action types.

In the process of understanding a given performance via an ideal type, the interpreter must start with his own perceptions of someone else's manifest act. His goal is to discover the in-order-to or because-motives (whichever is convenient) behind that act. He does this by interpreting the act within an objective context of meaning in the sense that the same motive is assigned to any act that repeatedly achieves the same end through the same means. This motive is postulated as constant for the act regardless of who performs the act or what his subjective experiences are at the time. For a personal ideal type, therefore, there is one and only one typical motive for a typical act. Excluded from consideration when we think of the personal ideal type are such things as the individual's subjective experience of his act within his stream of consciousness, together with all the modifications of attention and all the influences from the background of his consciousness which such experiences may undergo. Ideal-typical under-

46. For the sake of convenience we are dealing here only with acts, but our remarks can be applied *pari passu* to products of all kinds and to their generation.

standing, then, characteristically deduces the in-order-to and because-motives of a manifest act by identifying the constantly achieved goal of that act. Since the act is by definition both repeatable and typical, so is the in-order-to motive. The next step is to postulate an agent behind the action, a person who, with a typical modification of attention, typically intends this typical act—in short, a personal ideal type.

The conscious processes of the personal ideal types are, therefore, logical constructions. They are deduced from the manifest act and are pictured as temporally prior to that act, in other words, in the pluperfect tense. The manifest act is then seen as the regular and repeatable result of these inferred conscious processes. It should be noted that the conscious processes themselves are conceived in a simplified and tailored form. They are lacking all the empty protentions and expectations that accompany real conscious experiences. It is not an open question as to whether the typical action will succeed in being a finished act. Such success has been built into it by definition. The ideal-typical actor never has the experience of choosing or of preferring one thing to another. Never does he hesitate or try to make up his mind whether to perform a typical or an atypical action. His motive is always perfectly straightforward and definite: the in-order-to motive of the action is the completed act on whose definition the whole typification is based. This completed act is at the same time the *major* goal of the actor's typical state of mind at that time. For if the act were merely a means to another goal, then it would be necessary for the interpreter to construct for his ideal actor another typical state of mind capable of planning out that wider goal. This would mean that the wider goal would have to become the objective meaning-context of primary importance from the interpreter's point of view. In other words, the wider goal would be the one in terms of which the act would be defined. Finally, all this will hold true for the construction of the genuine because-motive. This must be postulated in some typical experience or passage of experience that could have given rise to the in-order-to motive we have already constructed.

The following, then, is the way in which a personal ideal type is constructed: The existence of a person is postulated whose actual living motive could be the objective context of meaning already chosen to define a typical action. This person must be one in whose consciousness the action in question could have been constructed step by step in polythetic Acts. He must be the person whose own lived experiences provide the subjective context of meaning which corresponds to the objective context, the action which corresponds to the act.

And now we see the basic reason why, in both the social sciences and the everyday understanding of another's behavior, we can ignore the "total action" in the sense that the latter concept includes the ultimate roots of the action in the person's consciousness. The technique of constructing personal ideal types consists in postulating persons who can be motivated by the already defined material ideal type. The manifest act or external course of action which the observer sees as a unity is changed back into a subjective context of meaning and is inserted into the consciousness of the personal ideal type. But the unity of this subjective context derives entirely from the original objective context of meaning, the context of meaning which is the very basis of the personal ideal type. And we cannot too strongly emphasize that this unity of "the other person's action" is only a cross-section which the observer lifts out of its total factual context. What is thus defined in abstraction as the unity of the other person's act will depend on the point of view of the observer, which will vary in turn with his interests and his problems. This point of view will determine both the meaning which the observer gives to his own perceptions of the act and the typical motive which he assigns to it. But for every such typical motive, for every such frozen cross-section of consciousness, there is a corresponding personal ideal type which could be subjectively motivated in the manner in question. Therefore, the personal ideal type is itself always determined by the interpreter's point of view. *It is a function of the very question it seeks to answer.* It is dependent upon the objective context of meaning, which it merely translates into subjective terms and then personifies.

It is precisely this point which the theory of ideal types overlooks. It fails to take into account the fact that the personal ideal type is *by definition* one who acts in such and such a way and has such and such experiences. Rather, it reverses the direction of the inference and, starting out with the personal ideal type as a "free entity," seeks to "discover" what the latter means by acting in such and such a manner. Moreover, it is naïve enough to suppose that the boundaries of the act can be objectively demarcated while the actor is at the same time free to give the act any meaning he chooses! Interpretation of this kind, whether carried on in everyday life or in sociology, has at least the advantage of a neat division of labor. While leaving to the personal ideal type the function of "attaching a meaning" to its action, it reserves to itself the privilege of saying what that meaning is. Contradictions are avoided by making sure that the personal ideal type is so constructed that it must subjectively attach to its acts precisely the meaning that the interpreter is looking for. The illusion consists in regarding the personal ideal type as a real person, whereas actually it is only a shadow person. It "lives" in a never-never temporal dimension that no one could ever experience. It lives through just the minimum number of subjective experiences to qualify it as the author of the given act. To be sure, it must be pictured as "free"; otherwise it could hardly bestow "its own" meaning to the course of action in question. However, its freedom is only apparent, because the original act which the social scientist or the common-sense observer takes as his datum already has ready-made and unambiguous in-order-to and because-motives built into it by definition. The ideal type of the actor is, then, that of the person who by definition experiences polythetically the act already conceived monothetically by the social scientist. And so anything the social scientist permits his ideal type to report about its actions is only a prophecy after the event.

The illusion of the "freedom" of the personal ideal type arises from the fact that we do ask what kind of future acts we can expect from a given personal ideal type. How behavior ascribed to a given ideal type will be carried out remains a matter of conjecture and of "wait and see." To all appearances the awaited action, already defined with respect to its in-order-to and because-motives, may or may not occur. Suppose I call *A*, a man I know, a miser, thereby identifying him with a personal ideal type. Still, it remains an open question whether he will give a donation to charity. However, strictly speaking, the real question here is not whether the ideal type's action is free and less than determinate. Rather, it is whether *A* is really a miser at all. To be sure, even the determination of the motives of the ideal type must be subjected to the test of indirect, and ultimately of direct, social experience. And even in direct social encounters, as we have seen, the interpretive schemes used in understanding the other person are constantly changing with experience. However, in the face-to-face relationship a real, free, enduring human being is present in person. But the contemporary appears to us in principle in the form of an ideal type with neither freedom nor duration. For, as we have seen, the mere fact that we can make only probable statements about a contemporary conceived under the heading of an ideal type does not imply that the ideal type itself is free. It is important to realize that the person so conceived is behaving *as* a type only insofar as he acts in the stipulated manner. In other situations his behavior need by no means be typical. When Molière involves Harpagon in a love affair, it does not follow that the latter's love behavior, whether individual or typical, can be predicted with accuracy from the fact that he is a tightwad. Rather, his love relationships will be in another category—they will be *type-transcendent*. Even so, once Harpagon is recognized as a typical miser, a number of interpretive schemes become immediately applicable to him. To put it in a more general way, the personal type can be, and usually is, constructed on the basis of other ideal types already known to the interpreter. Should the situation under interpretation change, the interpreter can always fall back on these ready-made ideal types in the background and substitute one of them for the ideal type with which he started. But he usually does this without full awareness; and because he uses the old name for the new ideal type, he tends naïvely to identify the new ideal type with the old. And suddenly it seems as if the ideal type has taken on a kind of freedom and has become a real person rather than an abstract, timeless concept. Suddenly it seems able to choose between alternatives, and the illusion is produced that one hardly knows what to expect of the ideal type. However, this illusion of ideal-typical conduct that is carried out freely cannot stand up under logical analysis. Wherever it turns up, it is a sign that the interpreter has not carried all the way the alteration in logical construct that is called for by his new problem. Of course, the illusion itself, arising as it does from the interpreter's confusion about what he is doing, can cause him to make real mistakes in action. The story of Pygmalion, whose statues came to life, is a parable illustrating the lengths to which such naïve interpretive ventures can go.

But this problem is by no means confined to interpretation of the world of contemporaries. The direct observer, and even more the participant in a social relationship, brings to the situation a whole armory of interpretive schemes for understanding others. Included will be schemes derived from his direct social experience, from his experience of his contemporaries, and from his experience of his predecessors. He will have on hand both personal types and course-of-action types. By constantly scrutinizing, shuffling, and juxtaposing these ideal types, he can keep up with the many changes occurring in the other person and thus grasp him in his living reality. (Of course this kind of personal understanding is usually possible only in the direct We-relationship and as a result of the living intentionality peculiar to that intimate situation.)

There are vast problems here for sociological research, but they are beyond the scope of this treatise. It is our hope to deal with them on a future occasion in a detailed study of the *sociological person*.

We can, however, briefly demonstrate the peculiar way in which the ideal types vary and shift in accordance with the observer's point of view, the questions he is asking, and the total complex of his experience. If I observe, or even hear about, a man tightening a nut, my first interpretive scheme will picture him as joining together two parts of an apparatus with a wrench. The further information that the event is taking place in an automobile factory permits me to place the operation within the total context of "automobile manufacturing." If I know in addition that the man is an auto worker, then I can assume a great deal about him, for instance, that he comes to work every morning and goes home every night, that he picks up his check every payday, and so on. I can then bring him into a wider context of meaning by applying to him the ideal type "urban worker" or, more specifically, "Berlin worker of the year 1931." And once I have established the fact that the man is a German and a Berliner, then all the corresponding interpretive schemes become applicable to him. Obviously I can increase indefinitely the number of the schemes I apply, depending on the questions I choose to ask and the particular kind of interest that lies behind them. Suppose, now, that my interest is in the worker's politics or in his religion. I can hardly extract such information from the purely factual and external interpretive schemes I have so far established. From this point on, lacking additional data, any ideal type I set up will be on shaky grounds. Suppose I say, "Workers of this kind typically vote Social Democratic." My judgment would be based on the statistical information that in the last election the majority of the Berlin workers voted for the party in question. However, what I do not know is that this particular worker belonged to the majority; all I have is a probability. The probability would increase if I knew that the worker was a union member or that he carried a party card. We have already noted that every interpretation based on ideal-typical construction is only probable. It is possible, for instance, that the man turning the nut in front of me is not a worker at all but an engineer or a student on a summer job. In this case, of course, all the deductions I have made about him by using the ideal type "Berlin worker" are false. But this only shows that every ideal-typical construction is determined by the limits of the observer's knowledge at the time. The example we have given shows clearly how meaning-context, interpretive scheme, and ideal type are correlated. They are all expressions of a common problem, *the problem of relevance.*

Now the ideal types that are continually being constructed in everyday life are subject to constant adjustment and revision on the basis of the observer's experience, whether the latter is direct or indirect. As for direct social experience, the knowledge of the contents of the other person's consciousness acquired in the We-relationship modifies the ideal-typical interpretive schemes whether the latter are positional or neutralizing. All our knowledge of our fellow men is in the last analysis based on personal experience. Ideal-typical knowledge of our contemporaries, on the other hand, is not concerned with the other person in his given concrete immediacy but in what he is, in the characteristics he has in common with others. To interpret the behavior of a contemporary as typical means to explain it as the behavior of a "man like that one," of "one of them." Orientation toward the world of contemporaries is necessarily and always "They-orientation."

39. Degrees of Anonymity in the World of Contemporaries. The Concreteness of the Ideal Type

THE THEY-ORIENTATION is the pure form [47] of understanding the contemporary in a predicative fashion, that is, in terms of his typical characteristics. Acts of They-orientation are, therefore, intentionally directed toward another person imagined as existing at the same time as oneself but conceived in terms of an ideal type. And just as in the cases of the Thou-orientation and the We-relationship, so also with the They-orientation can we speak of different *stages of concretization* and *actualization*.

In order to distinguish from one another the various stages of concretization of the We-relationship, we established as our criterion the degree of closeness to direct experience. We cannot use this criterion within the They-orientation. The reason is that the latter possesses by definition a high degree of remoteness from direct experience, and the other self which is its object possesses a correspondingly higher degree of anonymity.

It is precisely this degree of anonymity which we now offer as the criterion for distinguishing between the different levels of concretization and actualization that occur in the They-orientation. The more anonymous the personal ideal type applied in the They-orientation, the greater is the use made of objective meaning-contexts instead of subjective ones, and likewise, we shall find, the more are lower-level personal ideal types and objective meaning-contexts pregiven. (The latter have in turn been derived from other stages of concretization of the They-orientation.)

Let us get clear as to just what we mean by the anonymity of the ideal type in the world of contemporaries. The pure Thou-orientation consists of mere awareness of the existence of the other person, leaving aside all questions concerning the characteristics of that person. On the other hand, the pure They-orientation is based on the presupposition of such characteristics in the form of a type. Since these characteristics are genuinely typical, they can in principle be presupposed again and again. Of course, whenever I posit such typical characteristics, I assume that they now exist or did once exist. However, this does not mean that I am thinking of them as existing in a particular person in a particular time and place. The contemporary

47. [*Die Leerform*, literally, "the empty form."]

alter ego is therefore anonymous in the sense that its existence is only the individuation of a type, an individuation which is merely supposable or possible. Now since the very existence of my contemporary is always less than certain, any attempt on my part to reach out to him or influence him may fall short of its mark, and, of course, I am aware of this fact.

The concept which we have been analyzing is the concept of the anonymity of the partner in the world of contemporaries. It is crucial to the understanding of the nature of the indirect social relationship. We shall presently be discussing the important consequences of this concept for our over-all problem. But first we must deal with certain other meanings of anonymity.

Anonymity may mean the generality of the typifying scheme. If the scheme is derived from the characteristics of a particular person, then we speak of it as relatively concrete and rich in specific content. But if the scheme is derived from the characteristics of a previously constructed personal type, then we speak of it as relatively more anonymous. We can say, then, that the concreteness of the ideal type is inversely proportional to the level of generality of the past experiences out of which it is constructed. The deeper basis for this is the fact that, as the interpreter falls back on lower- and lower-level ideal types, he must take more and more for granted. He can hardly examine all these more general ideal types in detail but must take them in at a glance, being content with a vague picture. The more dependent he is on such ready-made types in the construction of his own ideal type, the vaguer will be his account of the latter. This becomes immediately obvious when we try to analyze such culture objects as the state, economy, law, art, and so on.

The degree of concreteness of an ideal type also varies directly with the convertibility of its corresponding They-relationship into a We-relationship. To the extent that I conceive the conscious states of my ideal type as belonging to one or more real persons with whom I could have a We-relationship, to that extent is my ideal type more concrete and less anonymous. It is the case, of course, that the conscious states of my contemporary are in principle mere objects of thought for me, not objects of lived experience. Nevertheless, the concreteness of my ideal type of him will be the greater depending on the ease with which I can convert the corresponding indirect orientation into a direct one, the ease with which I can shift from a merely conceptual and predicative understanding to an immediate grasp of the person himself. The personal ideal type is therefore less anonymous the closer it is to the world of directly experienced social reality. The following two examples should illustrate this point.

I think about N, my absent friend, assuming toward him the usual They-orientation. Knowing that he is at the moment facing a difficult decision, I construct from my past direct experiences of him the personal ideal type "my friend N" or a course-of-action type "how N acts in the face of difficult decisions." This ideal type is essentially They-oriented: "People *like* N act in such and such a way when facing difficult decisions." Nevertheless, the ideal type "my friend N" is still extremely concrete, and my indirect relationship to him can, technical difficulties aside, at any moment be changed into a direct one. The very validity of the ideal type, as well as its verifiability, is based on this possibility.

Our second example: My friend A tells me about X, a person he has recently met but whom I do not know myself. He "gives me a picture" of X, drawing upon his own direct experience to fashion an ideal type for me. Now of course the picture he sketches will be determined by the way in which he looks back on his meeting with X, and this in turn will depend on his interests and the modifications of his attention. But now I will take the ideal type A has constructed for me and make my own ideal type out of it on the basis of my own past experience. But since my interests and my modifications of attention will be radically different, so will my ideal type. Moreover, my friend A has made the judgment resulting in his ideal type in full and explicit clarity, whereas I necessarily have made mine only in a confused way.[48] I may even question A's judgment. Knowing that he is emotional, I may not accept his characterization of X, thinking, "That's the way A always sees people."

These two examples should be enough to indicate how complicated are the problems of indirect social understanding. Both involve relatively concrete typifications based on my direct experience of my fellow men. The direct experience involved is either my own or that of an intermediary. But in both cases the objective meaning-contexts which I use to understand N and X will show the effects of the original subjective meaning-contexts in the minds of those two real individuals.

Let us call an ideal type of this kind a "characterological" type. It should be distinguished from a "habitual" type, which defines a con-

---

48. This point is made by Husserl in his *Formal and Transcendental Logic*, pp. 51 and 52, where he discusses the "understanding-after" which characterizes our grasp of other people's judgments: "Accordingly, we must distinguish between another's non-explicit judgment indicated by an explicitly stated linguistic proposition on the one hand, and a corresponding explicit judgment or clarification of what was meant on the other hand. . . ." "If it is a matter of another person's judgment, and I do not share his belief, then what I have before me is a mere representation of that belief as 'the belief that such and such is the case.'"

temporary solely in terms of his function. The concept of a postal clerk, for instance, is a habitual type. The postal clerk is by definition "he who forwards the mail," or, in the example we used, *my* mail. A habitual type is therefore less concrete than a characterological type. It is based on a course-of-action type which it presupposes and refers to. The characterological type, on the other hand, presupposes and refers to a real person whom I could meet face to face. Furthermore, the habitual type is more anonymous. As a matter of fact, when I drop the letter in the box, I don't even need to have in mind the personal type "postal clerk" in the sense of thinking of an individual who has certain specific subjective meaning-contexts in mind as he goes about his work, such as thinking of receiving payment. The only thing relevant for me in this situation is the *process* of forwarding, and I merely "hang" this on the abstract type "postal clerk." And I don't even have to think of a postal clerk as such as I mail the letter. It is enough for me to know that somehow it will reach its destination.[49]

Under the heading of habitual types come those types which deal with the "behaving" or the "habit." [50] The fixation in conceptual form of external modes of behavior or sequences of action,[51] derived from either direct or indirect observation, leads to a catalogue of material course-of-action types, to which corresponding personal types are then adjoined. But these course-of-action types can be of different degrees of generality: they can be more or less "standardized," that is, they can be derived from behavior of greater or lesser statistical frequency. The ideality of the personal ideal type based on such frequency types (in other words, the irreducibility of the kinds of behavior to the conscious experiences of real other people) is, however, in principle independent of the degree of generality of the behavior itself.[52] On the other hand, the "standardization" of typified behavior can in turn refer back to a previously constructed personal ideal type. Let us take as an example Weber's "traditional behavior," "the great bulk of all everyday action to which people have become habitually accustomed," [53] which is already based on the previously constructed personal ideal type of the man who acts according to custom; and, as an additional example, let us take all behavior oriented to the validity of an order. This latter means,

49. Just as I can use the telephone without knowing *how* it works. See above, sec. 17, p. 88.

50. [Schutz has these words in English as "the 'behave' " and "the 'habit.' "]

51. For a critique of behaviorism as a sociological method see Mises, "Begreifen und Verstehen," *Schmollers Jahrbuch*, LIV, 139 ff.

52. We shall discuss this problem in greater detail when we take up the relation between causal adequacy and meaning-adequacy in Chap. 5. Cf. sec. 46, p. 234.

53. *Wirtschaft und Gesellschaft*, p. 12 [E.T., p. 116].

in terms of the constitution of ideal types of contemporaries, that the valid order functions as an interpretive scheme for them. It establishes as required conduct definite patterns of action and definite personal ideal types, to the extent that the person accepting such standard types and orienting himself to them can be assured that his behavior will be adequately interpreted by contemporaries oriented to the same order. However, every such interpretation by contemporaries

> must take account of a fundamentally important fact. These concepts of collective entities, which are found both in common sense and in juristic and other technical forms of thought, have a meaning in the minds of individual persons . . . as something with normative authority. This is true not only of judges and officials, but of ordinary private individuals as well . . . ; such ideas have a powerful, often a decisive, influence on the course of action of real individuals.[54]

This cursory observation, however, is by no means an exhaustive account of the situation which involves a valid order; for example, the coercive apparatus that goes along with every regulative order is of the greatest relevance from the point of view of sociology.[55] The point of importance for us here is that even behavior that is oriented to the validity of an order is, in our sense of the term, habitual behavior. Our concept of the habitual is, therefore, broader than that found in ordinary usage.

There are other ideal types that are characterized by a still greater degree of anonymity than the habitual ideal types. The first group of these consists of the so-called "social collectives," all of which are constructs referring to the world of contemporaries.[56]

This large class contains ideal types of quite different degrees of anonymity. The board of directors of a given corporation or the United States Senate are relatively concrete ideal types, and the number of other ideal types which they presuppose is quite limited. But we frequently use sentences in which ideal types like "the state," "the press," "the economy," "the nation," "the people," or perhaps "the

---

54. *Ibid.*, p. 7 [E.T., p. 102]. But cf. Kelsen's critique of this position in his work, *Der soziologische und juristische Staatsbegriff* (Tübingen, 1922), pp. 156 ff.

55. On this point see Voegelin's excellent study, "Die Einheit des Rechtes und das soziale Sinngebilde Staat," *Internationale Zeitschrift für die Theorie des Rechts*, IV (1930), pp. 58–89, esp. pp. 71 ff.

56. The fact that, in the notion of the social collective, concepts of a metaphysical, axiological, and epistemological nature are presupposed is something lying outside the scope of this study. On this point we can only refer the reader to Felix Kaufmann's "Soziale Kollektiva," in *Zeitschrift für Nationalökonomie*, which we have already quoted repeatedly.

working class" [57] appear as grammatical subjects. In doing this, we naturally tend to personify these abstractions, treating them as if they were real persons known in indirect social experience. But we are here indulging in an anthropomorphism. Actually these ideal types are absolutely anonymous. Any attribution of behavior we make to the type permits no inference whatever as to a corresponding subjective meaning-context in the mind of a contemporary actor. "For the subjective interpretation [58] of action in sociological work," says Max Weber,

> these collectivities must be treated as solely the resultants and modes of organization of the particular acts of individual persons, since these alone can be treated as agents in a course of subjectively understandable action. . . . For sociological purposes . . . there is no such thing as a collective personality which "acts." When reference is made in a sociological context to a "state," a "nation," a "corporation," a "family" or an "army corps," or to similar collectivities, what is meant is, on the contrary, *only* a certain kind of development of actual or possible social actions of the individual persons.[59]

In fact, every "action" of the state can be reduced to the actions of its functionaries, whom we can apprehend by means of personal ideal types and toward whom we can assume a They-orientation, regarding them as our contemporaries. From the sociological point of view, therefore, the term "state" is merely an abbreviation for a highly complex network of interdependent personal ideal types. When we speak of any collectivity as "acting," we take this complex structural arrangement for granted.[60] We then proceed to attribute the objective meaning-contexts, in terms of which we understand the anonymous acts of the functionaries, to the personal ideal type of the social collective. We do this in a manner that parallels our interpretation of individual actions by means of typical conscious experiences in the minds of typical actors. But when we proceed in this way, we forget that, whereas the conscious experiences of typical individuals are quite conceivable, the conscious experiences of a collective are not. What is lacking, therefore, in the concept of the "action" of a collective is precisely this subjective meaning-context as something that is even

---

57. For an analysis of such concepts we recommend Mises' critique of the concept of class (*Die Gemeinwirtschaft* [Jena, 1922], pp. 316 f.). [The English reader is referred to Mises' *Socialism* (New Haven, 1951), pp. 328–51, which is the translation of this, and to his *Theory and History* (New Haven, 1957), pp. 112 ff. and 142 ff.]

58. [*Verstehende Deutung.*]

59. *Wirtschaft und Gesellschaft*, pp. 6 f. [E.T., p. 101].

60. In connection with this problem see Kelsen's critique of Weber's views in his *Allgemeine Staatslehre* (Berlin, 1925), pp. 19 ff., pp. 66–79; and, for the concept of functionary, see pp. 262–70.

conceivable. That people should ever have been led to take such a metaphor literally can only be explained psychologically, that is, attributed to the fact that certain value systems have been at work here.

Needless to say, our reduction of statements about social collectives to personal ideal typifications does not foreclose a sociological analysis of these constructs. On the contrary, such an analysis is one of the most important tasks of sociology. Only a sociological theory of construct formation can bring to completion our previously postulated theory of the forms of the social world. Such a theory will have as its primary task the description of the stratification of social collectivities in terms of their relative anonymity or concreteness. Here it will be crucial to determine whether a social collectivity is essentially based on a direct or an indirect social relationship, or possibly on a relationship of both kinds, existing between the component individuals. It will also be necessary to study the exact sense, if any, in which a subjective meaning-context can be ascribed to a social collectivity. This will involve determining whether, by the subjective meaning-contexts of a collectivity, we do not really mean those of its functionaries. This is the problem of the responsibility of officials, a question of major importance in the fields of constitutional and international law.[61] Another question deserving investigation is whether and to what extent the concept of social collectivity can serve as a scheme of interpretation for the actions of contemporaries, since it is itself a function of certain objective standards common to a certain group. Such standards may be matters of habitual conduct, of traditional attitude, of belief in the validity of some order or norm, and they may be not only taken for granted but obeyed. Here, indeed, is one legitimate sense in which one can speak of the subjective meaning of a social collectivity. Even so, there are so many complexities in this way of speaking that we are in danger of confusing one problem with another and one type with another. This in turn may lead us once again into the illusion that we have discovered a type-transcending behavior and revive the discredited notion of a "free" type.[62]

What we have said about social collectivities holds true for languages as well. Here, too, a correlation can be set up between the product and that which produces it; we can hypostatize, for instance, an ideal anonymous "German speaker" corresponding to the German language. But here, as in the case we just discussed, we must beware

61. Cf. Kelsen, op. cit., pp. 48 ff., 65 ff., 310 f.
62. In his essay on Stammler, Max Weber demonstrated that in the concept "United States of America" there is a sixfold overlaying and confusion of types (Gesammelte Aufsätze zur Wissenschaftslehre, pp. 348 f.).

of treating this typical speaker as a real individual with his own subjective contexts of meaning. It is quite illegitimate, for instance, to speak of an "objective language spirit," [63] at least in the social sciences.[64] Whether such concepts are permissible in other disciplines is not for us to say here.

These observations apply as well to all culture objects. To the ideal objectivity of a culture construct there corresponds no subjective meaning-context in the mind of a real individual whom we could meet face to face. Rather, corresponding to the objective meaning-context of the culture object we always find an abstract and anonymous personal ideal type of its producer toward which we characteristically assume a They-orientation.

Finally, this applies also to all artifacts such as tools and utensils. But to understand a tool, we need not only the ideal type of its producer but the ideal type of its user, and both will be absolutely anonymous. Whoever uses the tool will bring about typical results. A tool is a thing-in-order-to; it serves a purpose, and for the sake of this purpose it was produced. Tools are, therefore, results of past human acts and means toward the future realization of aims. One can, then, conceive the "meaning" of the tool in terms of the means-end relation. But from this objective meaning-context, that is, from the means-end relation in terms of which the tool is understood, one can deduce the ideal type of user or producer without thinking of them as real individual people. In my opinion it is erroneous to speak, as Sander does, of the meaning of a tool in the same sense that one speaks of the meaning of an action.[65]

The artifact is the final member of the series of progressive anonymizations marking the typifying construction of the social world. We started out with the immediate grasp of another person which we have in the Thou-relationship, the experience upon which every ideal type is ultimately based. We then studied the characterological and habitual ideal types, the social collectivity, and, finally, the tool. Although these examples do not exhaust all the members of the series, they do illustrate their progressive anonymization and corresponding gradual loss of concreteness.

63. Cf. Vossler, *Geist und Kultur in der Sprache* (Heidelberg, 1925), pp. 153 f. [E.T., Oscar Oeser, *The Spirit of Language in Civilization* (London, 1932), p. 138.]

64. Felix Kaufmann, *Strafrechtsschuld*, p. 39.

65. "Gegenstand der reinen Gesellschaftslehre," *Archiv für Sozialwissenschaften*, LIV, p. 370: "By 'artifacts' we mean all physical things which owe their origin to human acts, which, in other words, are signs of a 'meaning' which they designate."

40. Social Relationships between Contemporaries and Indirect Social Observation

As SOCIAL RELATIONSHIPS in the face-to-face situation are based on the pure Thou-orientation, so social relationships between contemporaries are based on the pure They-orientation. But the situation has now changed. In the face-to-face situation the partners look into each other and are mutually sensitive to each other's responses. This is not the case in relationships between contemporaries. Here each partner has to be content with the probability that the other, to whom he is oriented by means of an anonymous type, will respond with the same kind of orientation. And so an element of doubt enters into every such relationship.

When I board a train, for instance, I orient myself to the fact that the engineer in charge can be trusted to get me to my destination. My relationship to him is a They-relationship at this time, merely because my ideal type "railroad engineer" means by definition "one who gets passengers like myself to their destination." It is therefore characteristic of my social relationships with my contemporaries that the orientation by means of ideal types is mutual. Corresponding to my ideal type "engineer" there is the engineer's ideal type "passenger." Taking up mutual They-orientations, we think of each other as "one of them." [66]

I am not therefore apprehended by my partner in the They-relationship as a real living person. From this it follows that I can expect from him only a typical understanding of my behavior.

A social relationship between contemporaries, therefore, consists in this: Each of the partners apprehends the other by means of an ideal type; each of the partners is aware of this mutual apprehension; and each expects that the other's interpretive scheme will be congruent with his own. The They-relationship here stands in sharp contrast to the face-to-face situation. In the face-to-face situation my partner and I are sensitively aware of the nuances of each other's subjective

66. In situations like this, the gradual transition from the world of direct social experience to the world of contemporaries is very visible. As a theatergoer, I am important to the actor only as a member of the public. The author who is publishing a book thinks of his reader only as the typical reader, choosing his expressive schemes according to what he imagines are the reader's preconceived ideas and interpretive habits. It would be the task of a theory of the forms of the social world to describe and elucidate all these situations with respect to their content, that is, the proportions of direct and indirect social experience to be found in them. The true precursor of such a theory was no doubt Wiese's theory of relationship.

experiences. But in the They-relationship this is replaced by the assumption of a shared interpretive scheme. Now, even though I, on my side, make this assumption, I cannot verify it. I do, however, have more reason to expect an adequate response from my partner, the more standardized is the scheme which I impute to him. This is the case with schemes derived from law, state, tradition, and systems of order of all kinds, and especially with schemes based on the means-end relation, in short, with what Weber calls "rational" interpretive schemes.[67]

These properties of social relationships between contemporaries have important consequences.

First of all, because of the element of chance that is always present, I cannot even be sure that the relationship exists until it has already been tried out, so to speak. Only retrospectively can I know whether my ideal type of my partner was adequate to him, either in the sense of meaning-adequacy or causal adequacy. This again differs from the face-to-face situation, where I can constantly correct my own responses to my partner. Another consequence is that the only in-order-to and because-motives of my partner that I can take into account in making my own plans of action are the motives I have already postulated for him in constructing my ideal type of him. To be sure, in the They-orientation, as in the face-to-face situation, I set up my project of action in such a way that my partner's because-motives are included in my own in-order-to motives; and I proceed in the expectation that his interpretive scheme of me as ideal type is adequate to mine of him as ideal type. If the partner in question is a postal clerk, for instance, the mere fact that my stamped letter lies before him will ordinarily become a genuine because-motive for his proceeding to forward it. Yet I cannot be sure of this. It may happen that there is a slip-up and that he will misdirect the letter before him, thereby causing it to be lost; to this extent he will fall short, of course, of my personal ideal type of a postal clerk. And this, in turn, of course, may have happened because he misinterpreted the address I put on the letter. All this results from the fact that we are not in direct touch with each other, as in the face-to-face situation.

In the face-to-face situation the partners are constantly revising and enlarging their knowledge of each other. This is not true in the same sense of the They-relationship. Certainly it is true that my knowledge of the world of my contemporaries is constantly being enlarged and replenished through every new experience from whatever part of the social world the latter may come. Furthermore, my

67. On this concept see below, Chap. 5, sec. 48.

ideal-typical schemes will always be changing in accordance with every shift in my situation. But all such modifications will be within a very narrow range so long as the original situation and my interest in it remain fairly even.

In the We-relationship I assume that your environment is identical with my own in all its variations. If I have any doubt about it, I can check on my assumption simply by pointing and asking you if that is what you mean. Such an identification is out of the question in the They-relationship. Nevertheless I assume, if you are my contemporary, that your environment can be understood by means of principles of comprehension drawn from my own. But even here the assumption is much less probable than it would be if we were face to face.

However, my environment [68] also includes sign systems, and in the They-relationship also I use these as both expressive and interpretive schemes. Here again the degree of anonymity is of major importance. The more anonymous my partner is, the more "objectively" must I use the signs. I cannot assume, for instance, that my partner in a They-relationship will necessarily grasp the particular significance I am attaching to my words, or the broader context of what I am saying, unless I explicitly clue him in. As a result, I do not know, during the process of choosing my words, whether I am being understood or not. This explains why I cannot immediately be questioned as to what I mean and possibly correct any misunderstandings. In indirect social experience there is only one way to "question a partner as to what he means," and that is to use a dictionary—unless, of course, I decide to go to see him or call him up; but in this case I have left the They-relationship behind and have initiated a face-to-face situation. As a matter of fact, any They-relationship characterized by a relatively low degree of anonymity can be transformed into a face-to-face situation by means of passing through various intermediate stages.[69]

In the world of direct social experience there is a radical difference between *participation* and *observation*. This difference disappears

68. In our sense of the word. See above, sec. 34, p. 170.
69. One example of such an intermediate stage is correspondence, which Simmel has so masterfully contrasted with speech: "One may say that, whereas speech reveals the secret of the speaker by means of all that surrounds it—which is visible but not audible, and which also includes the imponderables of the speaker himself—the letter conceals this secret. For this reason, the letter is clearer than speech where the secret of the other is *not* the issue; but where it *is* the issue, the letter is more ambiguous. By the 'secret of the other' I understand his moods and qualities of being, which cannot be expressed logically, but on which we nevertheless fall back innumerable times, even if only in order to understand the actual significance of quite concrete utterances" (*Soziologie*, 2d ed. [Munich, 1922], p. 286) [E.T., Kurt H. Wolff, *The Sociology of Georg Simmel* (Glencoe, Ill., 1950)].

when we get into the world of contemporaries. The reason is that in the latter we never encounter real living people at all. In that world, whether we are participants or observers, we are dealing only with ideal types. Our whole experience is in the mode of the "They." Nevertheless, the ideal type of an observer in the world of contemporaries necessarily differs from the ideal type of a participant in that same world. For, as we have noted, the ideal type varies with the interests of the person who constructs it. The latter's aim is always to visualize a certain objective meaning-context, which he already grasps, as someone else's subjective context of meaning. Now, the total context of experience with which the observer approaches the other person differs from that of the participant. Likewise his interests are radically different. His ideal type can be more or less detailed, more concrete or more formalized, of a greater or lesser degree of anonymity. Whatever the case, it will always be different.

Now, it may be that what is above all interesting to the observer of a social relationship among contemporaries is the conscious experiences of the two participants. Or it may be the course of the relationship. If the former is the case, the observer will either construct or draw from his past experience an ideal type equipped with those conscious experiences which anyone in such a relationship would necessarily observe in himself. The observer then "identifies" himself with this ideal type; he lives it out, imagining himself involved in just this situation. He can then imagine himself having all those experiences which are by definition proper to the ideal type in question. He can also make definite statements about the nature of the relationship he is observing and about the interrelations between the corresponding ideal types that are involved. He can do this quite easily because, as a human being, he is more than just an observer since he himself has in the past been involved in innumerable social relationships, direct and indirect. He may indeed have had such relationships with the very persons he is now observing. Indeed, he may even now be involved in a direct Thou-orientation with one of these persons. Such cases as the last are especially frequent.

Observation of the social behavior of another involves the very real danger that the observer will naïvely substitute his own ideal types for those in the minds of his subject. The danger becomes acute when the observer, instead of being directly attentive to the person observed, thinks of the latter as a "case history" of such and such an abstractly defined type of conduct. Here not only may the observer be using the wrong ideal type to understand his subject's behavior, but he may never discover his error because he never confronts his subject as a real person. Social observation thus tends to develop into second-order ideal-typical construction: the observed actor is himself an ideal type of the first order, and the presumed ideal type in terms of which the actor understands his partner is an ideal type of the second order. Both of these are logical constructions of the observer and are determined by his point of view.

This situation is very significant from the standpoint of every empirical social science involving indirect observation. Its ideal-typical concept formation underlies the principles of meaning-adequacy and causal adequacy which we have yet to discuss. Interpretive sociology, however, must go beyond this. It must construct personal ideal types for social actors that are compatible with those constructed by the latter's partners. This aim may be regarded as a postulate for interpretive sociology. Upon closer scrutiny, it reduces to a more basic principle—the postulate of meaning-adequacy. This postulate states that, given a social relationship between contemporaries, the personal ideal types of the partners and their typical conscious experiences must be congruent with one another and compatible with the ideal-typical relationship itself.

A good example of the type of clarification that is required lies in the field of legal sociology. This discipline encounters great difficulties when it seeks to formulate descriptions of legal relationships between various partners, e.g., legislator and interpreter of the law, executor and subject of the law. Legal sociology seeks to interpret these relationships in terms of the subjective meanings of the persons in question. But, in doing this, it confuses the ideal types in terms of which each of the persons imagines his real partner with the sociologist's own ideal types of the partner. There are only two possible ways to remedy this situation and make possible a genuine descriptive concept of the kind desired by legal sociologists. The first would be to fix from the beginning the standpoint from which the type is to be constructed. This would mean that the legal sociologist would identify himself with one of the actors, postulating as invariant not only the latter's acts but also his interpretive schemes of his partners. The sociologist would then have to regard the ideal-typical concepts so constructed as binding upon himself. If this were the procedure adopted, the kind of sociological concept used would be directly derived from the field of law itself: legislator, judge, lawyer, partner, verdict, execution, etc. The alternative would be to come up with a principle according to which these more general ideal types can be transformed into the individual ideal types which the partners have of each other in concrete situations.

In Chapter 5 we shall deal with the special systematic problems which arise when indirect social observation develops into social *science* as such.

[E] THE WORLD OF PREDECESSORS AND THE PROBLEM OF HISTORY

41. The Past as a Dimension of the Social World

THE WORLD OF predecessors does not present undue complications, and it can be dealt with briefly. Directness and indirectness of experience are to be found in this world, too, but in a fundamentally altered form. For instance, I may recollect a We-relationship or a They-relationship which I once had, and I may do so through step-by-step retracing or by total recall. If the original experience was that of a direct face-to-face relationship, it will remain such in reproduction. If it was indirect, it will remain indirect. But both of them will now bear the character of *pastness*. As a result, I now look at them from a different point of view. But there is a further modification which is quite important. When I was still undergoing these experiences, their future sections had not as yet transpired. I still was not sure how things would come out; I did not know, for instance, how my partner would respond to my actions. But now he has either reacted as I had hoped or he has disappointed me. His reaction, which I had anticipated in the future perfect tense, is now past, or perhaps it is taking place at this very moment. To be sure, it is still seen *as* an expectation but as an expectation *already* fulfilled or disappointed. As I say to myself, "I wanted such and such, but look what I got," it is obvious that the temporal structure is the same; but the temporal vantage point has shifted, and so has my interest in the situation.

We have already dealt with these problems, and it should not be necessary to recapitulate here the details of our conclusions.

What is of special concern to us, however, is that the line separating present social reality from the world of predecessors is fluid. Simply by looking at them in a different light, I can interpret my memories of people I have known directly or indirectly as if these memories belonged to the world of my predecessors. Yet such memories are not in the full sense experiences of my world of predecessors, for in each memory the sense of the simultaneity of the experiences of the partners in the We- or They-relationship is preserved. In other words, I remember that I was around at the time, that I was on the scene having my own experiences as my partner was having his.

I can define a predecessor as a person in the past not one of whose experiences overlaps in time with one of mine. The *pure* world of predecessors I can then define as entirely made up of such persons. The world of predecessors is what existed before I was born. It is this which determines its very nature. The world of predecessors is by definition over and done with. It has no open horizon toward the future. In the behavior of my predecessors there is nothing as yet undecided, uncertain, or awaiting fulfillment. I do not await the behavior of a predecessor. His behavior is essentially without any dimension of freedom and thus stands in contrast to the behavior of those with whom I am in immediate contact and even, to a certain extent, with the behavior of those who are merely my contemporaries. Relations between predecessors, since they are already past and hence fixed in themselves, require no further postulation of fixed ideal types in order to be understood.[70] I can, therefore, take up any kind of orientation toward my predecessors except one: I can never set out to influence them. Even the word "orientation" has a different meaning here: it is always passive. To say that an action of mine is oriented toward the action of one of my predecessors is to say that my action is influenced by his. Or, to put it another way, his action conceived in the pluperfect tense is the genuine because-motive of my own. I never influence my predecessors, they only influence me.[71] These remarks, of course, apply also to Weber's concept of traditional action.

In the world of predecessors, therefore, the distinction between social relationship and social observation does not apply. What at first glance may appear to be a social relationship between myself and one of my predecessors will always turn out to be a case of one-sided Other-orientation on my part. The cult of ancestor worship is a good example of such orientation toward the world of predecessors. But there is only one kind of situation in which I can meaningfully speak of a reciprocal interaction between myself and one of my predecessors. This is the situation in which he acts upon me and I respond by behaving in such a way that my conduct can only be explained as oriented to his act, having the latter as its because-motive. This would be the case, for instance, if he bequeathed some property to me.

There are corresponding peculiarities in the way in which we experience our predecessors. I can know a predecessor only if someone tells me about him or writes about him. Of course, this go-between can

70. To be sure, the world of predecessors can by its nature be known only through ideal types, but since past events are already completely fixed, the historical types in terms of which they are understood do not require a further act of fixing.

71. In the sense of the definition given above, sec. 30, p. 148.

be either a fellow man or a contemporary. For instance, my father may tell me about people now long dead and gone whom he remembers from his youth. The transition from the immediate present to the world of contemporaries is thus a continuous one. For my father is sitting across from me now, as he reminisces. His experiences, even though they are colored by pastness, are still the experiences of a person with whom I am now face to face. But for me those experiences are past beyond recall, because no moment of my life was contemporary with them; it is this which makes them truly part of the world of my predecessors. Even the past social experiences, direct or indirect, of another person are for me part of the world of predecessors, yet I apprehend them as if they were my own past social experience. For I apprehend them as the present subjective meaning-context of the person who is now telling me about them.

Second, I come to know the world of my predecessors through records and monuments. These have the status of signs, regardless of whether my predecessors intended them as signs for posterity or merely for their own contemporaries.

It is hardly necessary to remark that my orientation toward the world of my predecessors can be more or less concrete, more or less actualized. This follows from the structure of my experience (*Erfahrung*) of that world. Insofar as it derives from what my fellow men or contemporaries have told me, it will be determined in the first instance by the degree of concreteness that their original lived experience had. But it will then be further conditioned by the degree of concreteness of my own orientation toward them as narrators.

Since my knowledge of the world of predecessors comes to me through signs, what these signs signify is anonymous and detached from any stream of consciousness. However, I know that every sign has its author and that every author has his own thoughts and subjective experiences as he expresses himself through signs. It is therefore perfectly proper for me to ask myself what a given predecessor meant by expressing himself in such and such a way. Of course, in order to do this, I must project myself backward in time and imagine myself present while he spoke or wrote. Now, historical research does not take as its primary object the subjective experiences of the authors of source materials. Yet these sources refer throughout to the direct and indirect social experience of their authors. As a result, the objective content communicated by the sign has a greater or lesser concreteness. The procedure of historical research is at this point the same as that used in interpreting the words of someone who is speaking to me. In the latter case I gain through communication an indirect experience of what the speaker has experienced directly. In the same way, when I am reading a historical document, I can imagine myself face to face with its author and learning from him about his contemporaries; one by one his contemporaries take their places within my world of predecessors.

My world of predecessors is, throughout, the world of other people and not my world. Of course it contains within itself many levels of social experience of varying degrees of concreteness, and in this respect it is like my world of contemporaries. It also resembles my world of contemporaries in the sense that the people in it are known to me through ideal types. But this knowledge is in one important respect different.

My predecessor lived in an environment radically different not only from my own but from the environment which I ascribe to my contemporaries. When I apprehend a fellow man or a contemporary, I can always assume the presence of a common core of knowledge. The ideal types of the We- and They-relationships themselves presuppose this kernel of shared experience. That highly anonymous ideal type, "my contemporary," shares by definition with me in that equally anonymous ideal type, "contemporary civilization." Naturally this is lacking to my predecessor. The same experience would seem to him quite different in the context of the culture of his time. Strictly speaking, it is meaningless even to speak of it as "the same" experience. I can, however, identify it as "human experience": any experience of my predecessor is open to my interpretation in terms of the characteristics of human experience in *general*. In the words of Schiller,

> The uniformity and unchangeable unity of the laws of nature and of the human mind . . . constitute the reason why events of long ago happen again today, although in different circumstances, and the reason why from the most recent events light can be shed upon pre-historic times.[72]

What Schiller here calls, in the language of his time, the unchangeable unity of the human mind can be interpreted as the essence of human experience as such, something that necessarily transcends not only our own directly experienced and contemporary social worlds but the whole civilization of our times as well.

The schemes we use to interpret the world of our predecessors are necessarily different from the ones they used to interpret that world. If

72. In his essay, *Was heisst und zu welchem Ende studiert man Universalgeschichte?* Or, as Jacob Burckhardt has put it, "We, however, shall start out from the one point accessible to us, the one eternal centre of all things—man, suffering, striving, doing, as he is and was and ever shall be," *Weltgeschichtliche Betrachtungen* (Kröner-Ausgabe), p. 5 [E.T., *Force and Freedom*, ed. James H. Nichols (New York, 1943), pp. 81–82].

I wish to interpret the behavior of a contemporary, I can proceed with confidence on the assumption that his experiences will be pretty much like my own. But when it comes to understanding a predecessor, my chances of falling short of the mark are greatly increased. My interpretations cannot be other than vague and tentative. This is true even of the language and other symbols of a past age. To be sure, such objective sign systems are fixed by stipulation and therefore offer a relatively firm footing. However, I have no way of making sure that my own interpretive scheme coincides with my predecessor's expressive scheme when he made use of the signs in question. Satisfactory interpretation of signs used in the past is therefore always problematic. Think, for instance, how much controversy there has been over the "correct" interpretation of the works of Bach in terms of the "objectively given" system of musical notation. Even the history of philosophy is teeming with disagreements over the proper interpretation of terms used by philosophers in the past. This uncertainty is different in kind from the uncertainty we have about words and other signs used by our contemporaries, for we can always ask the latter what they mean and so settle the question once and for all.

While we can always get to know our consociates and our contemporaries better, this is not true in the same sense of our knowledge of our predecessors. Their experiences are over and done with, and we can get to know them better only in the sense of picking up more information about them. But the information was, so to speak, already there waiting to be picked up, and it is quite accidental that we have to acquire it bit by bit.

The main task of the science of history is to decide which events, acts, signs, and so on of all those found in the past are to be singled out for interpretation and systematized into something called "history." The famous discussion between Max Weber and Eduard Meyer [73] brought this whole problem to a head and, to a certain extent, clarified it. Since then the controversy over historicism has moved the entire theme into the foreground of interest.

Let us now point out some of the consequences of our findings concerning the world of predecessors.

The basic methodological problem of the historian is already set for him by that point of view which is his qua historian. This is the interest or purpose with which he approaches his task. History is thus

73. See Weber's *Gesammelte Aufsätze zur Wissenschaftslehre*, pp. 215–65. [Cf. "Critical Studies in the Logic of the Cultural Sciences, a Critique of Eduard Meyer's Methodological Views" in *Max Weber on the Methodology of the Social Sciences*, trans. and ed. by E. A. Shils and H. A. Finch (Glencoe, Ill., 1949), pp. 113–88.]

the same as any other field in that the angle of approach determines everything. The kind of interest the historian has depends, of course, on the time in which he himself lives and on his attitude toward his own age and toward the past age which is the object of his scrutiny. Just as the individual interprets his past experiences in different ways at different times, so the historian interprets past ages now in this way and now in that, looking at them from his own experience of the social world. This means that in the process of interpretation he will always be constructing new ideal types of both persons and actions, all in order to understand precisely the same facts. Into the historian's own picture of the social world, however, is incorporated his experience of the world of his contemporaries (or, as we say, the cultural context of his time) and also, indeed, his experience, whether prescientific or scientific, of his predecessors. Starting from this general picture as a vantage point, he focuses upon his specific problem, seeking to reconstruct what happened in the past. But he always seeks to "make sense" out of the past, that is, to describe it consistently with his total previous knowledge of the world of predecessors and of the world generally. Historicism is correct when it asserts that all of history conditions the point of view of the historian. But historicism falls into error when it gets out of its field and tries to reduce the nontemporal (or better, supertemporal) categories of ideal objects to historical categories. But these nontemporal categories are presupposed by the very objective contexts of meaning in terms of which we understand the world in general, including history. Historicism, when it goes to this extreme, simply cuts the ground from under its own feet.[74]

We can try to solve the problem of relevance by asking which acts were relevant to my predecessor, to his consociates, and to his contemporaries. But this approach only pushes the problem one step further back. For the historian can establish that a given act was the one regarded as relevant by someone in the past only if he resorts to a causal argument. That is, he must show that *since* the person had such and such a because-motive, *therefore* he must have regarded the act in question as relevant. But, as we have already shown, genuine because-motives are discovered as existing in the pluperfect mode, in other words, as preceding something else already known as past. But what is this something else? It can only be the actor's judgment of relevance itself! The historian, therefore, presupposes that he has already discovered the choice of goal. Now the historian can, in a

<hr />

74. For a treatment of the connection between historical writing and the concepts of the social sciences (and an accompanying critique of historicism) see Ludwig von Mises, "Soziologie und Geschichte," *Archiv für Sozialwissenschaften und Sozialpolitik*, LXI, 465–512, esp. 489 ff.

certain sense, identify himself with the personality out of the past whom he is studying and can ask what this person could have been intending to do just prior to the act in question. Or he can pose the more general question of how things would have turned out had event B occurred rather than event A. But what are the unspoken presuppositions lying behind such questions? The historian already knows perfectly well what the actor intended to do because he knows what he did in fact do. Furthermore, he knows the whole further course of historical events right down to the time he himself asked his question. Equipped with all this knowledge, he now projects himself back to a point of time prior to the moment of choice or prior to the moment of event A, as the case may be. Next he proceeds to ask, supposedly on the basis of his knowledge of the because-motive of the person "about to" act at that point, what purpose the latter could possibly have in mind. We encountered a similar problem before in our analysis of the problem of choice.[75] It will be remembered that we then identified as mere ex post facto explanations both the theory of a supposed choice between two open possibilities and the theory that the choice can be predicted from a knowledge of the genuine because-motive. We came to this conclusion as a result of our analysis of the nature of the genuine because-motive itself, during which we saw that the latter can be discovered only if we first know the whole course of events up to the immediate present. We must also have the same knowledge if we are to judge the relevance of a given event A for the later course of history. This is why only the past can be regarded as part of history, never the present. Whereas, in the present, all is pure process, every action is planned and takes place freely without any consciousness of a be-cause-motive on the part of the actor, there is in the past neither freedom nor probability, and it is at least in principle possible to discover any given action's genuine because-motive by seeking the latter in the events before that action.

If we look back at the stream of history, we shall see that it is a continuous manifold, similar in this respect to our own stream of consciousness. But in another respect the two are different, for history takes place in objective time, whereas consciousness takes place within the inner duration-flow of the individual.[76] The stream of history includes anonymous events, it knows coexistence and fixed loci in time. On the other hand, the stream of history *can* be reduced to the genuine experiences of other men, experiences which occur within the immediacy of individual streams of consciousness, experiences which

75. Sec. 11, p. 66.
76. Cf. G. Simmel, "Das Problem der historischen Zeit," *Philosophische Vorträge der Kantgesellschaft*, No. 12 (Berlin, 1916).

refer to consociates and contemporaries, experiences which take place within both We- and They-relationships. Meanwhile the cast of characters and the roles they play constantly change. As one generation gives place to the next, consociates become predecessors, successors become consociates. Some partners drop out of We-relationships and are replaced by others. In a sense, history itself can be regarded as one continuous We-relationship from the earliest days of mankind to the present, a relationship of variegated content and ever changing partners. This view of history is no mere metaphysics, although a metaphysics could no doubt be developed from it. Unless one accepts such a view, there is no reason to regard the world of our predecessors as one continuous world and in fact no reason to assert the unity of the social world. Indeed, our interpretation is the only one which leaves room for subjective meaning in history.

The starting point for historical interpretation may indeed be in the objective meaning of the human acts that have taken place. In that case, what we will have is a history of facts. But historical interpretation may also start out from the subjective meanings of actors in history, in which case the result will be a history of human behavior. The historian will seek a valid method and a relevant choice of data depending on which of these two starting points he has made his own.

In order to round out our picture of the social world, let us dwell for a moment on the world of successors. If the world of predecessors is completely fixed and determined, the world of consociates free, and the world of contemporaries probable, the world of successors is completely indeterminate and indeterminable. Our orientation toward our successors cannot amount to more than this: that we are going to have some. No key will open the door of this realm, not even that of ideal types. For the latter method is based on our experience of predecessors, consociates, and contemporaries, and there is no principle which permits us to extend it to the world of our successors. Of course, some of our consociates and contemporaries will outlive us, and we can assume that they will continue to act then as we know them to act now. In this way a kind of transitional zone can be set up between the two worlds. But the further removed the world of predecessors is from the Here and Now, the less reliable will such interpretations be.

This very point shows how erroneous in principle are all so-called "laws" of history. The whole world of successors is by definition nonhistorical and absolutely free. It can be anticipated in an abstract way, but it cannot be pictured in specific detail. It cannot be projected or planned for, for I have no control over the unknown factors intervening between the time of my death and the possible fulfillment of the plan.

5 / Some Basic Problems of
Interpretive Sociology

42. Summary of Our Conclusions to This Point

THE RESULTS SO FAR achieved are sufficient to allow us to state precisely and in conclusive form our theory of the understanding of meaning. We began by demonstrating the lack of clarity inherent in Max Weber's concept of intended meaning. We saw that, so long as action itself remains undefined, one cannot speak intelligibly of the intended meaning "which the actor attaches to his action." In order to reach a satisfactory definition of action, we found it necessary to make a detailed and exhaustive analysis of its constituting processes. We came, finally, to the conclusion that action is (1) a lived experience that is (2) guided by a plan or project arising from the subject's spontaneous activity and (3) distinguished from all other lived experiences by a peculiar Act of attention. We then saw that, on the basis of this definition, the formula "the actor attaches a meaning to his action" must be interpreted metaphorically. For the meaning is merely the special way in which the subject attends to his lived experience; it is this which elevates the experience into an action. It is incorrect, then, to regard meaning as if it were some kind of predicate which could be "attached" to an action. We further distinguished between the action (*actio; Handeln*) as an experience in process and the completed act (*actum; Handlung*), and we described the peculiar mode of constitution of the projected act, according to which it is anticipated in its own project in the future perfect tense.

Our next step was to formulate a preliminary definition of meaning applicable to every kind of lived experience. We said that the "meaning" of a lived experience can be reduced to a turning of the attention to an already elapsed experience, in the course of which the latter is lifted out of the stream of consciousness and identified as an experience constituted in such and such a way and in no other. Meaning in this initial sense is prepredicative and pertains to prephenomenal experience. We found it necessary to enlarge upon and enrich the concept in order to make it coincide with the object of our investigation, namely, the *specific meaning* which the actor "attaches" to his experience when he acts. It is this which is meant by "intended meaning." In order to analyze this concept of meaning, we examined the series of polythetically constructed Acts, which, according to a fundamental principle of phenomenology, can be taken in by a single glance of attention. We saw that every such series stands in a context of meaning, and we analyzed the constitution of the world of experience (*Erfahrungswelt*) as a total structure made up of different arrangements of such meaning-contexts. We then explained (1) the concept of schemes of experience (*Schemata der Erfahrung*), (2) the concept of the lower strata (*Unterstufen*) that are constituted as taken for granted, and (3) the concept of the "stock of knowledge at hand" (*Erfahrungsvorrat*). By studying the theory of attentional modifications we learned that it is *the interests of the subject* and his particular vantage point which defines the borderline between that which he takes for granted and that which is problematic for him. We thus gave the pragmatic element in thinking its due. As for the concept of action itself, we established (1) that a course of action is a polythetically constructed series of Acts (*Akte*) upon which, after their completion, one can direct one's attention in one "single-rayed" or concentrated shaft of attention within which they are seen as a deed or act (*Handlung*); and (2) that therefore action is itself a complex of meaning or meaning-context. At the same time we recognized that the specific meaning-context of an action is dependent upon the scope of the project which constitutes it as a single action. Therefore, if one is in earnest about seeking the subjective meaning of an action, one will find it in that which is the action's own principle of unity. The latter is always determined subjectively and only subjectively. It is methodologically inadmissible to interpret a given series of acts objectively as a unified sequence without any reference to a project and then ascribe to them a subjective meaning. We saw that Weber failed to distinguish the projected act from the completed act, leading him to confuse the meaning of an action with its motives. We, on the other hand, concluded that a series of complicated meaning-structures is already pregiven to the motive. We saw that the motive is really a context of meaning connecting that which motivates with that which is motivated. We drew the important distinction between the in-order-to motive and the genuine because-motive. Then, within the in-order-to motives of an action we pointed out various strata, and we showed that the in-order-to motive of an action is nothing more nor less than the act itself projected in the future perfect tense. We saw that it is for the sake of this act that the action is carried out step by step. We established all these points while our study was as yet limited to the stream of consciousness of the solitary Ego. We brought that study to a conclusion by introducing the concept of the "self-understanding" or self-interpretation of one's own act and of one's own action, which we saw to be an Act of synthetic recognition, the identification and ordering under mutually consistent schemes of experience of that which has already been grasped in the previous Act of attention.

We then turned to an analysis of the social world. Here the ego, as we saw, lights upon the alter ego, a being which, like itself, has consciousness and duration and which, also like itself, interprets its own lived experiences. But the fact that my partner *is* another self, the fact that he performs such and such acts whose external manifestations I can see—this is something I recognize solely by ordering and classifying my own perceptions of him within the total context of my knowledge. *But this is not yet knowledge of the other person as such.* All I am doing so far is ordering and classifying my own experiences of the social world just as if they were experiences of the natural world. But I can at any moment abandon this whole approach and adopt a new one. I can turn my attention away from the objective meaning-context into which I have ordered *my* experiences of the other person's experiences. For the perceived course of the other person's act which I perceive stands for him also within a context of meaning. This is because he sees in one glance of attention the polythetic phases which have gone to make up the whole act. It is only when I begin to grasp the other person's point of view as such, or, in our terminology, only when I make the leap from the objective to the subjective context of meaning, that I am entitled to say that I understand him.

We can attend to the subjective meaning-context of all sorts of human products and cultural objects, which can always be interpreted as evidence for what went on in the minds of their creators. Now, we have already seen that all knowledge of the subjective experiences of others must be obtained signitively. Among all the different kinds of products and indications we have considered, we have singled out for special attention signs, which stand in a context of meaning that is on the one hand an expressive scheme for the sign-user and on the other an interpretive scheme for the sign-interpreter. Both of these schemes can be interpreted as objective contexts of meaning if they are first abstracted from the living Acts and actions in which these signs were used and if the interpretation is confined to the signs themselves. However, we can start out from the external sign itself and, regarding it as a product, trace it back to the original actions and subjective experiences of its inventor or user. This is how, within the world of signs, the transition is made from the objective to the subjective context of meaning. The word *Verstehen* is generally used for the interpretation of both the subjective and objective meaning-contexts of products. This situation conceals the essential problem of knowledge of the social world. Only when the equivocation is identified does the problem come to light: that the meaning of one's own experiences is radically different from the meaning of the experiences of someone else and that consequently it is one thing to interpret one's own experience and quite another to interpret the experiences of someone else. It then becomes clear that the meaning attributed to a product, in contrast to the meaning attributed to a natural object, amounts precisely to this: that the product not only stands in a meaning-context for me—for the interpreter—but that it is also evidence for the further meaning-context in which it stands in the mind of you—its creator. It should here be emphasized that I, the interpreter, do not interpret alone and that your product as a thing in the world belongs not only to my private world but to the one intersubjective world common to us all. In this sense, the term "meaningful world" (*die sinnhafte Welt*), in contrast to the term "the natural world," carries within it an implicit reference to "the Other" who originated this thing that is meaningful. For, being-a-natural object and being-a-meaningful object are both conceptualized to the same degree in objective meaning-contexts by us, the interpreters, since we classify all our experiences in schemes of knowledge.

Our study of the social relationship and of observation in the social world has shown that we can have insight into the inner life of the other person by looking at it as subjective context of meaning. We found that all understanding of the Other is based on Acts of self-explication, that the objective meaning (*Sinn*) of a sign contains within it both actual and occasional meanings (*Bedeutungen*). We saw that we could distinguish the meaning-function (*Bedeutungsfunktion*) from the expressive function (*Ausdrucksfunktion*) of signs and that we could describe—even though only in outline—the special method by means of which the Other's interpretive schemes are comprehended. Our study of the context of motive in the social sphere showed us that all establishment of meaning was for the sake of interpretation and that all interpretation led back to the Act of meaning-establishment. At this point we finally gained access to the fields of "social action" and "social relationship."

An analysis of Weber's concept of social action revealed the nature of Other-orientation and of affecting-the-Other. This led in turn to the problems of orientation-relationship and of social interaction. We examined the general formal structure of these, for both participants and observers. In the process it became clear to us that the concepts of social action and social relationship undergo many modifications, depending on whether the object of the Other-orientation is an alter ego of the world of directly experienced social reality, the world of mere contemporaries, the world of predecessors, or the world of successors. We then turned to an analysis of these regions of the social world. Here we found that only in the direct social relationship as such can we have immediate awareness of the Thou's stream of subjective experiences in its living and present actuality. In contrast, we found that our own present subjective experiences at the moment of self-interpretation are in fact inaccessible to us and that the only experiences of our own that are open to self-interpretation are past ones. We analyzed the genuine We-relationship (*Wirbeziehung*), a relationship within which you and I can grasp each other's living stream of consciousness simultaneously and in one undivided glance. This We-relationship, too, is subject to manifold shadings: it occurs in different levels of actualization and concretization and can include lived experiences which lie close to, or further away from, the intimately grasped Thou of the face-to-face situation—in other words, lived experiences of greater or lesser proximity. On the other hand, we saw that in the world of mere contemporaries the other person is not given to me directly and bodily, but only indirectly. To a certain extent the Other has now become anonymous; we may even say that he has been replaced by an ideal type that has been constructed out of previously given experiences of certain courses of action. This ideal type, again, can be more or less removed from a real Thou, more or less concrete and full of content. We saw that the ego is oriented to the alter ego of the world of mere contemporaries in a special way: we called this the They-orientation (*Ihreinstellung*) because its object is not the thusness (*Sosein*)—or immediately apprehended qualities—of another person but rather his whatness (*Wie-sein*)—his being of such and such a general type (*Gleichsam-sein*). We have also analyzed the stratification of the They-relationships and have shown that they form a continuous series of ever increasing anonymization, beginning with the ideal type "my friend *N*" and culminating in the most general ideal type "one" or "someone" (*Man*), the originator of artifacts and objective sign systems. Hand in hand with the increasing anonymization of the previously given other person, there occurs for me a greater and greater self-distancing from his living personality. The more anonymous my partner, the less direct and personal the relationship and the more conceptualized must my dealings with him be. And the more I conceptualize my partner, the less can I regard him as a free agent. When I am face to face with someone, I immediately grasp him as a spontaneous and freely acting being: His future action is as yet open and undecided, and I can only hazard a guess as to what he is going to do. The ideal type, on the other hand, is, when rightly conceived, without any freedom; he cannot transcend his type without ceasing to be a mere contemporary and becoming a consociate of mine in direct experience. As for the world of predecessors, it is completely lacking in freedom. The world of successors, on the other hand, is free. We saw in section 11 that the problem of freedom, when rightly understood, is a *time problem*. Following our argument out to its conclusion, we now see that meaning in the social world is itself conditioned by time, a point that we had already proved with respect to the individual consciousness (see Chapter 2).

All the points made above we applied not only to the participant within the social relationship but to the observer as well. In the latter's case we found that the same basic distinctions can be drawn, namely, between observation of one's fellow men in direct experience, observation of those who are merely one's contemporaries, and observation of one's predecessors.

43. Indirect Social Observation and the Problem of Knowledge in the Social Sciences

WE SHALL NOW ATTEMPT to draw further conclusions about the modifications which Other-orientation and social relationship undergo in the four regions of the social world. Up to this point we have been concerned chiefly with the problem of how the man in the natural attitude, the man actually living in the social world, comprehends this world and interprets it. Only now and then, in connection with special points, did we make reference to the unique problem of social scientific knowledge. What is this problem? It consists in the fact that, although the social sciences start out from, and take for granted, the same social world in which we live from day to day, yet their methods of gathering knowledge are quite different from those of everyday life. For the social scientist organizes and classifies his data into quite different contexts of meaning and works them up in quite different ways.

In our introduction to Chapter 4, we referred to the relation between the knowledge we gain in everyday life and the knowledge we gain in the social sciences, and we showed how difficult it is to draw a sharp boundary between them. When in everyday life I think conceptually about my fellow man, I am actually taking up toward him the attitude of a social scientist. On the other hand, when I am engaging in social research, I am still a human being among human beings; in fact, it pertains to the very nature of science that it is not science for me only, but for everyone. Science always presupposes the experiences (*Erfahrungen*) of a whole scientific community, the experiences of others who, like me, with me, and for me, are carrying on scientific work.[1] And so the problem of the social sciences is already present in the prescientific sphere, and social science itself is only possible and conceivable within the general sphere of life in the social world. This is by no means to say that the social scientist may characterize as scientific that knowledge which he picks up in everyday life and in his ordinary associations. Our point has been merely to indicate the region where we must first look if we are to engage in a critique of the methodology of the social sciences.

What, then, is the specific attitude of social science to its object, the social world? Fundamentally, it is the same as the attitude of the indirect social observer toward his contemporaries. It is different, however, in one respect: no directly experienced social reality is pregiven to social science as such. The world of social science is simply not identical with the world of the social scientist, who is also a man living in the social world. But the world of predecessors is indeed pregiven to social science, and only this is pregiven to history. The whole context of knowledge of social science is therefore necessarily different from that of the indirect observer in everyday life.

With his usual acuity, Max Weber has also seen this problem. In his controversy with Münsterberg he speaks about the basic difference between scientific psychology and the psychology of the *Menschenkenner* or intuitive observer of others. In so doing, he sets himself in opposition to Münsterberg's assertion that the *Menschenkenner* either knows the whole man or does not know him at all. He replies: all he knows about him is what is *relevant for his immediate purposes* and nothing more.

> What is significant in a human being from one particular and limited point of view cannot for *logical* reasons serve as the basis of a pure psychological theory which seeks to express itself in the form of general laws. Actually, however, intuitive understanding takes into consideration the endless variety of human feeling and behavior—something which no theory can absorb into its "presuppositions." [2]

One must not allow oneself to be confused here by Weber's terminology. The distinction he draws applies, not only to intuitive versus

1. Cf. Husserl's *Formale und transzendentale Logik,* pp. 29 f. and 206.
2. Weber, "Roscher und Knies und die logischen Probleme der historischen Nationalökonomie," *Gesammelte Aufsätze zur Wissenschaftslehre* (1904), p. 81, obs. 3.

scientific psychology, but more generally and fundamentally to every-day knowledge as opposed to scientific knowledge.

It is to Husserl that one must turn in order to find a definitive statement of the distinction in question. As he showed in his *Formal and Transcendental Logic*, all scientific judgment has as its goal knowledge of the world with a maximum of explicit clarity and dis-tinctness. In scientific judgment no presupposition nor any pregiven element can be accepted as simply "at hand" without need of any further explanation. On the contrary, when I act as a scientist, I subject to a detailed step-by-step analysis everything taken from the world of everyday life: my own judgments, the judgments of others which I have previously accepted without criticism, indeed everything that I have previously taken as a matter of belief or have even thought in a confused fashion. Every social science, including interpretive sociology, therefore, sets as its primary goal the greatest possible clarification of what is thought about the social world by those living in it. Weber undertook the task of analyzing the processes of mean-ing-establishment as they occur in the social world—occur, of course, in a manner still lacking complete clarity. In so doing, he took as his basic theme the "intended meaning of human action," presupposing, at the same time, that the implicit meanings of everyday judgments in the social world can be rendered explicit by scientific means.

We shall be dealing shortly with the difficult question of how many social sciences there are and how their areas are to be marked off from one another. First, let us, with the aid of Weber's sociology, deal with the consequences resulting from the attitude of every social science to its object, in other words, from the attitude of whoever observes the world of mere contemporaries or the world of predecessors.

We have seen that the world of mere contemporaries is not given to the observer in any immediate and direct fashion and that the ego comprehends the contemporary alter ego only as an ideal type. When such ideal types are being constructed, the selection of their fixed and essential elements depends on the point of view of the observer at the moment of interpretation. It depends on his stock of knowledge at hand and upon the modifications of his attention to his knowledge of the world in general and of the social world in particular. Even the construction of scientific ideal types depends on the total context of scientific knowledge or, what is the same thing, on the total context of clear and distinct judgments about the world. All these judgments, however, insofar as they are scientific, must be ordered into those highest contexts of meaning which, to employ an image of Husserl's,[3]

3. *Logik*, p. 23.

comprehend in one expression all the axioms, fundamental principles, theorems, and deductions of a science. The interpretive schemes used by the observer in the social world to understand those who are his mere contemporaries are necessarily different from those of the social scientist, however. The indirect observer's knowledge is determined by his own direct experience regardless of whether what he knows is comprehended in Acts of judgment that are positional or neutralizing, explicit or vague, or are merely in the prepredicative "having" stage of the social world. This is true because of the living intentionality of the Acts (*Akte*) *in* which this individual lives. On the other hand, the complex of knowledge of the social sciences is based exclusively on explicit positional Acts of judgment, on constituted ideal objectifications, that is to say, on conclusions of thought, and never on prepredicative Acts of laying hold on (*in Selbsthabe erlebte Erfassungen*) the other person himself. Social science is through and through an explicit knowledge of either mere contemporaries or predecessors; it nowhere refers back to the face-to-face experience. Moreover, it must be recognized that scientific experience (*Erfahrung*) embraces the conclusions of all the sciences of the world and that the interpretive schemes of the social sciences must be compatible not merely with experience of the social world but with scientific experience as a whole. The original and fundamental scheme of science, the expressive scheme of its propositions, and the interpretive scheme of its explanations is, therefore, essentially that of *formal logic*. Accordingly, science is always an objective context of meaning, and the theme of all sciences of the social world is *to constitute an objective meaning-context either out of subjective meaning-contexts generally or out of some particular subjective meaning-contexts*. The problem of every social science can, therefore, be summarized in the question: *How are sciences of subjective meaning-context possible?* [4]

Our analysis of the social world of contemporaries has already partly answered this question. The fact that subjective meaning-contexts can be comprehended in objectivating and anonymizing constructions can be shown and described with the aid of the personal ideal types of the worlds of contemporaries and predecessors that are built up in the naïve natural point of view of everyday life. Since every social science starts out by taking for granted a social world which it sees as either a world of mere contemporaries or a world of predecessors, it can comprehend this world only by the method of ideal types,

4. Cf. below, sec. 49, pp. 275 ff. ["Wie sind Wissenschaften vom Subjektiven Sinnzusammenhang überhaupt möglich?" Cf. Kant, *Critique of Pure Reason*, B 20: "How is pure science of nature possible?" ("Wie ist reine Naturwissenschaft möglich?")]

whether course-of-action types or personal types. In other words, the social world is pregiven to each social science only indirectly and never with the immediacy of living intentionality. Now, since it is typifying experience, social science is an objective meaning-context whose object, however, is subjective meaning-contexts (to be precise, the typical subjective processes of personal ideal types).

We shall now describe the modifications which the laws of type-formation take on in the social sciences (as opposed to everyday life) due to the absence of direct social experience and the presence of the over-all scientific picture of the world.

We have seen that the observer of the world of contemporaries may, in order to understand the other person, appropriately construct only such ideal types as are in agreement with his past experience. The position of the social scientist is a parallel one. His ideal types must not only be compatible with the established conclusions of all the sciences but must explain in terms of motivations the very subjective experiences which they cover. To put the point in Weber's terminology, the ideal types constructed by social science, and, above all, by interpretive sociology, must possess at the same time both causal adequacy and meaning-adequacy. We shall presently examine the role played by these two concepts in interpretive sociology.

44. The Function of the Ideal Type in Weber's Sociology

IN ANALYZING a few of the categories of Weber's sociology, our source will be his great and, regrettably, unfinished work, *Wirtschaft und Gesellschaft*. Weber's views on methodology changed in important respects in the course of the years, as indeed one would expect in the case of a man of such outstanding intellectual integrity. We shall forego tracing these changes, first of all in order not to burden ourselves too heavily, and second because there are already a number of excellent works on this subject.[5]

5. Walther, "Max Weber als Soziologe," *Jahrbuch für Soziologie*, II, 1–65; Schelting, "Die logische Theorie der historischen Kulturwissenschaft von Max Weber und im besonderen sein Begriff des Idealtypus," *Archiv für Sozialwissenschaften und Sozialpolitik*, XLIX (1922), pp. 623–752; Hans Oppenheimer, "Die Logik der sozialwissenschaftlichen Begriffsbildung mit besonderer Berücksichtigung von Max Weber," *Heidelberger Abhandlungen zur Philosophie*, V (1925); Freyer, *Soziologie als Wirklichkeitswissenschaft*, pp. 145 ff., 175 ff., etc. For Weber's personal development see Voegelin, "Über Max Weber," *Deutsche Vierteljahrsschrift für Literaturwissenschaft und Geisteswissenschaft*, III, 177 ff., and, by the same author, "Gedenkrede auf Max Weber," *Kölner Vierteljahrshefte für Soziologie*, IX, 1 ff.; and, finally, the extensive and very important work of Marianne Weber, *Max Weber, ein Lebensbild* (Tübingen, 1926). [The reader is

Let us begin with a few quotations from Weber's main work:

Sociology is a science which attempts the interpretive understanding of social action.[6]

Sociology seeks to formulate type concepts and generalized uniformities of empirical processes. This distinguishes it from history, which is oriented to causal analysis and explanation of individual actions, structures and personalities possessing cultural significance.[7]

Among the various bases on which its concepts are formulated and its generalizations worked out, is an attempt to justify its important claim to be able to make a contribution to the causal explanation of some historically and culturally important phenomenon. As in the case of every generalizing science, the abstract character of the concepts of sociology is responsible for the fact that, compared with actual historical reality, they are relatively lacking in fullness of concrete content. To compensate for this disadvantage, sociological analysis can offer a greater precision of concepts. This precision is obtained by striving for the highest possible degree of adequacy on the level of meaning. . . . This can be realized in the case of concepts and generalizations which formulate rational processes. But sociological investigation attempts to include in its scope various irrational phenomena, as well as prophetic, mystic and affectual modes of action, formulated in terms of theoretical concepts which are adequate on the level of *meaning*. In *all* cases, rational or irrational, sociological analysis both abstracts from reality and at the same time helps us to understand it, in that it shows with what degree of *approximation* a concrete historical phenomenon can be subsumed under one or more of these concepts. . . . In order to give *precise* meaning to these terms it is necessary for the sociologist to formulate pure ideal types of the corresponding forms of action which in each case involve the highest possible degree of logical integration by virtue of their complete adequacy on the level of *meaning*. But precisely because this is true, it is probably seldom if ever that a real phenomenon can be found that corresponds exactly to one of these ideally constructed pure types. The case is similar to a physical reaction which has been calculated on the assumption of an absolute vacuum.[8]

Meaning (as the term is used in interpretive sociology) may be of two kinds. The term may refer first to the actually existing meaning in the given concrete case of a particular actor, or to the average or approximate meaning attributed to a given plurality of actors; or, secondly, to a

---

also referred to the above-named Alexander von Schelting's *Max Webers Wissenschaftslehre* (Tübingen: J. C. B. Mohr [P. Siebeck], 1934).]

6. *Wirtschaft und Gesellschaft*, p. 1 [E.T., p. 88].
7. *Ibid.*, p. 9 [E.T., p. 109].
8. *Ibid.*, pp. 9, 10 [E.T., pp. 109–110].

theoretically conceived *pure type* of subjectively intended meaning attributed to the hypothetical actor or actors in a given type of action.[9]

In all these cases, understanding involves the interpretive grasp of the meaning present in one of the following contexts: (a) as in the historical approach, the actually intended meaning for concrete individual action; or (b) as in cases of sociological mass phenomena, the average of, or an approximation to, the actually intended meaning; or (c) the meaning appropriate to a scientifically formulated pure type (an ideal type) of a common phenomenon. The concepts and "laws" of pure economic theory are examples of this ideal type. They state what course a given type of human action would take if it were strictly rational, unaffected by errors or emotional factors, and if, furthermore, it were completely and unequivocally directed to a single end, the maximization of economic advantage. In reality, action takes exactly this course only in unusual cases, as sometimes on the stock exchange; and even then there is usually only an approximation to the ideal type.[10]

The foregoing quotations are sufficient to give an adequate idea of the function within interpretive sociology of the ideal types as their creator conceived them. Since we have up to this point so often gone beyond the concepts of Max Weber and often found cause to disagree with them, the tremendous significance for all the social sciences of Weber's achievement cannot be sufficiently stressed. Again and again Weber refers to the problem of the ideal type as the central problem of all the social sciences. Our studies have shown how well founded this conception is. For the world of contemporaries and the world of predecessors can only be comprehended in an ideal-typical way. The individual episodes and events in this world are already abstracted from the concrete other person encountered in the face-to-face relationship. They are more or less anonymous and belong to typical courses of consciousness, which are to be found in all degrees of concreteness and richness of content, running from the type of an individual to the type of "someone."

Weber believes that he has taken care of all these manifold variations by dividing intended meanings into three classes: (a) the meaning intended by an individual actor in a historically given case, (b) the meaning intended on the average by a given group of several actors, and (c) the meaning of an ideal-typical actor. Weber's motives are clear; he is distinguishing the method of history and the method of statistics, on the one hand, from the method of interpretive sociology, on the other. The distinction is abundantly justified as long as the

9. *Ibid.*, p. 1 [E.T., p. 89; "subjectively intended meaning" has been substituted for "subjective meaning" in the Henderson-Parsons translation].
10. *Ibid.*, p. 4 [E.T., p. 96].

sciences in question are understood as sciences dealing with objective meaning-context and therefore with the external course of the act quite apart from any concern with the conscious experiences of the actor. This premise being granted, history (at least in Weber's conception of it) does have to do with the particular actions of individuals, statistics with the average actions of masses, and sociology with the action of a pure ideal type.[11] However, Weber's distinction turns out to be without foundation to the extent that these sciences are interpreted in terms of intended meaning—to the extent, that is, to which attention is turned away from the external course of action to the subjective context of meaning. For, since what is thematically pregiven to sociology and every other social science is the social reality which is indirectly experienced (never immediate social reality)—a social reality which can only be comprehended in the They-relationship and therefore typically—it follows that *even when social science is dealing with the action of a single individual, it must do so in terms of types.* Weber saw that clearly enough, for he expressly allows that all three methods of understanding meaning (*Sinn-Verstehens*) are valid for interpretive sociology. However, if we look more deeply into these distinctions, we will find that to each of the three modes of understanding there corresponds a different degree of verifiability of the external behavior. The boundaries, of course, are fluid. However, it can be said that the ideal type of an individual's behavior, say that of the behavior of a friend of mine, is derived from a very intimate acquaintance with his personal characteristics, that acquaintance which I enjoy in the We-relationship. This acquaintance is much greater than is the case with a personal ideal type constructed to fit a given piece of behavior. We have already explained this phenomenon in the preceding chapter. He who lives in the social world is a free being: his acts proceed from spontaneous activity. Once the action has transpired, once it is over and done with, it has become an act and is no longer free but closed and determinate in character. Nevertheless, it was free at the time the action took place; and if the question concerning the intended meaning refers, as it does in Max Weber's case, to the point in time before the completion of the act, then the answer must be that the actor always acts freely, and this is true even though I am able to know him only indirectly and in ideal-typical fashion. On the other hand, the personal *ideal type* that is correctly constructed, that is, one which is nontype-transcendent, is essentially unfree. This is true whether his action is regarded as now occurring or

11. With respect to Weber's concept of history and statistics, see Mises, "Soziologie und Geschichte," *Archiv für Sozialwissenschaften und Sozialpolitik,* LXI, 465–512.

whether (after its occurrence) it is interpreted as an already constituted ideal objectivity.

Let us remember the important distinction between the construction of the ideal type and the application of this type as an interpretive
scheme to real concrete actions. Let us take a case of interpreting a
future action by means of an ideal type. Our ideal type will be defined
as having definite and invariant motives, and from these motives we
will be able to deduce invariant acts and sequences of acts. Suppose
that our ideal type is that of a bureaucrat. Applying the type to a
concrete person, I can say, "N is a typical bureaucrat; therefore we
may expect him to be visiting our office regularly." Or else, "N has just
performed action *a; a* corresponds to ideal type *A; a'* is also characteristic of *A;* we may, therefore, expect N also to perform action *a'.*"
Now, how reliable are such judgments? Since action *a'* is still in the
future and therefore free, I cannot be certain that N will perform it.
The application of a personal ideal type to a future action of another
person is something that can only be done with the assumption that it
is *probably* correct. If the person does not act as predicted, we must
assume that we have applied the wrong ideal type to the person in
question. We will therefore look around for *another* personal ideal type
which *will* make his action comprehensible. This principle will hold
regardless of whether N is immediately experienced or is himself
known only as a type. Now, the more freedom N has, the less anonymous he is, the closer to the We-relationship he stands, the less
likelihood will there be that he will behave "according to ideal type."
But if N himself is no more than an ideal type, if his actions are
controlled by his observer, then the ideal type must *always* receive
positive verification, must always "come out right" insofar as it was
constructed according to a correct methodology, that is to say, in a
manner that is both adequate on the level of meaning and causally
adequate.

Now, what does it mean to construct an ideal type according to
both these criteria? In Weber's thought this does not mean the applicability of the ideal type to future actions. Rather it means the selection
of certain acts of one or more persons as typically relevant. An act is
defined as "typically relevant" if it originates from motives that can be
established as constant and invariant in the actor in question. But this
means merely that the act is repeatable, in other words, that the ideal
type derived from it has the ideality of the "and so forth," of the "again
and again." Therefore, the concept of adequacy on the level of meaning and causal adequacy applies to the correct choice of motive and
only implicitly to the acts that are postulated as following from these
motives. And, in fact, it is above all the in-order-to motive which is

thus postulated as constant. For the search for the genuine because-motive takes place, so to speak, in the pluperfect mode, on the basis of in-order-to motives posited as already given.

But how can we know the motives of another person? According to Weber, a motive is a context of meaning which appears either to the actor or to the observer as the meaningful ground (*als sinnhafter Grund*) of behavior. Now, we have already shown that this definition fails to distinguish between two quite different situations. In direct social observation, the observer assumes that the meaningful ground of the action was the project which was fulfilled by the already completed act. In this case the observer starts out by tacitly assuming that the action was really projected or planned. But he can, any time he wishes, simply question the actor and possibly discover that the latter intended to do something quite different. In other words, the actor can tell the observer just what the "span of his project" was. It is precisely this span which the observer cannot determine *merely* by observing. But in indirect social observation the situation is quite different. Here there is no distinction between the meaning-context of the observer and that of the actor. The reason is simple: if there is a real person corresponding to the observer's postulated ideal type, then he will by definition intend what the observer has in mind. However—and this is the basic postulate of social *science*—the motives ascribed to the ideal type must be both causally adequate and adequate on the level of meaning.

Before we proceed further, let us try to obviate a confusion that may arise from our own terminology. When sociology undertakes to interpret a concrete action, it has the act already given to it as a datum. From the act it tries to draw inferences about the motives that would be typical of a person acting in this way. In the process, recourse is had to a personal ideal type. For purposes of abbreviation, we shall not in the following paragraphs refer to the personal type as such, but merely to the typical motive. However, it should be quite clearly understood that by "typical motive" we mean the motive of an individual person who is comprehended via the ideal-typical method.

Let us now find out exactly what Weber means by the two terms "causal adequacy" and "adequacy on the level of meaning."

45. Causal Adequacy

WEBER MAKES THE distinction between the two concepts quite clear at an early point in his *Wirtschaft und Gesellschaft*:

We apply the term *adequacy on the level of meaning* to the subjective interpretation of a coherent course of conduct, when, and insofar as according to our habitual modes of thought and feeling, its component parts, taken in their mutual relation, are recognized to constitute a typical complex of meaning. It is more common to say "correct." The interpretation of a sequence of events will, on the other hand, be *causally adequate* insofar as, according to established generalizations from *experience,* there is a probability that it will always actually occur in the same way. An example of *adequacy on the level of meaning* in this sense is what is, according to our current *norms* of calculation or thinking, the correct solution to an arithmetical problem. On the other hand, a causally adequate interpretation of the same phenomenon would concern the statistical probability that, according to verified generalizations from experience, there would be a "correct" or "erroneous" solution of the same problem. This also refers to currently accepted norms, but includes taking account of typical errors or of typical confusions. Thus causal explanation depends on being able to determine that there is a probability, which, in the rare ideal case, can be numerically stated, but is always in some sense calculable, that a given observable event (overt or subjective) will be followed or accompanied by another event.

A *correct* causal interpretation of a concrete course of action is arrived at when the overt action and the motives have both been correctly apprehended, and at the same time their relation has become *meaningfully* comprehensible. A correct causal interpretation of typical action means that the process which is claimed to be typical is shown to be both adequately grasped on the level of meaning and at the same time the interpretation is to some degree causally adequate. If adequacy in respect to meaning is lacking, then no matter how high the degree of uniformity and how precisely its probability can be numerically determined, it is still an *incomprehensible statistical* probability, whether dealing with overt or subjective processes. On the other hand, even the most perfect adequacy on the level of meaning has causal significance from the sociological point of view only insofar as there is some kind of proof for the existence of a *probability* that the action *in fact* normally *takes* the course which has been held to be meaning-adequate. For this there must be some degree of determinable frequency of approximation to an average or a pure type.

Statistical uniformities constitute understandable types of action in the sense of this discussion, and thus constitute "sociological generalizations," only when they can be regarded as manifestations of the understandable subjective meaning of a course of social action. Conversely, formulations of a rational course of subjectively understandable action constitute sociological types of empirical processes only when they can be empirically observed with a significant degree of approximation. It is unfortunately by no means the case that the actual likelihood of the occurrence of a given course of overt action is *always* directly proportional to the clarity of subjective interpretation.[12]

We shall now seek to bring these remarks of Weber into accord with the requirements of our own theory. Let us begin with the concept of causal adequacy. A sequence of events is causally adequate to the degree that experience teaches us it will probably happen again. The concept of causal adequacy relates, therefore, to that objective context of meaning which is social science itself. That certain acts are followed by certain other acts is a generalization founded (1) in everyday life in my interpretation of my own experiences and (2) in social science, in a scientific complex of knowledge. In both cases the generalization is achieved through a synthesis of recognition. But this should in nowise be identified with knowledge of the conscious experience of the other person or with knowledge of the "intended meaning" of his action. A sequence of events is, therefore, causally adequate if it is in accord with past experience. Here it is immaterial whether the events in question add up to a human action or whether they are nothing more than a series of happenings in the world of nature. As a matter of fact, the concept of causal adequacy was first advanced by the physiologist Johannes von Kries [13] in connection with certain problems involved in the calculating of probabilities. His aim was to make a contribution to the theory of legal accountability in criminal law, but he introduced the idea as a general concept independent of any specific application. There are weighty objections against the use of the word "causal" in sociological discourse. For when we formulate judgments of causal adequacy in the social sciences, what we are really talking about is not causal necessity in the strict sense but the so-called "causality of freedom," which pertains to the end-means relation. Therefore, one cannot really speak of a causal relation in the general sense postulated by Kries [14] so long as one confines oneself to the external event, the objective context of meaning, and so forth. However, if one interprets the concept in Weber's sense, then the

12. Weber, *Wirtschaft und Gesellschaft*, pp. 5–6 [E.T., pp. 99–100].

13. "Über den Begriff der objektiven Möglichkeit und einige Anwendungen desselben," *Vierteljahrsschrift für wissenschaftliche Philosophie* (1888), pp. 180 ff.; on the concept of causal adequacy, see esp. pp. 201 f. With respect to Max Weber's concept, cf. the essay devoted to this theme in *Gesammelte Aufsätze zur Wissenschaftslehre*, pp. 78 ff.

14. A critique of this concept, for which we do not have the space here, would show that its universal validity is quite doubtful. Cf., with respect to its usefulness in criminal law, Felix Kaufmann, *Die philosophischen Grundprobleme der Lehre von der Strafrechtsschuld* (Leipzig and Vienna, 1929), pp. 78 ff.

postulate of causal adequacy is identical with what we have previously called "the postulate of the coherence of experience." A type construct is causally adequate, then, if it is probable that, according to the rules of experience, an act will be performed (it does not matter by whom or in what context of meaning) in a manner corresponding to the construct.

But this formulation is still lacking in precision. If I start out from a real action as my datum, then every ideal-typical construct that I base on it will already be in itself causally adequate. This is because the objective meaning-context of the act with which I start itself discloses the typical subjective meaning-context which corresponds to the act or, more strictly speaking, *can* correspond to it. Therefore, if I am going to construct a personal ideal type in a scientifically correct manner, it is not enough that the action in question probably take place. Rather, what is required in addition to this is that the action be *repeatable* and that the postulate of its repeatability not be inconsistent with the whole body of our scientific knowledge. This is a good time to repeat our previous observation that Weber starts out with an external action and seeks to connect with it an intended meaning without accounting for the fact that even the concept of the unity of the action presupposes a subjective foundation once we ask what the intended meaning is. However, this error turns out to be harmless if we follow his further train of thought. Causal adequacy is for him above all a category of the *social sciences;* hence, only sociological and historical understanding is bound by it. However, such understanding takes place via the construction of personal ideal types derived from a course of external behavior that has been isolated arbitrarily by the social scientist. If we set it down as a requirement that such constructs be derived only from acts occurring with a certain known frequency, then what we really have here is a heuristic principle based on the economy of thought. It means simply that a construct is appropriate and to be recommended only if it derives from acts that are not isolated but have a certain probability of repetition or frequency. If the postulate of causal adequacy is conceived in this way, then it is by no means a principle essential to all the social sciences. It would be binding upon sociology only and not upon history, since it derives from the basic approach of the sociologist toward his problems. But this would then leave everyone at liberty to decide whether he wanted to carry on the scientific study of the social world qua sociologist or qua historian.

But Weber's postulate of causal adequacy means something more than this. For reasons we have yet to discuss, the sociologist prefers the interpretive scheme of the *rational* action (specifically, either that of the action oriented to an ordinary purpose, or the action oriented to an absolute value [15]) to all other interpretive schemes. Every ordinary purposive action takes place within the means-end relationship. Establishing the pattern of such an action simply means seeking out how typical ends and typical means are related. In other words, the actor's choice of goals, his in-order-to projects, is determined via ideal-typical construction. Once this is done—that is, once the actor's goal is defined—it is only a matter of selecting those means for him that experience has shown to be appropriate. We can now interpret Weber's postulate of causal adequacy in the following way: In a type construct of ordinary purposive action, the means must be, in the light of our past experience, appropriate to the goal. Later, when we discuss rational action and rational method, we shall explain in detail what we mean by this second concept of causal adequacy.

An ideal-typical construct is said to be causally adequate when it turns out to predict what actually happens, in accord with all the rules of frequency. But this does not mean that what it predicts must always happen. Weber himself gives as an example the probability of a typical error in calculation. Let us suppose that we wish to multiply a given number by a two-digit number. Then, instead of placing the second partial product one point to the left of the first, we place it one point to the right. It would be causally adequate to conclude that we are going to come out with the wrong answer. But this conclusion would not be correct for all cases in which the above procedure was employed; for instance, if the two digits of the multiplier are the same, it does not matter whether the second partial product is moved to the left or to the right of the first. Here, as a matter of fact, we have Weber's ideal case of numerically assignable probability, for, out of ten such operations, nine will be incorrect and one correct. However, if we look more closely, we shall see that causal adequacy, or agreement with past experience, is based on typically comprehended meaning-adequate relations, in this case the laws of arithmetic and number theory as applied to the operation of multiplication. We can even go further and make the general statement that all causal adequacy which pertains to human action is based on principles of meaning-adequacy of some kind or other. For such causal adequacy means the consistency of the type construct of a human action with the total context of our past experience. Furthermore, we can come to know a human action only by ordering it within a meaning-context, whether objective or subjec-

15. [See *Wirtschaft und Gesellschaft*, p. 12; E.T., p. 115.]

tive. Causal adequacy, then, insofar as it is a concept applying to human behavior, is only a special case of meaning-adequacy.[16]

Our position on this point will immediately become more intelligible as we proceed to our analysis of the nature of meaning-adequacy.

46. Meaning-Adequacy

ACCORDING TO WEBER, a continuous course of behavior is meaning-adequate, or adequate on the level of meaning, to the degree that the relation of its constituent parts is affirmed by us as a typical meaning-context in accordance with average habits of thought and feeling. Here again we encounter the paradox that dominates Weber's whole philosophy of social science. He postulates as the task of social science the discovery of intended meaning—indeed, the intended meaning of the actor. But this "intended meaning" turns out to be a meaning which is given to the observer and not to the actor. In our terminology, Weber is saying that an action is meaning-adequate when it can be ordered under an objective context of meaning. We have already shown that such objective interpretation is quite a different thing from discovering what the actor himself has in mind. Our next question must therefore be whether meaning-adequacy is attained through objective interpretation or whether we have to go further and show without contradiction how the actor could himself have subjectively intended a certain meaning. We shall have to decide in favor of the second alternative, as we shall see.[17]

This distinction is by no means irrelevant for Weber's theory of meaning-adequacy. For him, behavior is meaning-adequate if it is in accord with "*average* habits of thought and feeling." What he means by this afterthought is not at all clear. For average habits of thought and feeling are a matter of causally adequate, not meaning-adequate, interpretation. It seems contradictory to set up the sociologist as judge of what is meaning-adequate, unless we mean by "knowledge of average habits of thought and feeling" the knowledge the social sciences

16. But not, of course, in the case of the natural sciences. The phenomena of nature are in principle beyond interpretive understanding and have no "meaning," since they fall outside man's consciousness and belong to an objective spatiotemporal order. This is not the place to investigate more deeply the distinction between the natural and the cultural sciences.

17. Since only a conscious experience can be meaningful (*sinnhaft*), we need not, in speaking of meaning-adequacy, distinguish between its application to cultural and its application to natural objects, as we did in the case of causal adequacy.

have of all conceivable subjective experiences whatsoever. It is enough for the meaningful interpretation of another's behavior that I assume that my ideal construct stands in a context of meaning *for him*. This suffices even if such a meaning-context clashes with my own knowledge. For instance, I can regard the totemistic interpretation of the behavior of a primitive tribe as meaning-adequate even though the whole totemistic way of thinking is foreign to the "average habits of thought and feeling" of our culture, or at least of the sociologists of our culture. But that is not at all what Max Weber means. For he is very conscious of the fact that these "average habits of thought and feeling" refer back to given personal ideal types. He knows also that it is a matter of our experience, that is, of the experience of the social sciences, whether certain meaning-contexts can be ordered under a definite personal ideal type in a way that is typically adequate rather than type-transcendent. And so our attempt to discover a criterion for what is meaning-adequate has come down to this: we are back once again at the subjective meaning-context and the personal ideal type, which in turn have to be constructed in terms of the postulate of causal adequacy.

On the other hand, we can regard an ideal-typical construct as adequate for a given action if the corresponding subjective meaning-context can really be ascribed to the actor in question without contradicting what else we know about him. Of course this person whose subjective experiences we are interpreting may appear to us as more or less determinate depending on how well we know him. Thus understood, the problem of meaning-adequacy pertains only to the interpretation of a concrete action via already constituted ideal types. On the other hand, the sociologist would have a completely free hand in the construction of a personal ideal type, because he so equips the latter's ideal consciousness that it is quite capable of having the subjective experiences appropriate to the typical behavior in question.

Our analysis has thus shown that, so far as Max Weber is concerned, the two concepts of causal adequacy and meaning-adequacy are convertible. Any interpretation which is meaning-adequate must also be causally adequate, and vice versa. The two postulates really require that there be no contradiction to previous experience. As soon as one assumes that there is a definite stock of such experience at hand—in other words, as soon as only one person is making the interpretation, and from only one point of view—then either both of the postulates will be fulfilled or neither of them will. If it appears otherwise, that is only because a number of interpreters are introduced or because a number of temporal vantage points are assumed, in which, for instance, one interpretation already meaning-adequate in itself conflicts causally with another, later one.

For even where a given instance of behavior seems incomprehensible to the observer, for instance, behavior which is on the one hand causally adequate but on the other seems lacking in meaning-adequacy, meaning-adequacy may well exist, even in such cases, from the point of view of the actor himself. Suppose, for instance, that an observer who is quite ignorant of the use of linguistic statistics in historical research comes on a man counting the frequency of certain words in the works of Plato. In terms of "average habits of thought and feeling" he will simply not know what to make of such behavior. He will begin to make sense out of the man's actions only when it is explained to him that in different periods of his life a person shows a preference for certain words and that, therefore, by studying the frequency of given words in his writings one will have made a start toward establishing a chronology for them. What was merely causally adequate then becomes meaning-adequate as well and therefore fully intelligible. We shall presently see how Weber's concept of meaning-adequacy really derives from the in-order-to motive of rational action and how his concept of intelligibility (*Verstehbarkeit*) is closely bound up with his notion of an action oriented to an ordinary purpose.

At this point we must add a remark on the situation underlying the distinction between causal adequacy and meaning-adequacy. The postulate that an ideal-typical construct must be both causally adequate and adequate on the level of meaning implies that it must be formulated as a *pure* construct without any admixture of type-transcending behavior.[18] Furthermore, it must be compatible with our experience of the world in general and therefore with our experience of other people in general and of the particular person in general whose acts we are seeking to understand by means of the construct. Another demand of the postulate is that the construct be based only on repeatable behavior. So much for the demands of the postulate of adequacy insofar as it deals with the *formation* of ideal-typical constructs. What are its requirements so far as the application of these types to concrete acts is concerned? Here the postulate of adequacy states that the type must *be sufficient to explain the action without contradicting previous experience*. But an action is sufficiently explained via an ideal type only when its motives are understood as typical ones; the explanation must, therefore, be meaning-adequate. To say that the motives must be causally adequate means merely that the motives could have brought about this action and, more strictly, that they probably did so. We must now examine the concept of probability.

18. With respect to this concept, see above, p. 191.

47. Objective and Subjective Probability

WEBER DISTINGUISHES between two kinds of probability, subjective and objective. Objective probability consists in the fact that certain behavior can be conceived with both causal adequacy and adequacy on the level of meaning without regard to the subjective experiences of the actor. *Objective* probability is, therefore, a category of *interpretation*. Subjective probability, on the other hand, is predicated only of the subjective meaning-context, in other words, of the "intended meaning." Subjective probability looks forward into the future from the vantage point of the actor. It pictures something in that future as already over and done with, or, as we have expressed it, in the future perfect tense. Subjective probability is synonymous with expectation in the broadest sense; above all, therefore, it is predicated of the project and of the protentions directed toward the latter's goal. Accordingly, for any actor, only a subjective probability can be attributed to each project as he plans the action to carry it out. Furthermore, all in-order-to motives have subjective probability, a fact which is already implied when we say that all actions are "oriented."

On the other hand, a genuine because-motive can have only objective probability. That is just another way of saying that the because-motive can be regarded as operative only if it has been so constructed in terms of meaning-adequacy and causal adequacy that it could have been operative. Here the position of the external observer and the position of the actor are in principle the same. The actor can discover his genuine because-motives only through a process of self-observation. Either his completed act or his in-order-to motive is then taken as datum, and he tries to picture in the pluperfect tense just what lived experience still further back in the past could have led him to plan such and such or do such and such. In search for such an experience, he uses, of course, the criterion of adequacy, which involves an objective meaning-context. It is, then, a question of objective probability whether the real because-motive of the act has been identified.

As for subjective probability, when we say that it is predicable of the in-order-to motive, we mean that every projected act calls for fulfillment through real action and that the actor counts on such fulfillment. But this assumption that the act is going to be carried through is based on the knowledge available to the actor at the time he formulates his project. This knowledge is largely a matter of his past experience as to whether things like this "can be done." He thus brings his planned action into a context of meaning, namely, certain previous projects of a similar nature that are now imagined in the pluperfect tense, judged as to whether they were successfully carried through and thus made the standard of "adequacy."

We must center our attention on the relation between the concept of probability and those ideal types that are constructed scientifically, that is, according to the postulates of adequacy.

As far as the construction of the ideal type is concerned, the postulate of adequacy required that it be probable that a real person would behave in the manner specified by the type. Objective probability and adequacy with respect to type are, therefore, correlative as far as behavior that has already transpired is concerned. But if the type construct is to be applied to future action, then the criterion of meaning-adequacy is different. Here the observer must postulate an action of such a nature that the *actor* would *think* its performance probable. In short, what is here called for is subjective probability. Projects have a positive degree of subjective probability if those who formulate them expect to be able to carry them out.

Probability, whether objective or subjective, involves potentiality. Now, we have known ever since Husserl's *Ideas* [19] that potentiality can originate from two different sources. First of all, it can derive from positionality, in other words, be the result of thetic positing acts. Second, it can result from the transformation into potentiality of neutralized contents of consciousness.[20] The concept of objective and subjective probability, when applied here, embraces both these categories. The difference is this: in the case of thetic potentiality, the judgments are made with relative explicitness and in clarity, whereas, in the case of neutralized contents of consciousness transformed into potentiality, the probability of their proving true remains from the subjective standpoint quite undecided or else is taken for granted. But all this depends on the actor's original mode of attention, which is antecedent to all contexts of meaning. If, however, his mode of attention is properly established as a typical and invariant way in which the Ego regards its own lived experiences, the subjective probability originating from the neutralizing experiences of consciousness can then be left out of account, and the probability originating from thetic positionality can be brought to light. It can then be assumed that the actor makes a series of positive judgments (*thetische Setzungsakte*) about his goal, its possibility of attainment, and the means available to him. Since these judgments are explicit and clear, he is said to be acting *rationally*.

19. Pp. 228 ff. [E.T., pp. 313 ff.]
20. With respect to this concept cf. sec. 11, p. 67.

The clarification of this notion of rational action will be the final step in our study of Weber's basic concepts.

48. Interpretive Sociology's Preference for Rational Action Types

LET US RECALL once again our definition of action. Action is behavior based on an antecedent project. Since every project has an "in-order-to" or "for-the-sake-of-which" structure, it follows that every action is rational. Without such a project, one does not "act"; one merely "behaves" or "has experiences." Every action can, in its turn, be placed in a higher context of meaning, within which it is merely a means to a further end. Now, this end or higher goal may be clearly pictured, while the action leading up to it is carried out in a confused and uncertain manner. Or conversely, the goal may be vaguely conceived, while the action leading to it is well thought out. An example of the first situation would be a direction like "The post office is that way," in contrast to "Take your first right, then after two blocks a left." An example of the second situation would be a chemist carrying out careful experiments on a newly discovered substance whose nature is as yet unknown. Both of these situations are alien to the kind of ideal type that is constructed in the social sciences and, as a matter of fact, in all indirect knowledge of social reality. The ideal type proper to such indirect social experience is one in which both ends and means are clearly conceived. For, since within these types the in-order-to motive is fixed and invariant, the corresponding ends and means must be assumed to have a maximum of meaning-adequacy and the action itself a maximum chance of being carried out. An action type of this kind is, according to Weber, a *rational* action.[21] It does not matter whether the rational action is oriented to an ordinary purpose or to an absolute value. This latter distinction really pertains to the genuine because-motive which can be coordinated to the typical in-order-to motive. Whether an act is oriented to an ordinary purpose or to an absolute value depends upon the interest of the actor; the same may be said for the problems he sets up for himself and the experiences he selects as relevant to their solution.[22]

This means-end relation can be thought of in an objective context

21. For an analysis of the concept of rational action see Hermann J. Grab's valuable monograph *Der Begriff des Rationalen in der Soziologie Max Webers* (Karlsruhe, 1927). Needless to say, my agreement with Grab can only be partial, since he presupposes Scheler's concept of objective values.

22. For the derivation of the two types of action in question see Mises, "Soziologie und Geschichte," p. 479.

of meaning and its objective probability estimated. With a suitable choice of type, the objective meaning-context of the means-end relation can be treated as a subjective meaning-context and the objective probability as a subjective probability. This will be true the more universal are the problem situations which are the genuine because-motives corresponding to the typical in-order-to motives in question. For this reason interpretive sociology—but in this it is by no means alone—prefers rational action types. Irrational action (namely, action whose ends or means are confused or uncertain) is interpreted as a variant function of rational action. This is done by postulating a rational action type and then making certain changes in its in-order-to motives; the result is a deviant type. We must keep in mind the fact that sociology is concerned primarily with social interactions and that the latter involve reciprocal orientations in which the calculation of means and ends plays a large role. It is precisely because of the centrality of this calculation that rational action is such an important concept for interpretive sociology. But this does not by any means imply that interpretive sociology neglects irrational action. Weber has again and again stressed that the latter is part of the subject matter of sociology. His works on the sociology of religion, for instance, make exemplary use of categories of irrational, emotional, and traditional action.

This preference for rational action types we must very sharply distinguish from the so-called "rational method" of interpretive sociology. Sociology can claim no monopoly on rational method. The methodologies of all true sciences are rational, involving, as they do, the use of formal logic and interpretive schemes. All true sciences demand the maximum of clarity and distinctness for all their propositions. There is no such thing as an irrational science. We must never cease reiterating that the method of Weber's sociology is a rational one and that the position of interpretive sociology should in no way be confused with that of Dilthey, who opposes to rational science another, so-called "interpretive" science based on metaphysical presuppositions and incorrigible "intuition."

It is true that the postulate of such an interpretive science arose historically from the necessity of breaking through the barriers that were erected between the rational special sciences and the understanding of living human experience. But it was forgotten by those proposing this new approach that life and thought are two different things and that science remains a matter of thought even when its subject matter is life. It cannot, therefore, base itself on some vague and confused empathy or on value presuppositions or on descriptions lacking in intellectual rigor. It was this point and nothing else that lay at the center of Weber's insistence on the objectivity of the knowledge attained in the social sciences. And it was Weber who first raised interpretive sociology to the rank of a science.

49. Objective and Subjective Meaning in the Social Sciences

HAVING COMPLETED our analysis of the most important basic concepts of interpretive sociology, we must now try to answer the questions we formulated in section 43 concerning the relationship between the meaning-endowing acts of everyday life and their interpretation by the social sciences. Our answer is this: *All social sciences are objective meaning-contexts of subjective meaning-contexts.* We shall now try to clarify what we mean by this statement.

All scientific knowledge of the social world is indirect. It is knowledge of the world of contemporaries and the world of predecessors, never of the world of immediate social reality. Accordingly, the social sciences can understand man in his everyday social life not as a living individual person with a unique consciousness, but only as a personal ideal type without duration or spontaneity. They can understand him only as existing within an impersonal and anonymous objective time which no one ever has, or ever can, experience. To this ideal type are assigned only such conscious experiences as are required to accompany motives already formally postulated. We have already outlined the methodology involved in this postulation. We have seen that it must take place in a manner that is both meaning-adequate and causally adequate. This means that there must be constant recourse to pregiven knowledge of the social world and of the world in general. It means that the motives postulated must not be incompatible with those of the observer's previously constructed ideal types.

Since the social sciences qua social sciences never actually encounter real people but deal only in personal ideal types, it can hardly be their function to understand the subjective meaning of human action in the sense that one person understands another's meaning when he is directly interacting with him. However, we saw that the nature of subjective meaning itself changes with the transition from direct to indirect social experience. In the process of ideal-typical construction, subjective meaning-contexts that can be directly experienced are successively replaced by a series of objective meaning-contexts. These are constructed gradually, each one upon its predecessor, and they interpenetrate one another in Chinese-box fashion, so that it is difficult to say where one leaves off and the other begins. However, it is precisely this process of construction which makes it possible for the social scientist, or indeed for any observer, to understand what the actor means; for it is this process alone which gives a dimension of objectivity to his meaning. Of course, this process of constitution can only be disclosed to the interpreter by means of his own typifying method. What he will thus come to know is only a conceptual model, not a real person.

We have already seen that there can be personal ideal types of all degrees of anonymity or concreteness. By studying a given cultural product we can gain some insight into what its creator had in mind, regardless of the anonymity of the ideal type we are employing. Accordingly, the different social sciences deal with subject matter of very different degrees of anonymity and concreteness. This should be obvious enough when we consider that the social sciences include, according to our own concept, such widely separated disciplines as individual biography, jurisprudence, and pure economics. And here we should add that not all the social sciences have as their goal the interpretation of the subjective meaning of products by means of personal ideal types. Some of them are concerned with what we have called course-of-action types. Examples of such social sciences are the history of law, the history of art, and political science. This latter group of disciplines simply takes for granted the lower stages of meaning-establishment and pays no attention to them. Their scientific goal is not to study the process of meaning-establishment but rather the cultural products which are the result of that meaning-establishment. These products are then regarded as meaningful in themselves (*als sinnhafte Erzeugnisse*) and are classified into course-of-action types.

At this point an obvious objection will be raised. It will be pointed out that the existence of the so-called law-constructing (or nomothetic) social sciences contradicts our assertion that all social sciences are type-constructing in nature. These law-constructing social sciences, it will be said, are able to provide us with universally valid knowledge prior to all experience. Let us look closely at these sciences and their attitude toward the subjective and objective meaning of the social world, using as our example pure economics.

The Austrian marginal utility school, the Anglo-American scholars working along similar lines, and the mathematical economists as well all claim to have an exact theoretical science, the principles of which are universally valid for all situations in which economic activity occurs. Among the more recent writers of this orientation, Mises can be regarded as the most significant advocate of the pure a priori character of economics. In his treatise "Soziologie und Geschichte," which we have already quoted repeatedly, he takes up a position opposed to that of Weber on the problem of the contrast between theoretical and historical social science. For Mises economics is only a part of sociology, though, to be sure, the most highly developed part. In his polemic against Weber, Mises asks "whether the concepts of economics actually have the logical character of ideal types." His conclusion is:

> This question must be answered quite flatly in the negative. In fact, our theoretical concepts "can be empirically discovered nowhere in reality in their pure conceptual form." Concepts can never be encountered in reality; they belong not to the realm of reality, but to that of thought. They are the intellectual means with which we seek to grasp reality on the level of thought. But one cannot say of these economic concepts that they are formed "by the one-sided accentuation of one or more points of view and by the synthesis of a great many diffuse, discrete, more or less present and occasionally absent *concrete individual* phenomena, which are arranged according to those one-sidedly emphasized viewpoints into a unified *analytical* construct (*Gedankenbild*)." [23] Rather, they are acquired by means of abstraction, which aims at selecting for conceptualization certain aspects of each of the individual phenomena under consideration. [24]
>
> Max Weber's basic error lies in his misunderstanding of what is meant by saying that the sociological principle is universally valid. The economic principle, the fundamental laws of the formation of rates of exchange, the law of profit, the law of population and all other such propositions are valid always and everywhere when the conditions presupposed by them are present. [25]

No doubt Mises' criticism is valid against Weber's earliest formulations of the concept of ideal type, and it is these to which Mises is here referring. According to this earliest view of Weber's, the ideal types would in principle be applicable only to historical data. They would stand in contrast to the concepts of theoretical sociology derived by abstraction from aspects of *each* of the individual phenomena under consideration. However, the theory of ideal types which I have set forth in the present work—a method which is, in my opinion, already

23. Quoted from Weber's "Die Objektivität sozialwissenschaftlicher und sozialpolitischer Erkenntnis," *Gesammelte Aufsätze zur Wissenschaftslehre* (1904), p. 191. [Cf. *Max Weber on the Methodology of the Social Sciences*, trans. and ed. by Edward A. Shils and Henry A. Finch (Glencoe, Ill., 1949), p. 90, from which our translation of the above quotation is taken.]

24. Mises, "Soziologie und Geschichte," p. 474.

25. *Ibid.*, p. 480.

foreshadowed in Weber's later works [26]—is an entirely different one, so far as its deduction is concerned. According to our view, ideal types are constructed by postulating certain motives as fixed and invariant within the range of variation of the actual self-interpretation in which the Ego interprets its own action as it acts. To be sure, this postulation of certain motives as invariant does refer back to previous "experience" (*Erfahrung*). But this is not the "experience" of shallow empiricism. It is rather the immediate prepredicative encounter which we have with any direct object of intuition.[27] The ideal type may, therefore, be derived from many kinds of "experiences" and by means of more than one kind of constituting process. Both "empirical" and eidetic ideal types may be constructed. By empirical we mean "derived from the senses," and by eidetic we mean "derived from essential insight."[28] The manner of construction may be abstraction, generalization, or formalization, the principle of meaning-adequacy always, of course, being observed. Our own theory of ideal types, therefore, covers the concepts and propositions of the theoretical social sciences, including those of pure economics. For even the examples cited by Mises—the economic principle, the basic laws of price formation, and so forth—are in our sense ideal types. Of course these principles must be based upon a thoroughgoing formalization and generalization of material that has already been postulated as fixed and invariant. It is this formalization and generalization which give the ideal types universal validity.[29] Such ideal types do not refer to any individual or spatio-temporal collection of individuals. They are statements about anyone's action, about action or behavior considered as occurring in complete anonymity and without any specification of time or place. They are precisely for that reason lacking in concreteness.[30] Mises [31] is right when he criticizes Weber for interpreting the marginal utility theory in too narrow a fashion, so that it appears to describe an economy run entirely according to the calculations of entrepreneurs.

26. Max Weber's well-known formulation of the concept of ideal type, made in 1904, which he himself calls "sketchy and therefore perhaps partially incorrect" is indeed fragmentary because it has in mind chiefly the ideal type of his theory of history. It must be strongly emphasized that once Weber's thought makes the transition to sociology, the conception of the ideal type itself undergoes a thorough change. Unfortunately, this fact is only hinted at in a few statements in *Wirtschaft und Gesellschaft*, e.g., on page 10 [E.T., p. 110]. Cf. Walther, "Max Weber als Soziologe," *Jahrbuch für Soziologie*, II, 1–65.

27. [See the first chapter of Husserl's *Ideas*.]

28. [See *ibid.*, esp. § 3 (E.T., p. 54).]

29. These two points are merely expressed in a slightly different way by Mises when he says that the theoretical propositions are universally valid *under the stipulated conditions*.

30. In the sense of our discussion in sec. 39; see above, p. 195.

31. *Op. cit.*, p. 486.

He justly remarks that Weber is here confusing the marginal utility model with that of classical political economy. The latter, he points out, has in mind a more concrete and less anonymous concept of "economic man." Modern theoretical economics,[32] on the other hand, starts not from the behavior of the businessman but from that of the consumer, in other words, from the behavior of anyone and everyone. Such behavior, of course, can serve as the basis of an ideal type of a higher degree of anonymity. It is because of this, in turn, that the principles of catallactics possess a higher degree of generality. Here, as Mises repeatedly emphasizes, is to be found the basis of the objectivism and objectivity of the propositions of catallactics.[33] But this "objectivity" of Mises is, therefore, the same as the concept of objectivity we ourselves put forward in our discussion of the objective and subjective contexts of meaning. The law of marginal utility, then, turns out to be a stipulation that merely marks out the fixed boundaries of the only area within which economic acts can by definition take place.[34]

In our view, pure economics is a perfect example of an objective meaning-complex about subjective meaning-complexes, in other words, of an objective meaning-configuration stipulating the typical and invariant subjective experiences of anyone who acts within an economic framework. Of course the word "typical" takes on a special meaning here, as Mises comes to admit when he emphasizes that an action running contrary to the "principle of marginal utility" (and therefore in our sense "atypical") is inconceivable. But that holds true only so long as one conceives the principle of marginal utility as a definition of the purely formal action as such. Excluded from such a scheme would have to be any consideration of the uses to which the "goods" are to be put after they are acquired.[35] But once we do turn our attention to the subjective meaning of a real individual person, leaving the anonymous "anyone" behind, then of course it makes sense to speak of behavior that is atypical—atypical in relation to standardized economic goals. To be sure, such behavior is irrelevant from the point of view of economics, and it is in this sense that economic principles are, in Mises' words, "not a statement of what usually happens, but of what necessarily must happen." [36]

32. [The reference here is to the marginal utility school emanating from Jevons, Menger, and Böhm-Bawerk.]

33. *Op. cit.*, pp. 482, 486.

34. Cf. Felix Kaufmann, "Logik und Wirtschaftswissenschaft," *Archiv für Sozialwissenschaften*, LIV, 614–56, esp. 650.

35. We need not here pursue the problem of the reduction of the concept "economic good" to less anonymous and more concrete psychological concepts. Cf. Mises, *op. cit.*, p. 476; also Kaufmann, "Logik und Wirtschaftswissenschaft," p. 628.

36. Mises, *op. cit.*, p. 484.

Mises' criticism therefore does not rule out the applicability of ideal types as such to economic activity. For how could ideal types be excluded from this area, since all scientific knowledge is essentially ideal-typical in character? On the contrary, Mises' argument really turns out to be a defense against the intrusion of ideal types of too great concreteness and too little anonymity into economics. And with this we must agree. At the same time, we must state that the very objectivity of economic knowledge consists in the ordering of subjective meaning-contexts (such as subjective valuations) into the objective meaning-context of scientific knowledge.

Let us now see how the contrast between objective and subjective meaning exhibits itself in a science that is methodologically of a quite different character, namely, the "pure jurisprudence" of Hans Kelsen. Here we find our problem cropping up in the following way:

> Is a constitution republican, for instance, merely because it announces itself as such? Is a state federal merely because its constitution calls it such? Since legal acts usually have a verbal form, they can say something about their own meaning. This fact alone betrays an important difference between the subject matter of jurisprudence, indeed of the *social sciences* as such, and the subject matter of the natural sciences. We need not fear, for instance, that a stone will ever announce itself to be an animal. On the other hand, one cannot take the declared legal meaning of certain human acts at their face value; to do so is simply to beg the question of whether such declared meaning is really the objective legal meaning. For whether these acts are really legal acts at all, if they are, what their place is in the legal system, what significance they have for other legal acts—all these considerations will depend on the *basic norm* by means of which the scheme that interprets them is produced.[37]

> Jurisprudence must pronounce that certain acts standing at the outer boundary of the legal system are, contrary to their own claim, *invalid acts.* The root of the problem is that the human acts which are the subject matter of jurisprudence have their own immanent subjective meaning which may or may not coincide with the objective meaning that accrues to them in the legal system to which they belong, *and by the basic norm postulated by the theory governing the system.*[38]

It would be hard to find a more penetrating formulation of the true relation of the social sciences to their subject matter, which we have defined as the ordering of subjective meaning-contexts within an objective meaning-context. According to Kelsen, the subjective meaning

37. Kelsen, *Allgemeine Staatslehre* (Berlin, 1925), p. 129; italics ours.
38. *Ibid.,* p. 278.

which the individual legal acts have for those enacting or performing them must be ordered within an objective meaning-context by means of what *we* should call ideal-typical constructions on the part of the interpreting science of jurisprudence. The ideal-typical construction that we find in jurisprudence is carried out through formalization and generalization, just as in pure economics. In pure economics the principle of marginal utility is the defining principle of the whole field and presents a highest interpretive scheme which alone makes possible the scientific systematization of the subjective meaning-contexts of individual economic acts. Correspondingly, in the realm of pure jurisprudence, as Kelsen himself clearly recognizes, application of a presupposed basic norm determines the area of invariance for all those subjective meaning-contexts of legal acts which are relevant for jurisprudence or which, to use technical terminology, bear the mark of positivity.[39] In another work Kelsen formulates this thought in the following way:

> While positivism means that only that is law which has been created by constitutional procedure, it does not mean that everything which has been thus created is acceptable as law, or that it is acceptable as law in the sense which it attributes to itself. The assumption of a basic norm which establishes a supreme authority for the purpose of law-making is the ultimate presupposition which enables us to consider as "law" only those materials which have been fashioned by a certain method. The above described interpretation of legal material has actually long been in use by legal science. If it is correct, and if this imputation of an objective meaning is possible (without which there can be no legal science), then it must be the basic norm itself which gives the significance of law to material produced by a certain procedure. It must, moreover, be possible to ascertain from this basic norm which part of the material is valid "law," and also the objective meaning of the legal material, which actually may conflict with its own subjective meaning. The hypothesis of the basic norm simply expresses the assumptions necessary for legal cognition.[40]

39. [Cf. Kelsen, *General Theory of Law and State* (Cambridge, Mass., 1945), pp. 114 ff.: "Law is always positive law and its positivity lies in the fact that it is created and annulled by acts of human beings, thus being independent of morality and similar norm systems" (E.T., Anders Wedberg).]

For a discussion of the concept of "basic norm" see Felix Kaufmann, "Juristischer und soziologischer Rechtsbegriff," in the anniversary volume for Hans Kelsen, *Gesellschaft, Staat und Recht: Untersuchungen zur reinen Rechtslehre* (Vienna, 1931), pp. 14–41, esp. pp. 19 ff. and 30 f.

40. Kelsen, "Die philosophischen Grundlagen der Naturrechtslehre und des Rechtspositivismus," *Philosophische Vorträge der Kantgesellschaft* (Charlottenburg, 1928), pp. 24 f. [E.T., "Natural Law Doctrine and Legal Positivism," by Wolfgang Kraus in Kelsen, *General Theory of Law and the State*.]

There is nothing to add to these ideas from the standpoint of the theory being advocated here. Kelsen quite clearly indicates that his basic norm is the principle by which are constructed those ideal-typical schemes which alone make it possible to interpret subjective meaning-contexts as objective meaning-contexts of law.

In these two examples we have shown how the two most advanced "theoretical" social sciences—pure economics and jurisprudence—make use of ideal-typical constructs (in our sense) in order to delimit their subject areas and establish an objective context of meaning. What is true for the "theoretical" social sciences is generally true for all the social sciences.[41] Subjective meaning-contexts are comprehended by means of a process in which that which is scientifically relevant in them is separated from that which is irrelevant. This process is made possible by an antecedently given highest interpretive scheme which defines once and for all the nature of the constructs which may be used.

It would require a treatise in itself to define the specific problems of each social science—especially the historical disciplines—and the methods peculiar to each of them and then, on the basis of these determinations, to attempt a classification of the sciences in question. As the principle of classification we should, first of all, put forward the degree of anonymity of the ideal constructs used in each social science, in other words, the fundamental attitude of each science to the subjective meaning-context with which it deals. Furthermore, the social sciences fall into two classes. First, they can be *pure theories of the form* of the social world, which deal with the constitution of social relationships and social patterns, the act-objectivities and artifacts in the conscious processes of individuals who live in the social world, meanwhile comprehending all these things by a purely descriptive method. However, the social sciences can also take as their subject matter the *real-ontological content* of the social world as already constituted and study the relationships and patterns in themselves—the already given historical or social acts and the artifacts as objects independent of the subjective experiences in which they were constituted.

There is still a word to be said about the field and method of interpretive sociology. The primary task of this science is to describe the processes of meaning-establishment and meaning-interpretation as these are carried out by individuals living in the social world. This description can be empirical or eidetic; it can take as its subject matter the individual or the typical; it can be performed in concrete situations of everyday life or with a high degree of generality. But, over and

41. Cf. the discussion in sec. 28.

above this, interpretive sociology approaches such cultural objects and seeks to understand their meaning by applying to them the interpretive schemes thus obtained.

50. Conclusion: A Glance at Further Problems

WE HAVE NOW ARRIVED at the end of our study, which, of course, could deal with only one aspect of the complex problem of the interpretation of meaning in the social world. There are many other tasks lying ahead for a sociology which is based on phenomenological principles and which is willing to take as its starting point our analysis of duration and of the latter's connection with meaning. The group of problems which held the center of our attention in this work was that which was concerned with the *sociological person*. We have by no means clarified to a sufficient degree the questions which we discussed under the heading of the Thou-orientation and the They-orientation, the We-relationship and the They-relationship, of the physically present alter ego and the personal ideal type. A crucial question which we never faced up to was that of interpretive sociology's right to make valid assertions about the form of social relationships, regardless of whether the entities involved in such relationships were one or more individuals, a personal ideal type, or a social collective. If we recall what we said about the relation of the individual to the ideal type, we shall find that even here the boundaries are fluid throughout, that the individual in his physical reality can be just as easily comprehended in terms of the content of all the possible ideal types of him as, on the other hand, each ideal type can be comprehended as a statement about an individual considered under an anonymous function. Every statement about the action of a personal ideal type removes the latter to some extent from the They-relationship and places it within a We-relationship. Every statement about an individual removes him from the direct We-relationship out of his concrete thusness into a like-thatness, into a typical relationship in the world of contemporaries.

A second group of problems reaches far beyond the boundaries of the subject matter of the social sciences. It is the whole *problem of relevance*, which has kept cropping up again and again in the present study. The definitive clarification of this problem will be possible only through an over-all phenomenological analysis, which nevertheless can be begun within the field of the social sciences. Whether we take our departure from the ideal type, from the existence of in-order-to and because-motives, from the "projected" character of the act, from the possibility of reproduction, even from the mere distinguishability of our lived experiences, repeatedly we come up against the same problem. This is the question of why these facts and precisely these are selected by thought from the totality of lived experience and regarded as relevant. The settling of this question is of crucial importance for all categories of social science which are based on the tacit assumption that the observer's interest situation and the statement of the problem which is determined by it were already satisfactorily deduced through the clarification of the problem of relevance.

A third group of problems would include the *constitution of the Thou* as such, the illumination of the intersubjective structure of all thinking, and the constitution of the transcendental alter ego from the transcendental ego. Hand in hand with the solution of this problem will come the solution of the intersubjective validity of our experience of the world in general. In his *Formal and Transcendental Logic*, Husserl has already laid the foundation for the solution of this problem. He has announced a future work which will make the whole question the center of attention, a question whose conclusion solution will probably give us for the first time an ontology of the human being on a phenomenological basis.[42]

The other two basic problems, namely, the problem of the sociological person and the problem of relevance in the social world, can be taken on by interpretive sociology working closely along the lines originally set down by Max Weber.

42. Husserl's *Cartesian Meditations* have already in part fulfilled his promise.

Selected Bibliography

A. Writings of ALFRED SCHUTZ

Der sinnhafte Aufbau der sozialen Welt. Vienna: Springer, 1932. 2d ed., 1960.

Collected Papers. The Hague: Nijhoff. Vol. I, *The Problem of Social Reality,* edited, with an Introduction, by MAURICE NATANSON, 1962. Vol. II, *Studies in Social Theory,* edited, with an Introduction, by ARVID BRODERSEN, 1964. Vol. III, *Studies in Phenomenological Philosophy,* edited by ILSE SCHUTZ, with an Introduction by ARON GURWITSCH, 1966.

B. Writings of other authors which are frequently referred to in this work or which restate positions here referred to

BERGSON, HENRI. *Essai sur les données immédiates de la conscience.* Paris: F. Alcan, 1938. English translation by R. L. POGSON, *Time and Free Will.* New York: Macmillan, 1913.

———. *Durée et simultanéité.* Paris: F. Alcan, 1923.

HEIDEGGER, MARTIN. *Sein und Zeit.* Halle: Niemeyer, 1927. English translation by JOHN MACQUARRIE and EDWARD ROBINSON, *Being and Time.* New York: Harper and Row, 1962.

HUSSERL, EDMUND. *Logische Untersuchungen.* 4th ed. Halle: Niemeyer, 1928. An English synopsis of this work is included in MARVIN FARBER, *The Foundation of Phenomenology.* New York: Paine-Whitman, 1962.

———. *Ideen* (or *Ideen I*). 3d ed. Halle: Niemeyer, 1928. English translation by W. R. BOYCE GIBSON, *Ideas.* New York: Macmillan, 1931; London: Allen & Unwin, Ltd., 1931.

———. *Vorlesungen zur Phänomenologie des inneren Zeitbewusstseins.* Halle: Niemeyer, 1928. English translation by JAMES S. CHURCHILL, *The Phenomenology of Internal Time Consciousness.* Bloomington: Indiana University Press, 1964.

[251]

HUSSERL, EDMUND. *Formale und transzendentale Logik.* Halle: Niemeyer, 1929. French translation by SUZANNE BACHELARD, *Logique formelle et logique transcendentale.* Paris: Presses Universitaires de France, 1965.

————. *Méditations cartésiennes.* Paris: Colin, 1931. German text: *Cartesianische Meditationen* in *Husserliana,* Vol. I. The Hague: Nijhoff, 1950. English translation of the German text by DORION CAIRNS, *Cartesian Meditations.* The Hague: Nijhoff, 1960.

MISES, LUDWIG VON. "Soziologie und Geschichte," *Archiv für Sozialwissenschaften und Sozialpolitik,* Vol. LXI, pp. 465–512.

————. *Human Action.* New Haven: Yale University Press, 1963; Chicago: Regnery, 1966.

SCHELER, MAX. *Wesen und Formen der Sympathie.* 2d ed. Bonn: Cohen, 1923. English translation by PETER HEATH, *The Nature of Sympathy.* New Haven: Yale University Press, 1954.

SIMMEL, GEORG. *Soziologie.* 1st ed. Munich, 1903; 2d ed., 1922. Parts of this work are included in *The Sociology of Georg Simmel,* translated and edited by KURT H. WOLFF. Glencoe, Ill.: The Free Press, 1950.

WEBER, MAX. *Wirtschaft und Gesellschaft.* 1st ed. Tübingen: 1922. English translation by A. M. HENDERSON and TALCOTT PARSONS, *The Theory of Social and Economic Organization.* Glencoe, Ill.: The Free Press, 1957.

————. *Gesammelte Aufsätze zur Wissenschaftslehre.* Tübingen: J. C. B. Mohr (P. Siebeck), 1922. A partial English translation of this work is included in *Max Weber on the Methodology of the Social Sciences,* translated and edited by EDWARD A. SHILS and HENRY A. FINCH. Glencoe, Ill.: The Free Press, 1949.

Index